Malaysian politics under Mahathir

Economic success and authoritarian government have been the hallmarks of Mahathir Mohamad's administration. Since Mahathir became prime minister in 1981, the Malaysian economy has grown dramatically and Mahathir has remained firmly in control of the political scene throughout.

Malaysian politics have been decisively shaped by Mahathir and this book provides a balanced and detailed account of his character, ideas, and temperament. The social and political scene in Malaysia is examined, as are the Prime Minister's successes such as the careful management of ethnic tensions between Malays and Chinese, the program of modernization and industrialization, and his emergence as a champion of Third World causes. Mahathir's faults are also honestly examined, including his preference for grandiose projects and his failure to check corruption. The abrupt dismissal from office, arrest and trial of Anwar Ibrahim, Mahathir's deputy, in late 1998, and their implications, are assessed.

The recent economic crisis in Asia has had a major impact on certain Southeast Asian states including Malaysia. *Malaysian Politics under Mahathir* considers these recent developments and their implications for Malaysia's, and Mahathir's, future.

R.S. Milne is Emeritus Professor and has held professorships at the University of British Columbia, Singapore University, London University and Victoria University, New Zealand. **Diane K. Mauzy** is Professor of Political Science at the University of British Columbia. Both have published widely on Malaysia and Southeast Asia.

Politics in Asia series
Edited by Michael Leifer
London School of Economics

Malaysian Politics under Mahathir

R.S. Milne and Diane K. Mauzy

London and New York

First published 1999 by Routledge
11 New Fetter Lane, London EC4P 4EE

Simultaneously published in the USA and Canada
by Routledge
29 West 35th Street, New York, NY 10001

Typeset in Baskerville by Routledge
Printed and bound in Great Britain by
MPG Books Ltd, Bodmin

British Library Cataloguing in Publication Data
A catalogue record for this book is available from the British Library

Library of Congress Cataloguing in Publication Data
A catalogue record for this book has been requested

ISBN 0–415–17142–3 (hbk)
ISBN 0–415–17143–1 (pbk)

**To Portia and Alexa, whose quantum leaps have
helped us to extend the bounds of knowledge**

Contents

Foreword

Ever since he became Prime Minister of Malaysia in July 1981 at the age of 56, Dr. Mahathir Mohamad has exercised an extraordinary dominating influence over his country's public life. An economic modernizer without fear of registering a scepticism of democracy and human rights, he has bent the politics of Malaysia to his will and in the process has successfully subordinated the constitutional monarchy, the judiciary and the predominant political party, the United Malays National Organization (UMNO) which he has led continuously despite a major challenge in 1987 which was only narrowly defeated. His sustained political dominance was demonstrated in the way in which he removed his deputy, Anwar Ibrahim, from national and party office in 1998. Indeed, in so doing, he effectively rewrote the rules of Malaysian politics.

Dr. Mahathir is exceptional as a Malay leader in contrast to his three predecessors as Prime Minister. He is not only authoritarian but also highly combative and confrontational and adept at open invective. Such behaviour is out of keeping with Malay cultural style and indeed with the notion of "Asian values" which Dr. Mahathir has espoused. It may be that his medical training as well as his personality has been a factor in shaping a political style that brooks no opposition to his diagnoses and prescriptions. His sense of rectitude in telling Malaysians that they should swallow the equivalent of so many pills a day in their own interest conjures up the image of medical infallibility translated to politics.

In locating Dr. Mahathir at the centre of their impressive study of Malaysia's politics, Professors Stephen Milne and Diane Mauzy have acknowledged a fact of life which will not go away. They bring to this study considerable first-hand experience of Malaysia's politics and its personalities and the text is informed by a deep understanding of its complexities. The role and political conduct of Dr. Mahathir is treated in a sober and balanced manner with credit given where it is due, while his early chequered political career is taken into full account. His accomplishments in economic modernization and his tolerant management of ethnic and religious matters as well as achievements in foreign policy are accorded full acknowledgement. Matching sober treatment is provided of his idiosyncracies and love of power. Indeed, it is pointed out that for him "power is a necessary food". In this context, the authors discuss political succession and his chequered relationship with his one-time political heir presumptive, Anwar Ibrahim. In addition, the shortcomings of governance in Malaysia under his rule are also addressed, including the rise in the incidence of corruption. Correspondingly, the reader is provided with an insight into his fixations, including a so-called edifice complex and characteristic angry xenophobic response to the onset of economic crisis from the second half of 1997. One depiction of Dr. Mahathir in this volume is as "innovative, eccentric and icono-clastic". The fact of the matter is that Malaysia's politics have never been the same since he assumed office and power nearly two decades ago. Professors Milne and Mauzy have captured the essence of the man and of the political context which he has shaped and conditioned in a scholarly and highly readable way. As such, they provide a unique insight into a distinctive political era in Malaysia.

Michael Leifer
September 1998

Acknowledgments

We have too many intellectual debts, to politicians, academics, diplomats, journalists, and other friends, incurred over more than thirty-five years of research in Malaya/Malaysia, to attempt to acknowledge them here. Many will be apparent from the references. However, some academics with whom we have had discussions since this book was underway merit our special thanks: Harold Crouch; Jomo, K.S.; Johan Saravanamuttu; Zakaria Haji Ahmad; and also, in Canada, Richard Stubbs and Frank Langdon. Also, we would like to thank M.G.G. Pillai for organizing, and listing us on, the <sangkancil@malaysia.net> Internet list, which has been very helpful and informative.

Libraries which were particularly helpful were: the library of *The New Straits Times* in Kuala Lumpur; the libraries of the Australian National University of Canberra; and the library of the Institute of Southeast Asian Studies in Singapore, especially the Librarian, Ch'ng Kim See.

We are also grateful to Nancy Mina of the Department of Political Science, University of British Columbia, for typing the manuscript on the computer, and for her diligence and patience in deciphering a myriad of inked-in alterations.

The Consulate of Malaysia in Vancouver, Canada kindly permitted us to consult its holdings of Malaysian newspapers.

Diane K. Mauzy would also like to thank the University of British Columbia for an HSS Small Grant that has helped to defray some of the research costs.

Concerning publication, we are especially grateful to Michael Leifer and Victoria Smith, not only for their guidance and understanding, but for having divined, in the first place, that we were willing and ready to write our book on Mahathir. Kate Hopgood, the Desk Editor, was delightful, and refreshingly non-bureaucratic, to work with.

Some of the material used in the book has been adapted from R.S. Milne, "The Mellowing of Mahathir?", in Bruce Matthews (ed.), *Le recueil, intitulé identities, territoire et environnement en Asie du Sud-Est/Identities, Territory and Environment in Southeast Asia*, Québec City, Documents Du GÉRAC #13, Université, Laval, forthcoming in 1999.

Acronyms

2MP	Second Malaysia Plan
ABIM	Angkatan Belia Islam Malaysia – Malaysian Islamic Youth Movement
ACA	Anti-Corruption Agency
AFTA	ASEAN Free Trade Area
AMM	ASEAN Ministerial Meeting
APEC	Asia–Pacific Economic Cooperation
ARF	ASEAN Regional Forum
ASA	Association of Southeast Asia
ASEAN	Association of Southeast Asian Nations
ASEM	Asia–Europe Meeting
BMF	Bumiputra Malaysia Finance
CHOGM	Commonwealth Heads of Government Meeting
DAC	Declaration of ASEAN Concord
DAP	Democratic Action Party
EAEC	East Asia Economic Caucus
EAEG	East Asia Economic Group
EPF	Employees Provident Fund
EPU	Economic Planning Unit
EU	European Union
FELDA	Federal Land Development Authority
FLDA	*see* FELDA
FIMA	Food Industries of Malaysia
FUNCINPEC	Front Uni National pour un Cambodge Indépendant Neutre, Pacifique et Coopératif
GATT	General Agreement on Tariffs and Trade
HAKAM	National Human Rights Society
HICOM	Heavy Industry Corporation of Malaysia
ICA	Industrial Coordination Act 1975
IKIM	Institute of Islamic Understanding
ILO	International Labor Organization
IMF	International Monetary Fund
IMP	Independence of Malaya Party

INA	Indian National Army
IRG	Islamic Republic Group
ISA	Internal Security Act
ISIS	Institute of Strategic and International Studies
JUST	Just World Trust
MAF	Malaysian Armed Forces
MARA	Majlis Amanah Rakyat
MCA	Malayan/Malaysian Chinese Association
MCP	Malayan Communist Party
MIC	Malayan/Malaysian Indian Congress
MPAJA	Malayan People's Anti-Japanese Army
MPHB	Multi-Purpose Holdings Berhad
MSC	Multimedia Super Corridor
MTUC	Malaysian Trade Union Congress
NAFTA	New Zealand and Australia Free Trade Agreement
NAM	Non-Aligned Movement
NCC	National Consultative Council
NDP	National Development Policy
NEAC	National Economic Action Council
NECC	National Economic Consultative Council
NEP	New Economic Policy
NGO	Non-governmental organization
NIE	Newly industrializing economy
NOC	National Operations Council
OIC	Organization of Islamic Conference
OPP2	*Second Outline Perspective Plan*
PAC	Political action committee
PAP	People's Action Party
PAS	Partai Islam Se-Malaysia
PBDS	Parti Bangsa Dayak Sarawak – Party of the Dayak Peoples of Sarawak
PBS	Parti Bersatu Sabah (United Sabah Party)
Perkim	Pertubuhan Kebajikan Islam
PMC	Post-Ministerial Conference
PPP	People's Progressive Party
RIDA	Rural and Industrial Development Authority
SNAP	Sarawak National Party
SUPP	Sarawak United People's Party
TAC	Treaty of Amity and Cooperation
UDA	Urban Development Authority
UEM	United Engineers (Malaysia)
UMNO	United Malays National Organization
UN	United Nations
UNESCO	United Nations Educational, Scientific, and Cultural Organization

UNTAC   United Nations Transitional Authority in Cambodia
WTO   World Trade Organization
ZOPFAN   Zone of Peace, Freedom and Neutrality

Malaysian proper names and titles

Malays are not referred to principally by their patronymics. Rather, they are referred to by their given name(s), and their fathers' names are attached at the end after "bin" (for males) or "binte" (for females). Some Malays drop the use of "bin/binte, e.g., the third Prime Minister, Tun Hussein Onn, son of Dato Onn bin Jaafar. When there are two given names and the first is "Abdul," either the person is referred to by both given names (e.g., Abdul Rahman), or the "Abdul" is dropped (e.g., the second Prime Minister, Tun Razak – otherwise known as Tun Abdul Razak bin Dato Hussein). Similarly, if the first of two given names is "Mohamed" (or one of its variations), it is sometimes dropped.

Malaysia's Chinese generally have three names, and the usage is simple and consistent. The family name comes first and is followed by two given names. For example, in the name "Lim Kit Siang," "Lim" is the family name; friends would call him "Kit Siang". The only exception for Chinese names occurs when a person uses a Christian first name, then the family name appears last, as for the Chinese politician, Michael Chen, who would otherwise by known as Chen Wing Sum.

Some descendants of royalty have the title of "Tunku" or "Tengku" (Prince) which is spelled differently in different states. The word "Haji" or the feminine "Hajiah" in a name indicates that the person has made the pilgrimage to Mecca.

Non-hereditary titles may be conferred by a ruler or governor at the state level, or by the Agung at the federal level. In most cases the nomination would come from the appropriate minister. The most usual state title is "Dato" or "Datuk," the latter is now becoming the more frequent spelling. Longer forms are "Datuk Seri" or "Datuk Amar." The feminine form is "Datin," although a woman who acquires the title in her own right, and not by marriage, is a "Datuk." At federal level the corresponding title is "Tan Sri." A higher federal rank, rarely conferred, is "Tun." Men without a title are referred to as "Encik" (Mr.). The feminine equivalent is "Che."

Key dates

Background

The first British territory acquired on the Malayan peninsula was the island of Penang, leased to the British East India Company by the Sultan of Kedah in 1786. Early in the Twentieth Century, the British government controlled all Malaya. It exercised the greatest control in the three "Straits Settlements," Penang, Malacca and Singapore. In four "federated states" its rule was less direct, and in five "unfederated states" it was even less direct.

Some important dates concerning Malaysia, and Mahathir, in the last half-century or so, are given below:

1925	Mahathir Mohamad born in Alor Setar, Kedah. His father, half-Indian, half-Malay, was a school principal. His mother was Malay
1942–5	Japanese invasion and occupation of Malaya
1946	United Malays National Organization (UMNO) formed
1946	Malayan Indian Congress (MIC) formed
1946–8	Malayan Union formed then abrogated
1948	*Federation of Malaya Agreement* on Malaya's constitutional future
1948–60	Communist rebellion (the "Emergency")
1948	Partai Islam, later Partai Islam Se-Malaysia (PAS), founded
1949	Malayan Chinese Association (MCA) formed
1951	Independence of Malaya Party formed
1953	The Alliance Party formed
1953	Mahathir awarded a medical degree by the University of Malaya, Singapore
1955	General election decisively won by the Alliance
1957	Malaya becomes independent, with a new Constitution. Tunku Abdul Rahman becomes the first Prime Minister
1957	Mahathir starts a new medical practice in Alor Setar
1963	Malaysia formed
1963	"Confrontation" by Indonesia against Malaysia
1964	Mahathir elected to Parliament
1965	Singapore separated from Malaysia

1966	Democratic Action Party registered
1967	Malaysia becomes a founding member of the Association of Southeast Asian Nations (ASEAN)
1969	Ethnic riots in Kuala Lumpur
1969	Mahathir denounces Tunku's leadership
1969–71	State of Emergency exists
1970	Mahathir publishes *The Malay Dilemma*, in Singapore
1971	Tun Razak succeeds Tunku as Prime Minister
1971	The New Economic Policy (NEP) announced
1974	The Barisan Nasional (National Front) replaces the Alliance
1974	Official relations established between Malaysia and the People's Republic of China
1975	Mahathir elected a vice-president of UMNO
1976	Tun Razak dies and is succeeded as Prime Minister and as president of UMNO by Tun Hussein Onn. Mahathir becomes Deputy Prime Minister and deputy president of UMNO
1981	Upon Hussein's resignation, Mahathir becomes Prime Minister and president of UMNO. Mahathir announces his "Look East" policy
1982	Anwar Ibrahim, standing as an UMNO candidate, wins a seat at the general election
1983–4	Mahathir leads UMNO in a campaign to limit the power of the Agung and the rulers
1983	Privatization policy announced
1985	Economic growth for the year negative
1986	Musa Hitam resigns as Deputy Prime Minister; replaced by Ghafar Baba
1987	Razaleigh and Musa challenge Mahathir's leadership of UMNO, unsuccessfully
1987	Razaleigh founds a breakaway party, but Mahathir's UMNO defeats it at the general elections of 1990 and 1995
1988	The Lord President of the Supreme Court and other high-ranking judges removed from office
1989	Mahathir has a successful coronary bypass operation
1991	The National Development Policy announced
1991	Mahathir launches his "Vision 2020" policy
1993	Anwar replaces Ghafar Baba as deputy president of UMNO and Deputy Prime Minister
1996	Razaleigh dissolves his party and rejoins UMNO
1997	An economic crisis severely affects Southeast Asia, including Malaysia
1998	Mahathir dismisses Anwar as Minister of Finance and as Deputy Prime Minister; Anwar expelled from UMNO, arrested and his trial begins

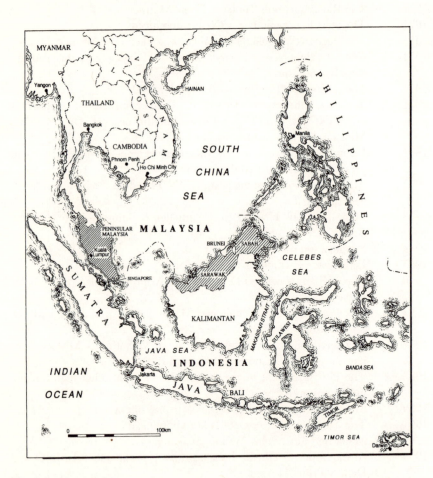

Map 1 Southeast Asia

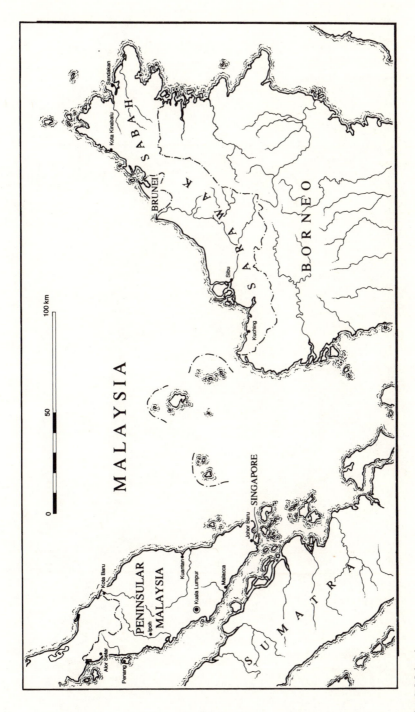

Map 2 Malaysia

Introduction

Leadership in Malaysia

The theme of this book should be stated at the outset. Indeed, it has already been affirmed, or suggested, in the title; "under" not only refers to a period of time, the years in which Mahathir has been in power – from 1981 to the present (1998) – it also conveys the high degree of control, almost of domination, that he has exercised. The structure and functioning of government, outlined below, is conducive to a high degree of control. However, Mahathir's assertiveness and strong political will not only made the most of the structures he inherited, but they also laid an imprint on them of increased prime ministerial authority, and strengthened the control that can be wielded by his successors, provided that they also have the necessary political will.

This chapter is intended to make the role of leadership more easily understood. In particular, it will demonstrate the weakness of any checks and balances on the leader, as compared with the national leaders of many other countries, especially those in the West.

There is a federal system of government, although the power of the states is limited, and the system was adopted initially only because the royal rulers of the Malay states were retained to make the acceptance of British colonial rule easier. Two of the states, Sarawak and Sabah on the island of Borneo, were combined only in 1963 (Singapore was also a component, 1963–5) with Malaya to constitute "Malaysia".

Politics in Malaysia are still dominated by ethnic considerations. The Malays constitute just about half the population. Together with other indigenous peoples they are classified as Bumiputera – sons of the soil – who enjoy certain privileges, primarily in employment and education. The remainder of the population consists mainly of Chinese (30 percent) and Indians (10 percent). Neither of these groups is homogeneous, being made up of persons with varying languages and religions. The Malays are all Muslims, but differences in the degree to which they attribute importance to various aspects of Islam complicate the pattern of politics. Ethnicity is the main factor, but social class also has an effect. However, while the majority of Malays belong to an umbrella-like inter-ethnic Barisan Nasional (National Front), a main opposition party, PAS (Partai Islam Se-Malaysia), which controls the state of Kelantan, receives considerable Malay voter support in the four northern states. Among other salient features is the dominating role of the Barisan in the political system, and the preeminence of the United Malays National Organization (UMNO) at its core.

The power of UMNO and its leader: the armed forces

The leading role of UMNO and its president, Dr. Mahathir Mohamad, who is also prime minister, can best be appreciated, not by listing formal constitutional powers, but by considering the relative weakness of other institutions. The situation resembles its British counterpart very little, in spite of the fact that the Constitution was modeled on the British. The counterpart should not be mistaken for an equivalent. The Barisan has never been defeated in a general election. Its percentage of winning votes is exaggerated when converted into seats, mainly because the Malay vote, where the Barisan tends to have an advantage, is strongest in constituencies that contain relatively fewer electors. The Barisan has much more money to spend than the other parties, and has more patronage to dispense. Because of the Barisan's usual large majority of seats and firm party discipline, Parliament is weak. Government-introduced bills usually pass as a matter of course, while other bills are seldom successful. The opposition parties have little power. It used to be asserted that civil servants in some developing countries exerted so much authority that these states could be described as "bureaucratic polities."[1] But, although some bureaucratic inertia still persists, in Malaysia Mahathir does not give the bureaucrats much chance to resist his will. The power of the rulers in the states and of the Agung (King), elected in rotation for a five-year term by and from among the rulers, was substantially reduced soon after Mahathir's succession. So were the powers of the judiciary in 1988, after a "battle" with the Prime Minister. Two other institutions are markedly weaker in Malaysia than they are in some other countries, especially Western ones: the press and interest groups. Additionally the rights of the citizen are weak in Malaysia. The government has, and has sometimes used, powers of detention without trial.

Unlike some countries close to Malaysia, such as Thailand or Indonesia, the armed forces are not prominent in politics. Malaysia has enjoyed forty-one years of unbroken civilian rule. There has never been a coup attempt in Malaysia, nor any hint that the military might seek a political role for itself. There are a number of reasons that the military has stayed out of politics.[2] First, the Malaysian military was trained in the British tradition of a professional corps whose role and duties did not include intervening in the political process. It helped that independence was gained peacefully, and that the role and limits of the Malaysian Armed Forces (MAF) were spelled out clearly in the Constitution. The governing elite in Malaysia differs from that in several neighboring countries, because in Indonesia, etc., the governing elite prevails over military elites, and in Japan it prevails over the bureaucratic elite.[3] Second, it probably helped that the expansion of the MAF was very gradual and that until the 1980s, the para-military federal police was a larger force than the army. Third, there has tended to be strong familial connections between the ruling elite and senior MAF officers.

All of Malaysia's prime ministers have placed relatives or in-laws in important senior positions in the MAF. In a country where feudal traditions persist, strong family loyalties provide additional insurance of good civilian–military relations. However, it is ethnic factors that provide the single most important reason that the MAF has stayed in the barracks. The combat services are overwhelmingly Malay. The premier corps, the Royal Malay Regiment, is entirely Malay. There has been a close coincidence of interests between the Malay civilian political elite and the Malay senior military officers on the political rules of the game in Malaysia; namely, ensuring that the ethnic status quo is not disrupted to the disadvantage of the Malays and that there are no threats to Malay political hegemony. Given the convergence of these factors, the military has stayed out of politics despite the demonstration effect of military rule in the region.

Nowhere in the Constitution is it stated that the Prime Minister must be a Malay or a Bumiputera, yet to violate this understanding would be unthinkable. One consequence is that the Malay Prime Minister, in order to be fair, must act in the interests of all ethnic groups; he must behave as a "Supra-communal Arbiter".[4] He is responsible for seeing that the national "pie" is shared out equitably, not just for material allocations, but also symbolically, in terms of ethnic esteem.

Other institutions, for example those at state level, which have less power than the Prime Minister, are not to be regarded as negligible or ineffective. They are important agencies through which power is exercised but only in accordance with the plans, or visions, of the leader. They are a means of ensuring that the leader can get the people in the society to do what he wants them to do.

The nature of leadership

Generalizations about leadership, taken from books on psychology, business administration and so on, are sometimes platitudinous. Some useful generalizations, especially in the field of international relations, are cited by Richard Stubbs.[5] Some recent examples rightly affirm that the most important leadership traits are not discernible by looking at the leader alone but by looking at interactive leader–follower relations. However, although it may be true that a leader retains his status to the extent that he meets the expectations of other group members, is this enough? To be sure, it makes for acceptability that one should be able to "get along" with followers. But is this the crux of leadership? A more appropriate, though sterner, test is whether a follower trusts a leader enough to follow him if he embarks on an unusual course of action. This is a necessary qualification for a leader. As Mahathir remarked, "You have to lead. You should be sensitive to what your followers think. But if you do exactly what they want, you're not a leader."[6] In the long run, it must be supplemented by the leader evoking sufficient feelings of loyalty, and providing enough material benefits, to establish legitimacy.

To try to explore in more depth the "Malay" characteristics or special traits of leadership is not easy. It is enough, perhaps, to suggest a few ideas. Some key terms occur in Mahathir's early political testament, *The Malay Dilemma*: for example, "feudal," "adat" (custom), "authority," "ritual."[7] A description of "the Malay way," which, among other elements, indicates the desire to avoid conflict, would include: emphasis on traditional courtesy and good manners, wide consultation, avoidance of direct confrontation where possible, but leaving a role for innuendo. Consensus is sought in preference to imposing the will of a majority. Critics are wooed, rather than repressed, and defeated opponents are not victimized but a way is left open for future reconciliation.[8]

Some "coffee-house" conversation was reported during the UMNO split in 1987, during which four qualifications were suggested as being desirable in a Malay leader. The leader must fight for the Malay cause, should not be *sombong* (stuck-up), should have *tokoh* (style), and, preferably, should be of aristocratic birth. Other desirable traits or features were mentioned, such as tradition, harmony, and peaceful succession, while disapproval of impatience and ambition was expressed.[9] One difficulty in discussing Malay styles and values is that they may be becoming somewhat old-fashioned for younger urban voters.

Mahathir's style is not typically "Malay." While approving of Asian values such as consensus and deference, his own style is confrontational and, indeed, "Western."[10]

Malaysia's prime ministers

The first three leaders had features in common, which were not shared by the fourth, Mahathir. Some are very well known. They were all of noble birth, and Abdul Rahman, known to all affectionately as "the Tunku," was a prince of the Kedah royal family. All three studied law in England. All of them played golf,[11] and all were administrators in the government service. Mahathir was also briefly in government service, but engaged in his profession of medicine.

All four prime ministers had one feature in common: none of them was entirely Malay. Tunku had some Shan-Thai blood; Razak, some Bugis (Indonesian); Hussein, some Turkish; Mahathir, some Indian.

Clearly, Tunku had a good deal of the playboy in him. When he was in England, he was reputedly interested only in fast cars, fast women and not-so-fast horses. Tunku did not take his studies very seriously, but when he resumed them after the war he found time to revive the Malay Society of Great Britain, and became its president. This was one of his opportunities for making contacts. Tunku was naturally gregarious, which was a useful qualification for becoming president of UMNO (in addition to his being a prince).

The choice of Tunku as UMNO leader was quite fortuitous. He was proposed by his friend, Razak, who had been asked to allow his name to go forward, but who considered himself too young. The presidency was vacant because of the acrimonious departure from office of Dato Onn (p. 5). He worked well with the British during the transition to independence. In office as

Prime Minister, he looked and played the part. Tunku found it easy to delegate; he did not believe in working too hard. Consequently, when Razak succeeded him as Prime Minister, he was thoroughly equipped to carry out the job. It was said that, while Razak *preached* delegation, he did not practise it himself. He assumed too many portfolios and headed too many committees, and when dealing with one problem, his mind was partly busy with others.[12] He was a confirmed workaholic. His inclinations were perhaps reinforced when he learned (in 1970) of his serious illness (leukemia) and knew that he was working against time.

His achievements, both before and after becoming Prime Minister, were prodigious. As Minister of Education he produced a report for creating a national system of education with a common syllabus (1956). Some of his greatest achievements were carried out when he was Minister of National and Rural Development, 1959–69. He adapted some of the techniques used to fight the Communist insurgency, setting up a series of "operations rooms" to record which agricultural projects were proceeding as planned, and which were lagging. He promoted the entire range of rural development operations. He also reshaped FLDA, later FELDA (the Federal Land Development Authority), a government body that helped to put settlers on the land and train and equip them.

He traveled, on average, about 50,000 miles in a year. Officials in the field looked forward to his visits with trepidation. One administrator was so fearful that his work might be less than perfect that, as Razak's visit became due, he visited the lavatory three times.[13]

Razak was also used by Tunku as a trouble-shooter, for example, during the period of Confrontation with Indonesia in the mid-1960s, and during the brief discussions on the separation of Singapore.

However, this kind of record of Razak's activities would suggest that he was mainly an administrator, though a talented one. But he was much more than that. What is most misleading in regarding him primarily as an administrator is that it gives no hint of his genius for innovation. This gift was most evident in three of his achievements. Looking for a way to satisfy Malay grievances, which had contributed to the Kuala Lumpur riots in 1969, he launched a carefully prepared New Economic Policy to reduce poverty and to enable Malays to have an increasing share in the management and benefits of the economy. He extended the scope of the multi-ethnic Alliance Party when he formed the Barisan Nasional in 1974. He promoted the acceptance of the concept of "neutralization" in the region, helped to persuade China to endorse it, and established diplomatic relations with China also in 1974.

Hussein Onn was a man of principle, like his father, Dato Onn, who had had to leave UMNO, which he founded in 1946, because it would not follow his wish to make its membership multi-ethnic. Curiously, the temperaments of the two were dissimilar. The father had a mercurial personality, and he was over-confident, and surprised by UMNO's rejection of his plans to make it a multi-ethnic party. Hussein was surely born under the influence of a different planet. His temperament may have been a product of his military career before and after the Second World War; so, maybe, were his directness and discipline. When combined with legal training, the result was a passion for accuracy and for close attention to detail. In his student days, he read carefully, page after page, checking and counter-checking. He disliked taking action in response to demands or pressures.[14]

Hussein was Prime Minister only from 1976 until 1981, and for much of the time was not in good health. Yet he demonstrated his regard for the law and for the rule of law. He was a determined foe of corruption, and on becoming Prime Minister he believed that, if it were widespread, it could ruin a country. Razak, following "the Malay way," removed Datuk Harun as Menteri Besar (Chief Minister) of Selangor, but offered him a post as Malaysian ambassador to the United Nations. Harun rejected the offer, and then was arrested in November 1975 on sixteen charges.

In May 1976 Harun was found guilty and sentenced to two years' imprisonment. He appealed, and Hussein had to withstand pressures from his supporters that he should be pardoned or have his sentence remitted. However, true to his principles, Hussein stood his ground, and Harun served out his term.[15]

For his first two years as Prime Minister, Hussein suffered from having no strong political base. His return to the political scene had been too recent for him to have established as close political ties as other politicians of his age and seniority.[16] Factionalism was almost beyond his control. Hussein strengthened his position by a decisive victory at the 1978 general election, but, in his state of health, he failed to exercise much leadership before his resignation in 1981. Probably his most important, indeed fateful, decision was to select Mahathir as his successor.

As will become evident, Mahathir has been an eager and dedicated modernizer, the first Prime Minister who really strives for change, and usually acts as if its benefits outweigh its costs. Projects that are his "pets" are often designated as "national" projects, for instance the Proton automobile and the Bakun dam in Sarawak.

The power of the UMNO deputy president (Deputy Prime Minister) depends very much on the discretion of his superior. So do his prospects of promotion to the top job. Partly because the Prime Minister is expected to "arbitrate" so as to ensure the appropriate balance of ethnic interests, his deputy is expected to be a guardian of Malay interests. Both Razak and Mahathir, when they took over as deputy, were watched closely by non-Malays to see that they did not lean too much in this direction, and so was previous Deputy Prime Minister Datuk Seri Anwar Ibrahim, especially because of his former Islamic connections, but all these leaders acted fairly and dispelled these apprehensions. A somewhat similar pro-Malay role is played, and is expected to be played, by UMNO Youth. Its role is to defend the Malays, aggressively, against the demands of other ethnic groups. The attitude of its members resembles that of "shock troops." In 1979 it was so militant that it was said that it sought to ensure that UMNO controlled the government and not vice versa.[17]

Continuity of families: turnover of prime ministers

Now (1998), just over fifty years after the independence of Malaysia, there are already signs of possible political "dynasties" in Malaysia. A son of Razak, Najib, is a possible successor to Mahathir. Another already impressive achievement concerns the descendants of Dato Onn. His son, Hussein, held the prime ministership for six years, and Hussein's son, Datuk Hishamuddin Tun Hussein Onn, is already acting head of UMNO Youth and a deputy minister at the age of 37 (1998).

Any discussion of leadership raises the question: how long do, or should, leaders stay in power? Some Constitutions, notably that of the United States, set limits to the length of time that some leaders can remain in office, but Malaysia's does not. Two Malaysian prime ministers, Razak and Hussein, had their period of rule cut short by death or illness. The replacement of the first Prime Minister, Tunku Abdul Rahman, was more complex and gradual. Tunku felt that he had not done all that he could to prevent the ethnic riots in 1969. The establishment of the National Operations Council, headed by Razak, parallel to the cabinet under Tunku, symbolized a shift in power which was already occurring. By 1970 power had effectively been transferred. To effect a formal handover, a constitutional issue was invoked. The Sultan of Kedah, a nephew of Tunku, had been elected by the rulers to take over as Agung (King) in 1970, and it was thought to be inappropriate for Tunku, who would have to report to him as Prime Minister, to remain in that office.

Currently (1998) Mahathir is the most contentious case yet. He has served for over seventeen years, and, although he is still capable of ruling, impatience would be excusable in a probable successor. According to Lucian Pye, Asian leaders in general tend to cling to power. Objectively, continuity of leadership – up to a point – may be advantageous to good governance, as Mahathir does not neglect to point out. The leaders have "Asian," "traditional" notions about it, namely that leadership implies status but does not involve heavy responsibilities.[18] This does not seem to explain entirely Tunku's (mild) disinclination to give up power or Mahathir's rather stronger reluctance, which contributed to his decision to remove Anwar from office. One has the impression that, to Tunku, power had become a habit. Certainly, after giving up power he regretted that he was not consulted sufficiently often by his successor.[19] Mahathir is so interested in the completion of his favorite projects, and so doubtful that anyone else would pursue them as successfully as himself, that he seems noncommittal about giving up power. Nowadays it is hard to dislodge a Prime Minister who is determined to stay on.

In 1986 the retiring Italian ambassador to Malaysia, and dean of the diplomatic corps, paid the ultimate tribute to the intricacies of Malaysian politics. They were, he claimed, even more complex than political intricacies in Italy.[20] Since then, there has been a growing perception that the complexity is centered in the mind and policies of Mahathir.

1   Malaysia

How Mahathir came to power

When Datuk Seri Dr. Mahathir Mohamad became Prime Minister in 1981, Malaysia was still quite a new country. As Malaya, it had attained independence in 1957, becoming Malaysia when in 1963 it combined with two former British colonies on the nearby island of Borneo (and with Singapore, temporarily). Malaya, situated at the southern tip of the mainland of Southeast Asia, is only about two-thirds of the size of Malaysia, but contains about 80 percent of the population. It was here that the government structure was established, and was later extended with the addition of the Borneo territories. It was also here that, with independence approaching, the party system developed, including the chief party of the Malays, the dominant ethnic group, UMNO. In that party Mahathir began, and has continued, with only one brief interruption, his political career.

What follows is a brief political history of the country that Mahathir inherited. Malaya was small compared with its neighbors, Indonesia and Thailand, as regards area and population. However, it had resources conducive to economic growth – timber, tin deposits, and land suitable for rubber plantations. It was situated on several trade routes, which facilitated the exchange of goods. Under British rule, an effective civil service was created – a necessary condition for economic expansion.

However, Malaya had one great potential disadvantage. It was ethnically diverse, almost half the population being Malay, a third Chinese, and about 10 percent Indian. World-wide, there are many examples of ethnic differences leading to violence, which sometimes becomes endemic. Currently, the former Yugoslavia and several parts of central Africa come to mind. With two exceptions, Malaya/Malaysia has been free from major ethnic conflicts. One took place after the end of the Second World War and the departure of the Japanese, when there was a (mainly Chinese) Communist rebellion, which caused numerous casualties and disruptions and lasted, effectively, for about six years. The other occurred in the capital, Kuala Lumpur, in May 1969, when hundreds were killed or injured during a few days. Although the casualties were small compared with those incurred during the rebellion, the incidents made a deep impression on the government and the public. Since then, no general election has been held in a year ending with the number nine, and for several years afterwards rumors circulated about a recurrence of ethnic violence as the date, May 13, approached. As a direct response to the violence, the government not only took measures to tighten provisions to preserve order and curtail free speech, but it also acted so as to assuage Malay economic dissatisfaction, by launching a pro-Malay New Economic Policy.

Today, Malaysia's economic success seems truly remarkable. It has gone from depending on its natural resources to moving into manufacturing. Its annual economic growth until 1997 averaged about 8 percent for the previous decade or so. It has newly industrializing economy (NIE) status. Its smallness has become less of a handicap – from the economic or security point of view – through its membership of ASEAN (the Association of Southeast Asian Nations), which in 1998 contains nine states and about 500,000,000 people. It is also a member of the Asia-Pacific Economic Cooperation (APEC) forum and the World Trade Organization (WTO). Much of its prominence on the world stage and its reputation as a champion of the "South" (less industrialized countries, as opposed to the more industrialized "North") has been due to the energy and persistence of its Prime Minister, Mahathir.

From the sixteenth century onwards, the territories that later constituted Malaya, and the surrounding areas – especially the present Indonesia – produced spices, notably pepper, cinnamon, cloves, etc., which were greatly in demand by west European countries. These countries sought agreements and concessions from Southeast Asian rulers in order to secure their sources of supply. Portuguese expeditions were followed by Dutch and then by British ones. In Malaya, the British connection took the form mainly of "indirect rule." As the term suggests, the British exercised their power through local, Islamic, rulers, mostly known as "sultans," with whom the British concluded agreements, ensuring peaceful conditions for trade in and near the main ports. The rulers' powers were not removed; the British appointed "residents" to their courts who conveyed appropriate "advice." In some ways, the rulers' powers were actually strengthened. The British regarded the influence of Islam as a force for promoting stability, and the sultans were reinforced by recognition of their religious status and by the introduction of more elaborate ceremonials.

It would be tedious to provide a blow-by-blow account of constitutional and administrative developments. A distinction was made between "federated" and "unfederated" states. British control was tighter in the former, while the latter were less affected by the impact of colonialism, for example they were more likely to conduct some of their business in Malay rather than in English. Four more (northern) states, which had previously been under Siamese (Thai) rule, were added to the structure in the early 1900s. The closest British control was exercised over the three "Straits Settlements" – Singapore, Penang, and Malacca – ports that were the most vital for British trade. The whole complex was tied together through the Governor of the Straits Settlements in Singapore, who was responsible to the British Colonial Office in London.

By the early 1900s, major economic and social changes were occurring. Tin mines were being developed and rubber plantations were in production. Indeed, rubber was the leading export, and its role in the economy was now so dominant that its price had become the accepted measure of the condition of Malaya's economy. Social changes were also taking place. There was an increase in immigration to provide labor for the tin mines (mostly Chinese) and for rubber plantations (mostly Indian – although there were many Malay laborers). The expanding economy also provided other jobs for immigrants. Although these immigrants were needed, their rapid arrival altered the ethnic composition of Malaya, and ethnic competition led to occasional ethnic "incidents."

This broad ethnic picture needs amplification. For instance, Chinese immigrants were made up of several dialect groups, some not easily comprehensible by others, although geography dictated that nearly all the immigrants came from southern China. The majority of the Indians were from South India and Sri Lanka, and they were mostly Tamil-speaking. The Malays were more homogeneous, though not completely so. In fact, for administration purposes, government tended to lump groups together as "Chinese," "Indian," etc. The British accorded a special status to the Malays. They were regarded as the original inhabitants, although, as their name suggests, the fifty thousand or so *orang asli* ("aborigines") had been there longer. The British believed that they should offer "protection" to the Malays, thus supplementing the protective role of the rulers. This was thought to be necessary because the Chinese and the Indians were exceptionally competitive. They were compelled to be so, for them to have undertaken the journey to Malaya, survived and made the necessary adjustment to local conditions. Protection took the form of protecting the Malays' occupation of land and according them preference for some government employment and for acquiring various permits and licenses. The consequence was that the Malays, for the most part, continued to live in rural areas, while Chinese and Indians tended to concentrate in urban settlements, the main exception being the Indian plantation workers.

The Japanese occupation: the "Emergency"

After the Japanese occupation (1942–5), it was clear that the old days of white supremacy could never be restored. Apart from British "loss of face," the wind of change that prompted Britain to grant independence to many of its colonies also reached Malaya. An unintended consequence of the Japanese occupation was that it exacerbated ethnic divisions. The Japanese wooed some Malays to support them, a similar policy to the one that they pursued in Indonesia. On the other hand, Japanese–Chinese relations had been strained by the Japanese occupation of, and atrocities in, parts of China. Some Indians were attracted by Japanese support for the Indian National Army (INA), which was pro-Indian independence and anti-British, and they provided recruits for that army.

The most determined resistance offered to the Japanese in Malaya came from the Malayan People's Anti-Japanese Army (MPAJA), supported largely by the Malayan Communist Party (MCP). In 1948, the party had attempted unsuccessfully to infiltrate the trade unions, and, after that failed, resorted to "direct action," which took the form of armed attacks. The vast majority of the rebels were Chinese; very few were Malays or Indians. At its peak, the number of armed rebels, as opposed to sympathizers or those who helped by hiding arms, providing food, etc., was more than 10,000. There were several reasons that the rebellion (which the British, with characteristic understatement, officially termed the "Emergency")[1] lost its force in the mid-1950s and was declared to have ended in 1960. The rebels suffered from two main handicaps, which caused them to be less successful than their counterparts in Vietnam in the 1970s. There was no country bordering on Malaya that was sufficiently friendly to the rebels to facilitate the passage of men or arms. Also, for the very reason that the insurgents were mostly Chinese, the Malays and Indians were unsympathetic to the rebellion.

British schemes for restructuring government

Soon after end of the war, the British, who had been considering what to do about Malaya's future, produced a scheme called the "Malayan Union," which excluded Singapore. The aim was to streamline the complex pattern of rule, and to make it more "democratic." However, the scheme was strongly challenged by the Malays and by many of the British "old Malaya hands," who had been administrators there, and now wrote irate letters to *The Times* of London. In Malaya itself, for the first time ever, Malay women joined public UMNO demonstrations in the streets. The Malays and their supporters objected that the position of the rulers, of great symbolic value to the Malays, would be downgraded, and attacked political concessions to the non-Malays, in particular claiming that too many of them would be given the right to vote too soon. They also protested that some jobs that had hitherto been reserved for Malays by the British would now be opened to others. Also, the scheme was introduced in a coercive, rather than a consultative, manner. The Union was withdrawn and replaced by a "Federation of Malaya Agreement," again without Singapore. Most of the objections were met. Citizenship would not be as easy to acquire as was contemplated in the Malayan Union scheme, and the rulers' roles and the preference for Malays in certain positions would be less affected.

The Agreement differed from its unfortunate predecessor in two important respects: there was no direct attack on the position of the rulers, and provisions were made for discussion and consultation about implementation. The British acknowledged that they had tried to alter too abruptly the pattern that they had evolved for governing Malaya over the previous three-quarters of a century. The Agreement became law in 1948.

Discussions about, and criticisms of, the proposals tended to be phrased in ethnic terms, because they contained items that seemed to benefit or disadvantage either Malays or non-Malays. Ironically, although the British plans were devised to secure concurrence on the form that government should take, in a multi-ethnic society, the immediate effect was to strengthen ethnic sentiments and to stimulate political activity along ethnic lines.

Ethnicity

The disputes about what ought to be the future shape of government reflected the significance of ethnicity. There were fears that, after the changes culminated in independence, not only might some ethnic groups be worse off, but that also ethnic violence might break out.

Ethnicity, of course, is of interest not only to political scientists but also to social scientists in general. In broad terms, an ethnic group has a common ancestry and shared memories of history (real or imagined). From past experience it has derived certain symbols, such as geographical continuity, language, religion, etc., to which it has become attached and which contribute to its sense of "group worth."[2] Additionally, ethnicity entails that not only the groups themselves have a subjective feeling about their ethnicity, but they also seek recognition that other groups accept this feeling. The symbolic elements referred to may coincide, a situation sometimes described as "coinciding cleavages." In Malaya, for example, all Malays, by definition, are Muslims. The reverse is not true, although the authors' Malay cook, in Penang in 1974, impressed by the publicity given to Mohammed Ali, when he came to box in Malaysia, identified him as the second most famous Malay in the country, behind only Tunku Abdul Rahman, the country's first Prime Minister.

Of course, groups can be further refined into sub-groups; for instance, "Chinese" could be split into the main dialect groups. However, sub-groups, such as Cantonese or Hokkien, might be too small for a party to direct its appeal to just one, or two or three, of them. This might not appeal to a sufficiently large number of electors. When dealing with ethnic politics in Malaysia, it is usual to speak of the broader groups, conventionally Malays, Chinese, and Indians. Another category, although the definition of ethnicity given here does not quite apply, is "non-Malay," which is often used to apply to Chinese, Indians, and others. Who you are is defined by who you are not.[3] Use of the term has been encouraged by government policies which designate special benefits for Malays only.

Ethnicity is also related to occupation and location. At the time of independence (1957) most Malays were rural, working on the land or as fishers. Malays were also well represented in government service. Apart from mining and farming, Chinese tended to be urban, mostly employed in small family businesses or working for European firms. Rural Indians were often employed on rubber, or other, plantations. Those in professional occupations were likely to be non-Malays. A degree of separation actually contributed to ethnic harmony. One of the dangers of "modernization" is that it may bring different ethnic groups closer to each other under competitive conditions. The substantial movement of Malays to the towns stimulated by the New Economic Policy (NEP) (1970–90) may have had such a tendency. Much depends on the speed with which intermingling occurs and the extent to which the newcomers are seen as competitive rather than complementary. The early and gradual influx of, mostly male, Chinese into the Straits Settlements was followed by a high degree of peaceful assimilation. Most Chinese who arrived there were quick to pick up the Malay language, as well as Malay culture and a taste for Malay food. The later arrivals were not so easily assimilated.

A class approach

A supplemental approach in investigating causes of tension is through differences and conflicts between social classes. Indeed, in Kelantan, a state where practically everyone is Malay, it may be the only approach. However, it would be too simple to think that class explains everything.[4] Nor would it be correct to assume that only elites derive advantages from the status quo. Government parties, which confer benefits mainly on elites, may still provide limited but tangible benefits for non-elites even if they may occur only in the future.[5] These include patronage in the form of providing jobs, permits, licenses, expenses-paid trips, and loans, etc.[6] Sometimes the choice of an ethnic or a class approach may depend on the interpretation of a given situation by the beholder. A conflict between Malays and Chinese may be seen either in terms of ethnicity or of economic interest. An example might be the reactions of Malay rice producers to what they perceive as inadequate payment offered by Chinese intermediaries.

In his classic account of social class in Malaya/Malaysia, K.S. Jomo begins with the colonial period, but remarks that government efforts to create a really capitalist class had made little progress by 1969.[7] Consequently, if one is discussing an internal capitalist class, the choice of an ethnic or a class approach (or the appropriate "mix" between them) would seem to depend on the period under study. Failure to use an ethnic approach in considering, say, the mid-1960s, would be as unproductive as treating class divisions too lightly in studying the 1990s. In the former case, the ethnic approach is not just "conventional,"[8] it is also entirely appropriate. Even as recently as 1994, a voting study on Malaysia found that, although class differences were emerging as a potential force in differentiating attitudes, they were not as strong as political ethnic differences.[9]

Ethnicity and political parties

Given the salience of ethnicity in the early 1950s, it was only to be expected that most of the effective parties formed to contest the first federal elections in 1955 would be ethnically based. Even those that claimed not to be ethnically based found that their support came mainly from one ethnic group. Which parties were formed around this time, and to what extent were they "ethnic?" UMNO was an ethnic party *par excellence*, having been formed (1946) principally to resist the Malayan Union proposals aimed, it seemed, at the heart of Malay power and status, hitherto strongly backed by the British. Underpinning this specific reason for establishing the political organization, UMNO, were Malay nationalist sentiments. Some of these came from abroad – for example, from those who had studied in Britain, or in Egypt, or had been influenced by Indonesian nationalist feelings – or from inside Malaya, for example, from religious schools or Islamic literature. By the end of the 1930s, nationalism was starting to assume a political form.[10] Whatever the sources of nationalism which led to the creation of UMNO, there was little doubt about where it would have to look for leadership. In the virtual absence of a Malay middle class, or of a religious leader with extraordinary charismatic powers, leadership could come only from "aristocrats," in a broad sense. The founder of UMNO, Dato Onn Jaafar, and his successor, the Tunku, both came from this source.

A religious party, founded in 1951, later changed its name to PAS (Partai Islam Se-Malaysia). As the name suggests, it laid more emphasis on Islam than did UMNO, and also, having gained most of its following in the mainly rural northeast of the country, it campaigned hard for more development for the peasants. It came to power in the state of Kelantan in 1959.

The Malayan Chinese Association (MCA),[11] founded in 1949 with the assistance of well-off Chinese, was led by Tun Tan Cheng Lock, and later by his son, Tun Tan Siew Sin, who became Malaya's/Malaysia's able and responsible Finance Minister. The party was well supplied with money, but also wanted to make a wide appeal to the Chinese. One of its chief aims at the time of the Emergency was to counteract the communists efforts to increase their following. The MCA therefore launched a scheme to improve living conditions for those who had been relocated, at the time of the Emergency, in "New Villages," which originally had few amenities. The MCA's relations with the Chinese Associated Chambers of Commerce were good, but it did not get on very well with two Chinese educational bodies, the United Chinese School Teachers' Association and the All-Malaya Chinese Schools Management Association. Their programs for improving Chinese education were thought by the MCA to be unrealistic.

The standing of the Malayan Indian Congress (MIC) was suggested by a saying, current at the time it joined the Alliance (1954), that its initials stood for "May I come in?" Almost from the start, it was troubled by factionalism. However, its presence in the Alliance filled a gap, ethnically. Now all three main ethnic groups were represented.

Among the parties, not ostensibly ethnically based, which were founded in the 1950s, the most important were "socialist."[12] But, to avoid being harassed by the government, they had to try to distance themselves from communism, which they were often suspected of favoring, especially while the Emergency existed. Two parties founded in the early and late 1950s respectively, the Partai Rakyat (later the Partai Sosialis Rakyat Malaysia) and the Labour Party, suffered from this handicap. Because one was rural based and the other located mostly in urban areas, one's membership was mainly Malay and the other's mainly Chinese. They established a "Socialist Front," an Alliance-type structure, which, however, failed to ensure its survival.

The Constitution of 1957

The Constitution was intended to provide a viable basis for ethnic understanding and good government. Behind it there was a great deal of bargaining, mainly among ethnic groups and political parties. There are two basic points to keep in mind in order to understand the nature and significance of the political process at this time: ethnicity is the key; the Malays have been the strongest group, not only in terms of numbers, but also by virtue of the high positions they occupied under the British and would occupy unchecked by British constraints after independence. The Malays would control the executive – it was inconceivable that the Prime Minister would not be a Malay. The Malays would also hold most of the top posts in the judiciary and the civil service.

The Constitution[13] was the product of a conference held in London in the previous year. The draft was drawn up by a Constitutional Commission, with an English judge as chairman, and one member each from Britain, Australia, India, and Pakistan. Over a hundred individuals or organizations submitted memoranda. Obviously, more weight was given to the views of the Alliance Party (which had substantial backing from both Malays and Chinese) than, for instance, to those of the Central Electricity Board. The Commission's recommendations were mostly, but not entirely, accepted, and the Constitution took effect in August 1957.

Broadly, the Constitution followed that of Britain – except, of course, that Britain has no written Constitution – or India, but with variations to meet distinctive features of Malayan history, society, or culture. The "British" model was adopted in one important respect. A "parliamentary" system was chosen in preference to a "presidential" one, as used in the United States. After a general election, the Prime Minister and his chosen ministers would come from the party in Parliament that could command, possibly in a coalition, a majority of the seats. Ministers would be responsible to the lower, elected, House of Parliament. There would be an independent judiciary. The other differences from Britain were of two kinds. Sometimes a "translation" from the British model was made to fit Malayan conditions. For example, there is an appointed Upper House of Parliament, the Senate with limited powers, which has functions somewhat resembling those of the House of Lords. Finding the equivalent of the British monarch, who would be head of state and would be available to resolve constitutional conflicts, was more difficult, because in Malaya the rulers function only at state, not federal, level. A happy solution was found. Every five years, they were required to vote for one of their number to perform, in rotation, the duties of "King" (Yang di-Pertuan Agung).

A feature that departed from the British model was that the Malayan state was federal, not unitary. The explanation lay in the existence of the rulers. A unitary system would have entailed downgrading their powers and would have reminded Malays of the hateful Malayan Union scheme. In fact, the powers allocated to the states were very few. The only really important ones concerned land and Malay customs and religion. Another feature, taken from the United States, was that the courts had the power of judicial review; they could rule that a statute passed by Parliament was invalid.

Most clauses in the Constitution may be amended with the approval of at least two-thirds of the members of each house, although there are exceptions, e.g., where the powers of the rulers are involved. The Constitution is surely one of the most frequently amended constitutions in the world. It was amended fifteen times in the first fourteen years of its existence.

Some provisions in the Constitution do not amount just to "translations" of other constitutions, but are based on differences between British and Malayan society. The Constitution was drawn up with ethnic considerations explicitly in mind, and some of its clauses lay down basic rules on this. The Malay rights and privileges which are mentioned in the Constitution, or are based on these, are impressive. The privileged position of the Malays and the status of Malay as the national language are both of profound symbolic value. The well-known Article 153 provides that a proportion of positions in sections of the public service (including the military and the police) has to be filled by Malays. A similar provision applies to scholarships for Malays. The existing system of land reservations for Malays was continued. Anti-subversion powers of detention (Articles 149 and 150) also had a pro-Malay aspect, because they were directed mainly against those involved in the Emergency, very few of whom were Malays.

The Alliance Party: consociationalism

In the approach to independence, Malaya's main political problems could be easily seen (but less easily solved). To operate the system of government after independence, the main ethnic groups would have to work together, but the parties had been constructed along ethnic lines; the main exception, the Independence of Malaya Party (IMP), had been a noble aspiration but a disastrous failure. So what common ground did they have? The mere achievement of self-government would not, by itself, provide an answer. It was incorrect to regard self-government in a plural society as a way of bringing the races together. In plural societies self-government had to arise from a unity that was already felt.[14]

On the other hand, in the existing political and party context, unity could not be expected. One could only hope that ethnic parties, not being able to achieve unity except maybe in the very distant future, would work together towards it. The creation of the Alliance Party was fortuitous. In the 1952 Kuala Lumpur municipal elections, Dato Onn's IMP, which he formed after he failed to persuade UMNO to be multi-ethnic, seemed likely to be the winner. As a purely *ad hoc* tactic, the local leaders of UMNO and the MCA struck a deal. The two parties, intent on defeating the front-runner, decided not to put up candidates against each other. At that time there were many more Malay than Chinese electors, because not many Chinese had citizenship. So UMNO was allotted most of the seats. On the other hand, the better-off MCA contributed most of the money. The tactic was successful, and the election was won by nine seats to two. Success at this level for a limited time inspired the parties to repeat their arrangement at national level for an extended period. An Indian component was supplied when the MIC joined the Alliance in 1954. At the general election the next year, the party proved successful – it won fifty-one out of the fifty-two seats. The Alliance leader (and UMNO president), Tunku, became Chief Minister.

Although the formation of the Alliance was "accidental," some kind of inter-ethnic party would almost certainly have come into existence anyway. The British were anxious to hand over power to a party whose legitimacy would be recognized by substantial numbers of all major ethnic groups. It would not be enough just to win a numerical majority. The British had worked hard on this question by forming a Communities Liaison Committee to bring the ethnic groups together, paying particular attention to gaining Chinese participation in spite of the competing attraction of communism for some Chinese.

A realistic requirement for the successful formation of an Alliance-type party is that the leaders of the constituent parties should be prepared and able to work together, without losing the support of their followers. This the IMP had not managed to do, maybe because its structure did not contain an intermediate ethnic grouping to consolidate its appeal.

The Alliance-type system resembles the system of elite cooperation, described and analyzed by several authors,[15] often drawing on the experience of the smaller European democracies, and given the name of "consociationalism." The reliance of this kind of system upon elites has sometimes been seen as a disadvantage, because it appears not to be very democratic. On the other hand, the system seems to work quite well under certain conditions – moreover, some other quite successful political arrangements are not very democratic. The form it assumed in Malaysia differed from the "ideal" model in some respects. To take the writings of Arend Lijphart[16] as an example, his concept of consociationalism contains the principle of proportionality: the benefits received by the groups or parties in question should be roughly proportional to their numbers. The country should be relatively small, thus enabling leaders to get to know each other well and to communicate easily – this requirement is nowadays less difficult to meet, because of the increased ease of communication.

The Alliance system in Malaysia did not fulfill such "ideal" criteria. The country was indeed small, although it became larger with the addition of Sarawak and Sabah when Malaysia was formed in 1963. "Segmental isolation" of groups was desirable, in Lijphart's view, in order to lessen the prospects of ethnic competition. Initially it was quite marked in Malaya, but decreased with modernization. Proportionality was never a feature in Malaya/Malaysia, because of the existence of Malay privileges and, later, the pro-Malay features of the NEP. While Malay benefits have expanded, the main Chinese gain – concessions to make it easier for them to become citizens – was of decreasing significance over time. Again, according to Lijphart, consociationalism with several groups of not too disparate size is more viable than the situation in Malaya which contained only two main groups. Additionally, the Malay position had been buttressed by the British and had been included in the 1957 Constitution. Nor was another of Lijphart's recommendations present: a mutual veto was lacking. In one important respect, the working of the Alliance met the conditions for ideal consociationalism quite closely. Followers did indeed generally follow their leaders. When the Alliance candidate for a seat was chosen, for example, from the MCA, directions from UMNO leaders to UMNO followers that they should vote for that candidate were generally obeyed and they resisted any urges to vote for a Malay candidate from another party. Actually, some MCA leaders ran in seats with Malay majorities, and were returned principally by the votes of pro-UMNO electors.

The most outstanding breach of proportionality concerned the top levels of government. The Prime Minister will be a Malay for the foreseeable future, and so will be the Deputy Prime Minister. In the 1970s, the MCA made what seemed to be a reasonable proposal, that a second deputy would be appointed who would be Chinese. The request was refused, even when the person appointed would have been the eminent MCA leader, Tan Siew Sin. The other parties in the Alliance are represented in government and their views are listened to. But UMNO both proposes and carries through most major items of policy; it also disposes of proposals from other quarters with which it disagrees. As opposed to "ideal consociationalism," the arrangements adopted are best described as "hegemonic consociationalism."[17]

The 1957 Constitution: the bargain

Preliminary discussions about the provisions of the 1957 Constitution obviously had to include bargaining, particularly between UMNO and the MCA. It was never claimed that the bargain was completely embodied in writing although some of the bargain was made part of the Constitution.[18] Politicians sometimes have tried to summarize its terms very broadly. In essence, they think, it took the form of a trade-off between political and economic power. More specifically, the Chinese would acquire greater electoral strength, because more of them would become eligible to vote, through the more liberal requirements for becoming citizens. It also seemed to be assumed that the economic role of the Chinese under the British, significant except at the top levels of the economy, would persist. On the other hand, the Malays would keep their special position, through the retention of the rulers and their privileges on land and jobs enjoyed under British rule. What the Malays were to receive economically was never precisely stated, but the expectation was that their economic lot would be improved.

The actual terms of the bargain have become less relevant. Increasing numbers of Chinese, and other non-Malay electors, never brought non-Malay parties even close to a victory at a general election. Rural electors' votes had greater weight, which benefited the Malays. On the other hand, initially economic improvement came too slowly to match the Malays' expectations, so that when, after 1969, it was accelerated through the NEP, the effects were plainly visible – and to some non-Malays disturbing.

The formation of Malaysia: Singapore's exit

Malaya extended its territory and increased its population in 1963 when, together with two former British colonies, Sarawak and Sabah (the former British North Borneo), it formed Malaysia. Singapore joined as well, but political and economic tensions led to its peaceable expulsion in 1965. The motives behind the formation of Malaysia, announced by Tunku in May 1961, were complex but turned on compensating ethnically for the predominantly Chinese population of Singapore, perceived as a Southeast Asian Cuba. Indonesia reacted to an uprising in Brunei in December 1962 by adopting a policy of "Confrontation," which took the form of a series of small armed incursions, first into northern Brunei and then the Malayan mainland. The impulse to create Malaysia came from several directions. The British, who administered the two Borneo territories, wished to follow the current trend towards decolonization and give them independence. However, it feared that they might not be viable, even if they were combined. Together, their population amounted to little more than a million. They were not yet developed, economically, although they were rich in some natural resources, particularly timber. They were not very safe from the security point of view, especially given the contiguity of a radical Indonesia.

For some years, UMNO leaders had entertained the idea of joining Malaya with these two territories.[19] This possibility was supported by a report from its ambassador to Indonesia, Datuk Senu Abdul Rahman. In his opinion, the local inhabitants, excluding the Chinese, could be classified as "Malays," a somewhat simplistic view (later, when the territories were part of Malaysia, if anything went wrong in them, Tunku would jokingly put the blame on Senu). The third impulse favoring the creation of Malaysia came from Singapore. Successive chief ministers in Singapore had been advocating a Singapore–Malaya "merger." Economically, it made sense to revert to the "borderless" situation which existed under British rule until the Second World War.

Additionally, by 1961, a sense of urgency had been injected, because of political changes. Singapore Prime Minister Lee Kuan Yew raised the issue with the Tunku. Lee's People's Action Party (PAP) was in danger of being replaced as a government by a left-wing group which had seceded from it and formed the Barisan Sosialis party. Tunku's concern at the possibility of having a neighboring country that was governed by pro-Communists was compared to the contemporary United States' concern over Communist rule in nearby Cuba. There was another reason that the pieces in the Malaysia "jigsaw" now seemed to fit together. Without the inclusion of the Borneo states, a simple "merger" with Singapore would have upset the existing racial balance by adding more than a million Chinese to Malaya. But now, with the inclusion of the Borneo states, the impact would be neutralized by the inclusion of people most of whom, though not exactly "Malays," were certainly not Chinese.

After a series of negotiations, and a report by the "Cobbold Commission" established by the British government, which estimated that the degree of support that existed for Malaysia in the two territories was sufficient, the details of the proposal were worked out. As regards Singapore, among the most important details were the limited representation that it should have in the Malaysian Parliament, that it should have its own policies on education and labor, and the allocation of revenues between it and Peninsular Malaysia. In the Borneo states,[20] in addition to the financial aspects, the main issue was how to fit into the Malaysian framework two states that differed from Malaya in their stage of development and in their cultural heritage. The Malayan Constitution required very extensive amendments. The status of non-Muslim religions (more prominent in the new territories than in Malaya) received attention, as did how to designate natives who were not Muslims as beneficiaries from the special position accorded to Malays in Malaya. The advent of Malaysia prompted Indonesia to intensify Confrontation. Fortunately, partly as a consequence of unpublicized talks between Kuala Lumpur and Jakarta, and, later, the end of the Sukarno regime through internal upheaval, Confrontation was less actively pursued, and officially ended in 1966.

The formation of Malaysia did not proceed exactly as planned. Originally Brunei was to have been included. However, the small British protectorate, after negotiations, decided not to join, partly because it would not be left with as much of its large oil revenues as it wished to retain. It became independent eventually in 1984.

More seriously, Singapore remained in Malaysia for only two years.[21] Its government was discontented with the low share of customs duties it was receiving. Also, at a time when Singapore and Peninsular Malaysia were both industrializing, the latter resisted the formation of a common market between them because it feared the prospect of greater competition. On the other hand, the PAP took advantage of the "political common market" that had been created, by putting forward candidates in Peninsular Malaysia (not very many and with not much success) in the general election of 1964. The two issues were connected, because some Malayan Chinese business people, who would suffer from economic competition, felt challenged as MCA partners in the ruling Alliance coalition from the PAP's political foray.

Malay nationalists in UMNO, sometimes labeled as "ultras," made inflammatory speeches against Singapore and its government, and ethnic riots broke out in Singapore later in 1964. The Tunku reviewed the possible options when he was recovering from a particularly painful attack of shingles, and decided that separation was the only solution. As he remarked later, without separation there would have been "blue murder." Singapore separated in August 1965.[22] In spite of its limited natural resources, Singapore went on to prosper as an independent state. However, the disputes that arose between the two countries from time to time were exacerbated by memories of their previous tempestuous relationship.

The addition of the Borneo states did not make the task of governing the country much more onerous. Electoral consequences, of course, had to be taken into account, and were rather unpredictable, because of changing party membership and realignments in both Sabah and Sarawak. However, generally, the Prime Minister and his ministers gave the states close attention only when a political crisis arose, which seldom happened.

1969 and its aftermath

The crushing Alliance victory at the 1955 elections was not repeatable. The Alliance percentages of votes and seats fell at the 1959 election, but recovered in 1964 – perhaps because of the unifying effect of the threat from Indonesian Confrontation. However, in 1969 the Alliance secured only 48 percent of the votes and 66 percent of the seats (not including the Sarawak and Sabah elections, which had been postponed because of the "May 13" riots in Kuala Lumpur, described below). [23]

The drop of about 10 percent in the Alliance vote applied to both its Malay and non-Malay components, although the drop in seats was higher for non-Malays. The reduced Alliance majority was unexpected.

The occurrence of three minor racial "incidents" in various areas of Malaysia during the mid-1960s did not suggest that major ethnic riots were in prospect. Nevertheless, the election campaign was heated, and ethnicity and personalities were prominent topics. The result was not a loss of power by the Alliance, but, rather, a reduction in its margin of victory. Yet the public response was curious. The Alliance "winners" were depressed. The MCA, dejected after its losses, decided, perhaps too subtly, to "educate" the Chinese electors by withdrawing its representatives from the cabinet. The opposition Democratic Action Party (DAP) losers (the DAP was the successor party to the PAP in Malaysia) were elated, because they believed they had made a substantial breakthrough. The DAP and the Penang-based, mainly Chinese, Gerakan Rakyat Malaysia party (Gerakan) held "victory" processions, and the militant UMNO Selangor Menteri Besar, Datuk Harun Idris, launched a massive counter-procession.

The riots were limited almost entirely to Kuala Lumpur and its environs. Officially, 196 deaths occurred over a period of two and a half weeks, which may be an understatement. The ratio of non-Malay deaths to Malay deaths was about six to one. There were, officially, 409 injured.[24] The riots made a deep and saddening impression, and fear of making things worse had strange and sometimes inhibiting effects on the actions of some parties. The MCA reversed its earlier decision to withdraw from the cabinet for the sake of stability. The Gerakan party refused to join anti-Alliance groups which might have been able to form successful governing coalitions in Perak and Selangor, because the Malays in these three states were counting on the Alliance forming governments there, and might, in their frustration, have resorted to violence.

Apart from the epithets and abuse that accompanied the 1969 campaign and its aftermath, there were deeper criticisms of the status quo from both major ethnic groups. Malay criticisms, which the government took more seriously, were voiced by Deputy Prime Minister Razak and others, who believed that the Malays' economic grievances had not been sufficiently addressed.

Mahathir intervenes

Mahathir, elected to Parliament in 1964, lost his seat in 1969, but was already recognized as a coming man in UMNO, because of his ability and forcefulness.

To students of how power is acquired, as opposed to researchers on the causes of ethnic violence, a well-publicized letter from Mahathir to Tunku about the 1969 riots was perhaps more significant than the riots themselves. It might well have been entitled "J'accuse!" The letter was ostensibly confidential, but, according to Tunku, was circulated by the thousands.[25] It was in fact an open letter. Why should Mahathir want it not to be? It made two main points. It complained that the Tunku was out of touch with the opinions of most Malays, who were angry because the government had been weak in dealing with the Chinese and the Indians. Tunku, it claimed, had also lost the trust of the senior civil service, army, and police personnel, and he should resign as leader of UMNO.[26]

The letter originated from the question – should the MCA members of the cabinet who left it after the riots be readmitted or not? Mahathir made a statement on this, to which the Tunku replied, and the well-known Mahathir letter was in response to that reply. Mahathir's letter was doubly offensive, because, in addition to its anti-Tunku contents, the writer was from Kedah, the same state as the Tunku (the Prime Minister), and where the Sultan was Tunku's close relative.

Was Mahathir's action the product of passion or deliberation?[27] Part of the vehemence may have been engendered by Mahathir's loss of his seat at the elections and his feeling that he had received all, or nearly all, the Chinese vote in 1964, while in 1969 he won only about half. He attributed this drop to MCA opposition in 1969 because he had been chairman of FIMA (Food Industries of Malaysia), a government corporation, which had allegedly caused damage to certain Chinese business interests.[28]

What is not in dispute is that the letter acquired the status of an unimpeachable testimonial to Mahathir's credentials as a Malay nationalist. It reached many Malays, including university students, who were sympathetic to Malay nationalism and were eager to find a forthright exponent of their views.

The allegations against Tunku were repeated, though in a more moderate form, at the beginning of *The Malay Dilemma*,[29] written several months later, published in Singapore and banned in Malaysia – but not very effectively. The allegations of Tunku's appeasement of the Chinese and the failings of his government in general are repeated, but passion has been tempered with deliberation. Most of the book, with the exception of some excursions into "social Darwinism," constitute a serious inquiry into why the Malays were not economically better off. The failings of the Malays in conducting business are clinically dissected and the other side of the coin, the "Chinese dilemma" in Malaya, is fairly presented. Khoo Boh Teik's analysis of the book and of Mahathir's other writings could hardly be improved upon.[30]

Policy changes after May 1969

Major changes in government policy following the riots were in accordance with the Malay criticisms just summarized. Long-term changes embodied in the NEP are dealt with later (pp. 51–5). Apart from economic matters, the emphasis was on restoring law and order and clamping down on dissent. Some arrests were made. A State of Emergency was declared and an Emergency (Essential Powers) Ordinance was promulgated, delegating authority (usually exercised by the cabinet in the name of the Agung) to a director of operations, the Deputy Prime Minister, Razak. He was assisted by a National Operations Council (NOC), composed not only of politicians but also including civil servants and members of the military and the police. The cabinet remained; its functions overlapped with those of the NOC, but coordination was achieved through Razak's membership of both and by his daily reports on NOC activities to the Tunku. Other organizations were set up, including a non-elected partial substitute for the now suspended Parliament – the National Consultative Council (NCC), containing some representation from the Opposition, and a Department of National Unity, which produced a "National Ideology," the *Rukunegara*. The latter listed a number of unobjectionable precepts, such as promoting national unity, a just society, etc. The DAP leader, Lim Kit Siang, commented that few would disagree with them, just as few would disagree with the Ten Commandments.[31] Before Parliament met once again (in February 1971) some new restrictions on free speech were imposed. In Parliament itself, the use of words that were likely to promote feelings of ill will, etc., between the races was ruled out. (An Opposition member was said to have commented that members must now avoid four-letter words, and had to find equivalents consisting of three or five letters.)

Generally, the definition of sedition was enlarged, and it became a "seditious tendency" to question the rights and privileges of the rulers or of the Malays, including the reservation of positions or permits for the latter (Article 153 of the Constitution). The scope of that article was extended to apply also to the provision of places in educational institutions for Malays. The events of May 1969 and the provisions enacted to prevent their repetition and to remove some of their underlying causes, led to a basic change in the nature of the political system – as well as of the economic system through the NEP. There were other concessions to Malay sentiment. The implementation of the rules governing the acquisition of citizenship was tightened. A change in the use of languages used in English-medium secondary schools was announced; English would be replaced by Malay over a period of years.

As head of the NOC, Razak gradually took over power from the Tunku, although he sedulously observed constitutional niceties and showed respect for the Tunku, who resigned as Prime Minister in September 1971, and whom he then succeeded. Tunku's departure left the way open for the readmission of Mahathir to UMNO, with the backing of Razak, and for his subsequent rise in the party and the government.

The formation of the Barisan Nasional

Soon after the 1969 riots, Razak and a small group around him, consisting of politicians and civil servants (but not containing Mahathir), set their minds to devising policies that would supplement the NEP. Principally, they focussed on remodelling the party system so as to coopt other parties into an enlarged Alliance, thus removing some sources of opposition and enhancing national unity. To use a word often employed by Razak, he wished to minimize the amount of "politicking" in the system. The Barisan Nasional (National Front),[32] first mentioned in public in August 1972, was not formed officially until June 1974. It was originally presented as a "concept," but was realized, step by step, through arrangements with particular opposition parties. The main "hold-out" was the DAP, which had emerged as the only substantial non-Malay party. The first entrant was the Sarawak United People's Party (SUPP) which at one time had a left-wing reputation, but later became increasingly pragmatic. It entered the evolving Barisan in 1971 through a coalition with the Sarawak Alliance. Several parties on the mainland followed suit, including Gerakan based on Penang, and the PPP (People's Progressive Party), concentrated around Ipoh, Perak. The most important party to join was PAS, which held power in the state of Kelantan. This was a triumph for Razak, because PAS had always been a threat, partly because it was UMNO's main rival for the Malay vote, and also because of its strength, and potential for expansion, in the north of Malaya. The reasons that such parties were willing to join the Barisan were various, and sometimes there was more than one incentive. A powerful reason was that a party in the Barisan could qualify to receive patronage from the federal government, including paid membership on boards, commissions, etc. Other motives varied. Gerakan was plagued by internal dissension and its leaders needed federal support in order to contain it. The PPP wished to ensure that it maintained control of the Ipoh municipal council. PAS was attracted by the prospect of affirming Malay unity after the 1969 riots, and of cooperating to make the NEP a success.

In return, the Barisan recruited increased support for the implementation of its national policies, and strengthened its ability to obtain the two-thirds vote required for the enactment of changes in the Constitution. Most of the arrangements mentioned above were originally temporary, just as, at first, the Alliance agreement had been. However, as in that arrangement, entry into the Barisan usually was permanent. The exception was PAS, which left, after a party split, in 1977.

Razak once said that the Barisan was not much different from the Alliance, only larger. However, its operation was not quite the same. In the Alliance there were only three member parties, each based on an ethnic component. But, in the Barisan, some parties have more than one ethnic group supporting them, while an ethnic group may spread its support beyond one single party. This made it possible for party members to move to another party and still remain in the Barisan. Moreover, there was a difference in the role of the party leader. In the

Alliance it was less formal and more personal than in the Barisan. In the latter, the leader is less accessible, and can deal with leaders of the constituent parties on a one-to-one basis. If so inclined, he can play one off against another. In this respect, the power of prime ministers (including Mahathir) has grown appreciably.

How UMNO works: how Mahathir became Prime Minister

Mahathir's attack on Tunku in 1969 resulted in the latter's fall, though at the cost of Mahathir's sustaining a brief check to his own career. His rise to be UMNO president and Prime Minister in 1981 may be attributed to several factors. His rebellion effectively removed Tunku from power; Mahathir turned out to be not just a brave rebel, but also a *successful* one. To skeptics, in retrospect the end perhaps justified the means. Second, his behavior after readmission was exemplary. His combativeness had apparently been tempered. Also, he performed ably in managing successively two difficult portfolios, Education (often regarded as a necessary position to have held in order to qualify as a Prime Minister) and Trade and Industry. In the latter he demonstrated his skills by his management of the NEP. The third factor was that the succession process, in which two prime ministers, Razak and Hussein, played a major role, turned out to be unexpectedly favorable to his chances of advancement.

The General Assembly of UMNO meets every year, but votes for its office-holders every third year. (Until 1987, elections were held biennially; among other things, supporters of the change claimed that it would reduce "politicking.") There is no direct correspondence between prime ministerial appointments to the government and popularity as measured by voting in the General Assembly.

A few words about UMNO's structure may be in order. At the base are party branches, and, above them, divisions. The delegates who attend the annual conferences are chosen by divisions, and divisional chairmen are important people, as is indicated by the amount of money they can command in exchange for delivering votes. At the top of the structure, there is the president and the supreme council, which may make decisions overriding the decisions of all other UMNO bodies. Below that, there are the deputy president and five vice-presidents, three of them elected by the General Assembly. The other two are, *ex officio*, the heads of the Women's (Wanita) and Youth wings of the party, elected by their own separate assemblies. The supreme council, which has twenty elected members, also contains vice-presidents (*ex officio*) and several members appointed by the president. The party–government link is embodied in the president also being Prime Minister and the deputy-president being Deputy Prime Minister. No UMNO election has ever resulted in the president/Prime Minister being defeated, although the 1987 election was close.

The delegates to the General Assembly include many influential persons, notably ministers and Menteris Besar (or chief ministers in states without a ruler). The composition of the delegates has changed considerably over the past forty years. Previously, about half were teachers, but by early 1987 these amounted to only about a fifth. Almost a quarter were from the civil service. Business people now constitute about 30 percent. Two "waves" of business people have been identified, one that arrived before the NEP had started to take effect, before, say, the mid-1970s, and a later contingent, which brought to politics the aggressiveness of the business world.[33] This group is also prominent in UMNO Youth, already well known for its aggressive defense of Malay rights. The number of graduates who are delegates is also rising rapidly.

Another change is that delegates have shown less deference to authority than formerly, and there has been more disposition to be critical.[34]

An important procedural change occurred in 1975. Voting was made secret, which diminished the power of a Menteri Besar to impose a "block vote" on the delegates from his state and to verify that his wishes had been carried out. However, a Menteri Besar's influence still carries weight, and it is widely believed that, in order to become a vice-president, it is advisable to have the support of at least one Menteri Besar.

Money politics in UMNO

As deference has declined, the expenditure of money has soared. A distressing aspect of UMNO politics has been the prevalence of "money politics," more guardedly referred to as "lobbying," and more blatantly known as "vote-buying." "We've put an end to vote-buying in UMNO"[35] was the confident assertion of the head of a 1995 UMNO committee appointed to look into this question. Actually, the practice has been going on for years. Twenty years previously, the Tunku deplored the fact that lobbying was more common than in his day, adding, characteristically, that he didn't remember that there had been such a fuss made then about UMNO elections.[36] In the mid-1980s, Mahathir was lamenting the evils of money politics, saying that, if it continued, UMNO would no longer be a national party but a rich man's club.[37] Sizeable payments had gone far beyond the originally more common provision of free lunches. The success of the NEP in enriching some Malays was shown by the fact that in the mid-1980s, for the first time, the UMNO elections attracted more money from Malays than from Chinese.[38]

A major effect of the spread of money politics must be to increase the chances of the incumbents in UMNO's top offices being re-elected. In conjunction with the new rules giving greater security to incumbents in the two top offices (p. 154) and the funds available to them from UMNO's vast reserves, incumbents, unless blocked by other incumbents at a higher level, are almost unbeatable.

The fact that certain members win top UMNO posts at party elections strengthens the chances that they will also be appointed to high *governmental* positions. However, the flow of influence does not move only from the UMNO General Assembly to government. The Prime Minister/UMNO president has some discretion about government appointments, as will be seen from the last three paragraphs of this chapter. (Indeed his powers *vis-à-vis* the Assembly have grown ever since the establishment of UMNO. Some UMNO positions became appointed instead of elected.)[39] Moreover, as president, the Prime Minister is in a strong position to give the General Assembly convincing reasons that it should support candidates for office recommended by him. The classic example occurred at the 1975 General Assembly, which is worth looking at in some detail. The ultimate beneficiary, as it happened, was Mahathir, who emerged as one of three strong candidates for the presidency after the president and the deputy-president, both in bad health, would pass from the political scene.

Since UMNO's foundation, there had been hardly any question about the accession to the prime ministership. Razak's appointment of Ismail as Deputy, who unfortunately died in 1973, was uncontroversial, as was that of his next appointment, Hussein. However, by 1975 there was clearly a problem. Both Razak and Hussein were in bad health, although only Hussein's illness was then widely known. At the 1975 General Assembly, Razak and Hussein decided to express their views on the succession. The crucial election was for the three posts of vice-president, because the winners would constitute the obvious "pool" from which the successor to Hussein – or to Razak, if Hussein pre-deceased him – would be drawn. There were four "serious" candidates for the three posts. Alphabetically, they were: Ghafar Baba, senior vice-president, ex-Chief Minister of Malacca, with the disadvantage of not being fully proficient in English; Harun, ex-Menteri Besar of Selangor, a militant in 1969, and under suspicion of implication in corruption in Bank Rakyat; Mahathir, who had won the highest vote in the UMNO supreme council elections of 1972; and Razaleigh, currently a vice-president, a prince of the Royal House of Kelantan, a prime favorite of Razak's, and previously head of Pernas, a huge state trading organization.

Razak's purpose was to eliminate Harun from the running. His speech was carefully prepared, but some off-the-cuff remarks were inserted. He proceeded by saying that honesty should be an indispensable condition to qualify for election. He made references, understandable by those familiar with Malay folklore, to certain animals with evil traits, which should be shunned. He praised the achievements of all four major candidates, but his order of preference was clear. (Hussein's speech, among other things, warned his listeners against any modern "Robin Hood.") What effect these speeches had on the results is not known, but Razak's speech was acclaimed as a triumph. The results were: Ghafar, 838; Razaleigh, 642; Mahathir, 474; Harun, 427.

When Razak died in early 1976, Hussein, his successor, had already suffered a stroke in the previous year, and had not fully recovered, even after heart surgery, in 1981. He took time to nominate his deputy. The timing had to fit in with the requirements of his illness and his UMNO duties. Apparently, in addition to considering the three vice-presidents, he also gave some thought to Tan Sri Ghazali Shafie, an incumbent minister. After he selected from among Ghafar, Mahathir, and Razaleigh, he revealed that he had lost count of the number of times he had changed his order of preference, and that he had made his final decision only the night before the announcement. His predicament was under-standable. Choice of any of the three could be defended; equally it could be attacked. Ghafar was the senior vice-president, but did not project an image of modernity. Razaleigh, in spite of his political and administrative achievements, could be considered too young and was unmarried. Mahathir was the least senior, but had proved his administrative ability and also his dedication to the defense of the Malays. He was also a medical doctor. Mahathir was the final choice.

Comments on Hussein's decision were largely favorable, although, predictably, there were a few "no comments." The MCA had reservations, which was understandable in view of Mahathir's lack of sympathy for the party in 1969. However, it concluded that, as the leader of a nation and not just the Malays, he would be expected to act accordingly.[40] Mahathir himself said he was surprised by the choice, adding, perhaps unnecessarily, that he would not hesitate to express his opinions.[41] Hussein said that he did not expect 100 percent approval of his choice.[42] A later comment, denied by some, was that Hussein hoped he had made the right choice, but afterwards had said that he was sorry. Tunku's version is that Hussein visited him in 1981, soon after Mahathir became Prime Minister, sat for about twenty minutes without saying anything and then left.[43] In spite of Mahathir's qualifications for the post and some deficiencies on the part of the other contenders, many things could have happened to block his path to the prime ministership. Razak could have lived longer (and the longer he survived, the less Razaleigh's youth would have counted against him); Tun Dr. Ismail (Razak's first Deputy Prime Minister) could have lived longer; Hussein could have lived longer – and acquired more information on which to base his decision; Hussein could have died earlier, in which event the choice might have been the senior, Ghafar. Finally, by his own account, Hussein's near-decisions might have ceased their rotation at a different point – possibly to Mahathir's disadvantage.

2 Mahathir's assertion of executive power

Mahathir became Prime Minister in 1981. During his first year or so in power he strove to impress his personality, and priorities for governing, on his colleagues, the civil service, and the country generally. He wanted to run a "clean, efficient and trustworthy government", in the words of the Barisan Nasional election manifesto of 1982. He made ministers and civil servants wear name-tags, insisted on the observance of office hours, and stressed urgency, particularly in conveying information. Hard work and discipline were to be the order of the day. Government employees were not workaholics, but they ought to be.[1]

Concerning government policy, two main themes were stated and pursued. He made known his position on the role of Islam, which was a continuing theme (discussed in Chapter 4). The second theme (or, rather, slogan, as he himself suggested), was a more elusive concept which taxed the comprehension of some of his colleagues. As stated in Chapter 3 (pp. 55–6), it seemed to combine an emphasis on instilling in Malaysians some desirable economic values and practices current in Japan and South Korea, with increasing Malaysia's economic transactions with such countries. Khoo Boo Teik has discerned some aspects of "liberalism" in this early period of Mahathir's rule,[2] but they seem to have been substantially circumscribed.[3]

From about 1983 to 1990, Mahathir was engaged in three great contests for power. The first, against the Agung and the states rulers, was intended to make their powers more strictly defined and consequently more predictable. It did not end in a complete victory for Mahathir and the government, but some of the "magic of monarchy" was tarnished. The second was a struggle for the control of UMNO, partly explainable in terms of supply and demand. There were no longer sufficient rewards, in the form of power or money, to satisfy the growing number of educated Malays whose expectations had been raised by the operation of the NEP, particularly as the economic recession of the mid-1980s had decreased the supply of these rewards. Combined with personality differences and the rise of factions in UMNO, this led to a split followed by the creation of a new Malay party which contested the general election of 1990 against Mahathir and his adherents, who had successfully retained control of the UMNO name, as "UMNO Baru".

This conflict reached its climax in 1987, an *annus horribilis* for Mahathir. In order to retain power he engaged in a third contest – against the judiciary (pp. 46–9). He had Malaysia's highest judge and several of his colleagues dismissed, thus humbling and subordinating the judiciary. Concurrently, human rights suffered, most notably by arrests in 1987, and Mahathir's rule became increasingly authoritarian. By the 1990 election, which Mahathir won with relative ease,[4] the political scene was transformed. Three possible rival centers of power – the Agung and the rulers, his opponents in UMNO, and the judiciary – no longer presented a serious threat to his dominance. It is hard now to imagine the Malaysian political landscape without him. Outside Malaysia, age was endowing him with the familiarity and acceptability of Suharto or Lee Kuan Yew. He did even better at the 1995 election.[5] His mind then had time to meditate on broader problems than outmaneuvering opponents, although these were dealt with when necessary. He became more and more concerned about the plight of the relatively non-industrialized "South," and with visions of how Malaysia could become a less ethnically divided society. There were few signs of his relinquishing power, even though he had announced that Anwar Ibrahim would be his successor.

The constitutional crisis: UMNO versus the Agung and the rulers

Beyond ceremonial duties and symbolic privileges, the Malaysian Constitution provides the monarch with certain "powers." All bills passed by Parliament require royal assent (Article 66) before they can be gazetted as laws. Further, there are certain "entrenched" articles of the Constitution, which require the Agung's (and the Conference of Rulers') consent rather than assent. The Agung has discretionary power in the appointment of a Prime Minister, in the withholding of consent to a request for the dissolution of Parliament, and has a supposedly non-discretionary power in the declaration of a state of emergency (Article 150). For these political functions, the Constitution adds the phrase "upon the advice of the cabinet."

The problem with a "constitutional monarchy" is apparent in the title, which seems to embody a contradiction in terms. How can a monarch who rules, be bound by the will of the people? Likewise, how can the state preserve the prestige and important symbolic role of the monarch without also according him some genuine political power? In fact, while the monarch appears to exercise political power – in signifying royal assent to bills, making appointments, and so on – he is "above" politics and exercises no constitutional discretion. The rules (whether established by precedent or written) require that the monarch fulfill these functions on the "advice" of the elected government. However, there are two problems with this formulation. Does accepting "advice" really mean that, in effect, power rests not with him but with the elected government? Also, a situation might occur where he could be expected to act on his own discretion. For example, in the unlikely event of the Barisan Nasional's losing its absolute majority in Parliament after an election, and a three-party system arising, the monarch might play a role in the formation of a government. Where these rules are well understood, where the personalities involved do not clash, and where the relationship between the monarch and the governmental elite is based on trust and cooperation, the system works well. Where these conditions are not met, trouble is likely.

The Constitution assumes, but nowhere states, that the monarch *must* accept advice (except possibly on a few occasions) and *must not* withhold royal assent. Further, the Constitution seems especially open to different interpretations concerning emergency powers, saying, ambiguously, that the Agung must be satisfied that "a grave emergency exists...." Finally, the Constitution offers no clue as to how the government could overcome an impasse if the Agung did not accept advice or acted unilaterally. It is just "not done". But what if it *is* done? The courts are not empowered to rule on the constitutionality of an emergency declaration, and can rule only on parliamentary laws – not bills that have not received the royal assent.

The smooth functioning of this system in the past was due in part to the fact that the early prime ministers were from the aristocracy and their personal relations with the rulers were such that they could consult directly and as equals. In the early 1980s, Malaysian political leaders at the time (including Mahathir and his deputy, Musa) were almost all commoners, thus making easy rapport with royalty less likely than in previous years. Absence of friction was also due to the Agungs' accepting a "narrow" interpretation of their role and not challenging the government.

The problem

The immediate problem in mid-1983, from the government's perspective, was that at the forthcoming election of a new Agung in February 1984, the rulers next in line were from Perak and Johor – the former was then senior. They were considered "independent-minded." Both had records of interfering in state politics to the extent of exceeding their constitutional roles, and through obstructive tactics each had forced out the respective Menteris Besar of their states. (Other states had similar, but less serious, problems.)[6] These acts resulted in minor crises which did not become major, because the government gave in – highlighting the Malay quandary of how to say "no" effectively to a ruler. Further, the Sultan of Perak in 1982 and 1983, and the Sultan of Johor in 1983, clashed with the federal government over the date for the end of the fasting month of Ramadan, thus causing confusion and consternation to Malays and disrupting holiday timings. Finally, the Sultan of Johor had had a series of problems with the law in his youth and had been convicted on charges of causing hurt, for which he was fined, and on the charge of culpable homicide – he was pardoned by his father, the Sultan. He was removed as heir to the Johor throne in 1961 and was reinstated only in 1981, when his father, aged 86, was on his deathbed. "Understandings" might work quite well with rulers who were predictable, but either of those would be a risky choice. The Sultan of Johor inspired fear. He invited a government minister, along with his wife and young child, for lunch at the palace. The minister accepted the invitation for his wife and himself, but was afraid to put the child at risk.[7]

The "constitutional crisis" was precipitated by reports, received by Mahathir, that the Sultan of Johor stated at a gathering that when he was elected Agung he would unilaterally declare a state of emergency, and, with the aid of the army, throw out all the politicians.[8] Compounding this were stories that the Sultan was close to certain key military men, and that the army chief, General Tan Sri Mohd. Zain Hashim, had criticized Mahathir's approach and had questioned where the army's loyalty rested.[9]

The government saw trouble ahead and decided to take immediate action to close constitutional loopholes before the election of the next Agung.

The attempted solution

Apparently with the incumbent Agung's agreement, at least concerning Article 66, the Constitution (Amendment) Bill of 1983 went before Parliament on August 1, and quickly passed both houses. Hoping to avoid public debate on the issue, which might alarm the population, especially the Malays, the Bill's swift transit through Parliament was accompanied by a domestic press blackout. The Bill amended Article 64 to read that, if such bills were not assented to within fifteen days of being presented for assent, the Agung should be deemed to have given his assent, and the Bill would become law. Changes to emergency powers gave the Prime Minister alone the right to declare an emergency. In accordance with the Eight Schedule, provisions corresponding to the above would be inserted in the state constitutions.[10]

The Agung was upset when the Bill was presented to him because, apparently, he had not been briefed about the Eighth Schedule which provided that the amendment would also apply to the states. He consulted the rulers, and they told him not to give assent to the Bill.[11] He complied, and also withheld assent from two other important bills. The rulers felt insulted, and were united in their opposition, although some took a harder line than others. The very situation that the amendments had been designed to prevent, was occurring; indeed they had actually helped to bring it about. The government used intermediaries to try to overcome the impasse, but its efforts failed. Mahathir met with a frosty reception at the Conference of Rulers in October 1983, as well as having his proposals rejected. The government now perceived that a genuine crisis existed.

The crisis: strategies and alignments

The public was not aware that anything was seriously amiss until former UMNO minister Datuk Senu Abdul Rahman's "Open Letter" to the Prime Minister on October 3, 1983, opposing the amendments, was widely circulated in Malay and English. This was followed by a press report confirming that the

Amendment Bill was still awaiting royal assent. The reason, the report implied, was that the Agung was indisposed following a heart attack. After this, rumours were rife, for example that Mahathir had been assassinated, or that Malaysia would be turned into a republic.[12]

By the end of October the government had decided that, since the news was out and rumors were frightening people, it should begin a newspaper campaign to explain the government's position. There was a series of restrained and learned articles explaining the Constitution and the role of a constitutional monarch. Support also came from various sections of UMNO. The Menteris Besar urged the rulers to accept the Bill, despite the fact that this put them in very awkward and delicate positions in trying to govern their respective states.

The government then offered a compromise formula to the rulers, who agreed to consider it at their November 20, 1983 meeting. However, they swiftly rejected the new proposals, apparently to the shock and surprise of UMNO leaders, who thought the formula would resolve the crisis. At this point, the government hardened its position. The cabinet gave a unanimous mandate to the Prime Minister to take whatever steps were necessary to resolve the crisis. In the last week of November the government started a campaign to demonstrate the amount of public support it enjoyed, and to apply pressure. The first mass rally was held in Alor Setar, Kedah, where Mahathir told about fifty thousand people that he would not quit, and that he did not wish to abolish the monarchy but just wanted to make sure that the rights of the people were not violated. Further rallies were held throughout the country, featuring various UMNO ministers. At these rallies, listeners were reminded that in opposing the Malayan Union, UMNO had been more active than the rulers. During the rallies, the rulers were sometimes referred to in unflattering terms – a great shock to them after twenty-five years of being treated as sacrosanct. Exposés were presented of their extravagant lifestyles, their lavish expenditures on palace renovations and royal weddings, and, on the part of some, unbecoming personal conduct. Further, it was found out that the government was compiling dossiers on the rulers, and a year-long TV Malaysia program on the Constitution and the monarchy was being prepared. Finally, a not-too-veiled threat was conveyed. UMNO Youth passed a resolution asking the government to go ahead and gazette the bills – regardless of the royal assent. The rulers were angry, but could not think how to fight back effectively. They had been stunned by the wide support given to the government, as shown by the success of its rallies, and by the heavy press backing it received. They did, however, hold some rallies, which were better attended than press reports indicated.

Support among the Malays was almost evenly split, generally following traditional–modern and rural–urban divisions. UMNO was for the amendments in approximately 60:40 proportions. The split seemed to be roughly between politicians who aspired to lead a new politico-economic power elite, and older-style political figures, some with aristocratic connections, and their clients. One might have expected that, since the rulers and the Agung were symbols of "Malayness," the Chinese would feel little loyalty to them. Paradoxically, they were quite pro-royalty,[13] because they did not really trust Malay politicians. Indeed they viewed the Agung and the rulers as protectors of their vital interests. Further, Chinese business people believed that they understood the rulers and knew how to work with them. This feeling was reciprocated. Chinese business people quite often were mentioned in the honors lists of state rulers. Despite these feelings on the part of many non-Malays, however, they did not make a display of pro-ruler sentiments during the crisis. It was not deemed wise to offend the government, and non-Malays tended to view the debate as they view Islam – as a subject that is exclusively "Malay," which it is politic to stay away from.

The DAP, mainly a Chinese-supported party, opposed the amendments, both because they put emergency powers in the hands of the Prime Minister, and also because the amendments would actually increase the power of the Agung beyond what was proper for a constitutional monarch. He could then have functioned as a third house in the legislative process through his ability to delay legislation.

In the first week of December 1983, Mahathir reiterated that the government was willing to compromise, although it could not concede basic principles.[14] If no settlement were reached, his offer would be withdrawn. After Mahathir had rejected a counter-offer from the rulers, by a majority, they accepted his latest version for the amending legislation.

Resolution

The Deputy Agung signed the Constitution (Amendment) Bill 1983 and it was gazetted. The nation breathed a sigh of relief and the government elites seemed jubilant. At a rally in Malacca, Mahathir told the crowd of eighty thousand that the "feudal system was over."[15] However, some of the rulers were unhappy, and the Sultan of Johor told the press that UMNO was against the rulers. On December 20, 1983, the Chief of the Army, General Tan Sri Mohd. Zain Hashim, opted for early retirement in order to go into business. A wider "house-cleaning" also occurred, and there were about 500 dismissals and early retirements. The timing of this army shake-up could have been coincidental, or it could have been directed at weakening "religious extremism," or in order to improve efficiency. It might also have been made because, rightly or wrongly, the possibility of a conspiracy had existed.

On January 9, 1984, Parliament reconvened and passed the Constitution (Amendment) Bill 1984 in six hours by a margin of 141 votes to 10 (all DAP). It then passed the Senate and received the royal assent. The new act had the effect of repealing the 1983 amendments with respect to Article 150 and the Eighth Schedule. It also further amended Article 66. The Agung would have thirty days to assent to non-money bills or return the Bill to Parliament, stating his objections. Any Bill reconsidered and approved again in Parliament would automatically become law after another thirty days, if not given the royal assent. There were special provisions for money bills. Concerning the Eighth Schedule,

Mahathir said that he had a verbal understanding with the rulers that they would not withhold assent to state bills without reasonable cause. Regarding Article 150, on emergency powers, Mahathir said that there was no need for a verbal undertaking from the rulers, as they understood the implications of the original provision. It is believed that the rulers reassured him that, if an Agung tried unilaterally to declare an emergency, the rulers would remove him from office.[16] It is curious that a dispute that had occurred in order to clarify understandings was resolved, apparently quite happily, by leaving some of them in a state of imprecision.

While everyone was relieved that the crisis was over, some, including UMNO Youth, were critical, believing that the government had conceded too much.

The election of the new Agung: continuing irritants

Ten days before the date for the election of the new Agung, the odds-on favorite, the Sultan of Perak, died of a heart attack. He was succeeded on February 3 by Raja Azlan Shah, the Lord President of the Federal Court. Speculation was current that the rulers might "play safe" and appoint him Agung, thus bypassing the Sultan of Johor. He was an expert on constitutional law, had been an intermediary during the recent crisis, and his relations with the government elite were cordial. However, the Conference of Rulers chose the Sultan of Johor. Perhaps significantly, the customary congratulations were absent. Some sought to explain the rulers' choice as expressing their anger and their desire to have a "strong" Agung to protect their own position.

Quite soon, minor instances of eccentricity were evident. Photographs of the Prime Minister and Deputy Prime Minister were removed from government offices and buildings in Johor, and, on royal instructions, the national flag was removed during the Sultan's tour of Johor. There was a "war of wills" over his desire to wear a military uniform instead of the traditional costume for his official installation. The government did not like the image conveyed by a military uniform. However, the new Agung preferred it, especially the uniform of colonel-in-chief of his (Johor) private army, complete with sidearm, rather than Western dress or the Agung's formal dress, which he regarded as a "Kedah–Siamese" outfit – the Tunku had helped to design it. Consequently, for months after he began his duties, the official photographs of the Agung and his consort in government buildings, hotels, etc., remained those of their predecessors. However, on November 14, 1984 he was officially installed in the traditional dress of the Agung.

By far the most sensational and talked-about clash was the so-called "mosque incident." The Agung had not forgiven the Deputy Prime Minister, Musa Hitam, a Johor subject, for his remarks in speeches made during the constitutional crisis, which the Agung regarded as disloyal. The Agung would not grant an audience to Musa, and he did not want him to be at the airbase when he was first received by the federal government (the Prime Minister prevailed upon the Agung and the compromise was that Musa was at the airbase but not in the front where he should have been). At the end of June 1984, in the national mosque after Hari Raya (end of fasting month) prayers, the Agung, omitting the title of "Datuk", asked Musa to stand up (all others were kneeling) and make a public apology. Musa kissed the Agung's hand and apologized, and the congregation broke out in applause. TV Malaysia cut off its broadcast, but Radio Malaysia covered the entire incident live. Most newspapers did not report the event until it was reported in the *Star*.[17]

While some Malays applauded the Agung's actions, other Malays were appalled by it (especially since it took place in the mosque, which was apparently unprecedented), and many thought that Musa handled the confrontation with considerable grace. Some people interviewed just after the event believed that the Agung's motive was a conciliatory one, whereas others believed that it was confrontational and meant to put Musa "in his place." But all agree that, however regrettable, the incident helped the government get over a hurdle in that it made a working relationship between the Agung and Musa possible.

Fallout from the crisis

The crisis divided UMNO and the Malay community. Politically, the fallout had some effect on the UMNO General Assembly 1984 elections. It also influenced relations between some Menteris Besar and their respective rulers. There were also some new, but deeply etched, political alignments. For instance, it was clear that the Agung and the rulers were now bitterly opposed to Musa, Anwar, and some other UMNO leaders. There were other, related, factors, which played a part in the UMNO General Assembly elections of May 1984. The 1984 voting could be explained nearly as well in terms of "generational differences." In the most important contest in the UMNO 1984 election, Musa once again defeated Razaleigh for the position of UMNO deputy president,[18] Razaleigh had supported the government only reluctantly in the crisis. The third contestant, the formerly powerful Harun, considered a royalist, received only a handful of votes, while Anwar, not a royalist, easily won re-election to the presidency of UMNO Youth. In the contests for the three posts of UMNO vice-president, two were making their first bid, while the third was the incumbent, Ghafar Baba. For several years, observers had been preparing Ghafar's political obituary, convinced that his style did not fit in well with more modern political figures, but his role as intermediary during the constitutional crisis may have helped his re-election as vice-president.

For the twenty UMNO supreme council elected positions, sixteen of those elected represented the younger generation who were openly government supporters during the crisis. Four ministers lost their council seats, of whom at least two – Ghazali Shafie and Datin Padukah Aishah Ghani – were identified as "royalists:" all four were soon gone from the cabinet.

Another area of fallout from the crisis has been in the relationships between the rulers and the Menteris Besar. As most people acknowledge, an angry, over-acquisitive, and obstinate ruler can make the life of a Menteri Besar miserable.

One apparent victim of this fallout was Kedah Menteri Besar, Datuk Seri Syed Nahar Shahabuddin, who resigned on January 24, 1985.[19] Officially, he resigned for personal reasons, and it was widely known as early as 1982 that he wanted to step down. He had taken a firm and courageous stand on the government side during the crisis, thus finding himself uncomfortably in the opposite political camp from his uncle, the Tunku, and the rulers.

The future

When the crisis was officially over, all the protocol, propriety, and ceremonial required to sustain royalty were carefully observed. Personally, the Agung and the Prime Minister reached an accommodation which exceeded the minimum required. The Agung seemed to respect Mahathir. They enjoyed horseback-riding together. Also, the Agung seemed to raise no objection to the government's removal later of the Lord President of the Supreme Court from office because it objected to his comments on executive criticisms (p. 4).[20]

The longer-term question is whether modernization and the growth of a middle class is compatible with feudal institutions. The process of modernization tends to disrupt old customs and values and leads to a decline of deference, awe of majesty, and blind loyalty to myth and superstition. Traditionally, in Malay culture the worst of crimes was disloyalty to one's ruler.[21] The constitutional crisis may have been a watershed in altering the sacrosanct image of the rulers and undoing this feudal Malay tradition. Royal institutions are not easily accepted by either the rising technocratic-oriented young elites or "fundamentalists" who view the ideal Islamic society in more egalitarian terms (at least for males).

Malaysia is not likely to be a republic soon, even after the shocks it sustained during the crisis. Generally, especially in rural areas, the monarchy has become a well-loved institution, although, being less than a half-century old, it still lacks the deeper roots of the rulers. The Royal Houses have the advantage that they play a needed role in countering the destabilizing tendencies inherent in modernization. In the face of challenges from Islamic purists, traditional structures cannot be torn down without unleashing forces that would damage Malaysia's secular, multi-ethnic political style. The Royal Houses have had an important and positive role to play in helping to temper and direct change without impeding progress. But, to accomplish this difficult task and ensure their survival, the rulers must adjust, must exhibit philanthropic and exemplary behavior, must not challenge the agreed political boundaries, and must be aware that the feudal myths publicly repeated about themselves do not actually correspond to current reality.

Another, ominous trend (p. 38) is that the rulers and politicians in office sometimes get along *too well* together. Rulers are susceptible to the rewards that business can offer them and towards which government can guide them. Indeed, they are liable to create their own opportunities by putting pressures on Menteris

Besar to bend the law. From another perspective, politicians may resent such pressures and see the rulers as competitors for business opportunities.

Mahathir's role in the crisis

What exactly was the constitutional crisis all about? It did not seem to be driven mainly by a desire for constitutional perfection. Rather, it was fueled by the coincidence that the two most likely candidates to become Agung were "difficult." Actually, the Sultan of Perak, who died before the election for Agung, might best have been described as eccentric and temperamentally not ideally suitable for the job. Even the "more physical" Sultan of Johor did not turn out to be disastrous. Was Mahathir too eager to launch a preemptive strike? Except for some rural Malays (and, surprisingly, some Chinese), the rulers had acquired a legacy of opprobrium because of their ostentation and acquisitive behavior, and their interference with the operation of state governments. It could be argued that the "problem" of the rulers was not "constitutional" in the narrow sense, but, rather, that they impeded the operation of government by seeking too avidly their own profit.

The government did not win an overwhelming victory in the dispute; "understandings" still remained open to the possibility of being misunderstood.

Once Mahathir had initiated the battle, he appears to have enjoyed it. A populist role brought out the actor in him, and he seems, as perhaps a naturally shy person, to have appreciated the approval of crowds. He was also given the opportunity to voice his anti-feudal feelings, as he had in his letter in 1969. He had no great regard for the Malay rulers.[22] Yet the degree of support shown for the rulers during the crisis suggested that they still attracted the loyalties of many, even if their power to "protect" had lessened, while UMNO's had grown. Mahathir's object was surely not to abolish the monarchy; it was rather, in the short term at least, to put it in its proper place in his own scheme of things. He was certainly not an opponent of all varieties of monarchy, although the Malay monarchy may not have been the most likely to command his respect. Khoo, citing Adshead, makes the point that he found his heroes in modernizing sovereigns, such as Peter the Great, who operated on a grand scale.[23]

The rulers' powers were circumscribed further in early 1993. The Constitution (Amendment) Act 1993 withdrew the immunity of the rulers in their personal capacities, and also withdrew their power to grant royal pardons. A special court was set up to try rulers facing criminal charges. These changes followed an assault on a school hockey coach by the former Agung, the Sultan of Johor. When the rulers resisted the changes, there was a repetition of the press campaign unleashed ten years before. The rulers backed down, after having secured minor concessions.[24] Additionally, the government also decided to withdraw all privileges, allocations, and other entitlements from them, except for those provided for by legislation or other regulations. Other new restrictions provided that civil servants, federal or state, would no longer answer summons for duties at the various palaces, unless permitted to do so by ministers or the respective Menteris Besar. Since 1993, the heat engendered by the disputes between UMNO and the rulers over the last decade has faded somewhat.

The next struggle, in which Mahathir also played a leading role, proved to be an even more divisive contest. It concerned nothing less than a fight for the control of UMNO itself. Mahathir now showed that, in defending himself in a situation where he might lose all his power, he was playing the role for which he was preeminently suited, that of the authoritarian.

The battle to retain control of UMNO

Factions

A faction is a segment of a party, with views that are not entirely identical with the party's but which are close enough to prevent either from trying to end the arrangement. There have been numerous party factions in Malaysia; Means lists sixty-six entries for them in the index to his book on Malaysian politics.[25]

Many so-called "factions" are little more than cliques. This would be true of the "ultras" (radicals, or ultra-nationalists) during Tunku's prime ministership. There were only about half a dozen of these, including Syed Jaafar Albar, Syed Nasir Ismail, and, possibly, Mahathir and Musa. Tunku's own clique included Senu, Tan Sri Khir Johari, and Tan Sri Sardon Jubir. The clique surrounding Razak, when he was Prime Minister, was hardly much larger; it included Tun Dr. Ismail Abdul Rahman, Tan Sri Ghazali Shafie, Razaleigh, and Musa, and extended to Datuk Abdullah Ahmad, a Deputy Minister in the Prime Minister's Office.

Hussein, when Prime Minister, did not have a strong power base, and ruled principally by asserting his own views. There were factional skirmishes, leading Mahathir to comment that Malaysian leadership was in an unparalleled state of chaos. A bizarre element was injected by the arrest of six politicians (two of them deputy ministers, one of whom was Abdullah Ahmad) and a government journalist under the ISA (Internal Security Act) as pro-Communist.[26] Hussein himself declared that Malaysia could not afford factions.[27]

Several features of the UMNO 1987 split make it unique. Nearly all UMNO members aligned themselves with one side or the other and differences among leaders were transmitted to followers through the patronage system. There were few who were uncommitted, waverers, or switchers. The rival groups were nearly equal in numbers. Perhaps commentators realized that this was no ordinary example of a "factional" battle. Maybe this is why they dignified the event by referring to the groups as "teams."

Origins of the UMNO split

The split is generally considered to have begun in 1987, when Razaleigh and Musa formally joined forces to oppose Mahathir. Yet an earlier date could be considered: 1986. That was the year when Musa, then Deputy Prime Minister, dissociated himself from Mahathir's government, indicating that he might be receptive to invitations to join an anti-Mahathir coalition. Somewhat fancifully, the intricacies of the successive relationships among the members of the "triangle" – Mahathir, Musa, and Razaleigh – almost suggest that they were following the directions of a choreographer, interested in seeing how to produce the maximum number of variations on a theme.

First of all, Musa and Razaleigh had been opposed, with Mahathir officially neutral but actually favoring Musa. With Musa's election as Deputy Prime Minister, he and Mahathir became formally aligned. Then Musa quit as Deputy Prime Minister and after a while joined with Razaleigh. After Razaleigh and he suffered defeat, he rejoined UMNO, but without holding office – although he performed some important international assignments for the government. The contest was now between Mahathir and a weakened Razaleigh, but Razaleigh was eventually persuaded to rejoin UMNO, bringing his new party with him. Artistically, the end resembles the beginning – all three were back in UMNO. The difference was that Mahathir was still in office while the other two were not. The clue to these shifting alignments is that, in general, the participants were pursuing power. If not actively pursuing power, they were recuperating to summon up strength for the next power play, or had become disenchanted with the struggle. Musa believed that there was a typhoon loose in the country, and that there was nothing to do but lie low, survive, and wait for it to pass. Mahathir would win, and could not be stopped.[28]

When Mahathir became Prime Minister, he left the choice of the deputy president to the UMNO General Assembly, although he gave indications of his preference for Musa over Razaleigh. Several explanations are possible. Both Mahathir and Musa believed themselves to be "victims" of Tunku's adverse reaction to their "challenges" to his power in 1969. Both had reasons to believe that their fortunes would improve when Razak became Tunku's successor. Both had expressed their dislike of "feudalism" as exemplified by Tunku's prime ministership. Initially, Mahathir and Musa got on well together. They communicated freely and often. They were jointly known as the "two M" administration, although later Mahathir claimed that this stood for "Mahathir Mohamad."

However, by 1985 there were rumors of differences between them, at least in style and approach. Musa was the less confrontational of the two, and was sometimes thought to be the person behind any of the liberal measures taken – in particular, the release of detainees when he became Minister of Home Affairs. In 1986 Musa resigned as Deputy Prime Minister but retained his position as deputy president of UMNO, thus keeping some of his party connections and influence. The resignation was contained in a letter to Mahathir, which was also sent to all UMNO supreme council members. Musa claimed that Mahathir did not trust him, and had accused him of discrediting the Prime Minister in the eyes of others. He added that he had disagreed with some of Mahathir's policies, but accepted that he shared in the government's collective responsibility for them.[29] Some observers believed that Musa overreacted by resigning when he did. One eminent politician from outside Malaysia thought that Musa should have stayed on as Deputy Prime Minister, while showing suitable deference to Mahathir.[30] However, Musa felt too deeply about the issue and was so resentful of Mahathir's manner that he could not bear to work with him any longer.[31]

In spite of the previous rivalry between Musa and Razaleigh, exacerbated by Musa's unsuccessful attempt to persuade Mahathir to drop him from the cabinet, Razaleigh, like Musa, was not happy in his relationship with Mahathir. He had been moved from the Ministry of Finance to the Ministry of Trade and Industry, an important but less prestigious post. It was the first step downwards in a career, which, under his patron, Razak, seemed to hold almost infinite promise. Although, unlike Musa, he did not find dealing with Mahathir really difficult, he thought that he was not consulted very often, and that Mahathir originated bright ideas, rather than plans.[32]

Team A and Team B

Opposition to Mahathir was a strong incentive for Razaleigh and Musa to come to an agreement. As the April 1987 General Assembly approached, they decided that Razaleigh would fight Mahathir for the presidency, while Musa would defend his deputy presidential post. The two opposing groups were now commonly referred to as Team A, led by Mahathir and his chosen candidate for deputy president, Ghafar, and Team B, Razaleigh and Musa. The choice of these labels was said to have been made by the press, which is quite credible, because the label "A" would seem to have conferred a decided advantage and the press was strongly pro-Mahathir.

This was not the only respect in which the teams were unequal. It seems scarcely believable that Team A won the presidential race in the UMNO General Assembly by only 43 votes out of about 1,500. Team B was outnumbered in its share of UMNO office-holders. It had the support of only one of the three vice-presidents, Datuk Abdullah Badawi, eight out of twenty-five of the supreme council's elected members, and eight out of forty-two of the supreme council's total members. Above all, Team A benefited by being the team of the incumbents and from being led by Mahathir. It received more favorable coverage than Team B in the press and TV and also through Bernama, the official news agency. The police were more cooperative in issuing permits to it for holding political meetings, although the meetings that Team B did hold were well attended. Team B had to be resourceful in circumventing restrictions. Never before had the Tunku held so many "religious" meetings on his property.[33] It also resorted to using "flying letters," small pamphlets distributed in unorthodox ways. Menteris Besar and chief ministers pledged support for Mahathir, at his request, in February 1987. The leaders of the other Barisan Nasional parties also dutifully pledged support to him. The Agung, now Mahathir's friend, expressed public approval of Team A, regardless of constitutional propriety. Some prominent Team B supporters were harassed by the threat of bank loans being withdrawn and by the vexatious inquiries of the tax authorities. Additionally, Team A had control of UMNO's assets (until February 1988, ten months after the UMNO election, when access to them was blocked by the courts after UMNO was declared illegal). It was always in control of the allocation of government contracts, etc., and thus able to generate more funds.

The sources of Team B's revenues are not fully known. It may have been relevant that Razaleigh was financial adviser to the Sultan of Brunei, one of the richest men in the world. One rough estimate was that Team B spent between ten million and twenty million dollars by July 1988.[34]

Mahathir did not answer Team B's frequent criticisms of the government's "big" projects (pp. 64–8) by frequently extolling their virtues; instead he countered with the question: had Musa not known about these issues at the time, and had he not in essence "approved" of them by not resigning earlier? On April 13, 1987, Mahathir impressively – though maybe not with propriety – released confidential cabinet records on several of his projects to show that Musa and other cabinet members were aware of them and had not objected to them.[35] He also counter-attacked by criticizing actions taken by Musa when the Prime Minister was away from Malaysia (pp. 87, 100–1).

Other matters debated were charged with emotion. Each of the teams accused the other of trying to break up UMNO. Team A alleged that its rival had been motivated by greed and the lust for power. Team B's retort was that it was not it, but Mahathir, who should be denounced as having destroyed the party's unity: he had betrayed the Malay virtues of sincerity and togetherness.[36] Team B also deplored Mahathir's tolerance of corruption and extensive use of patronage. Mahathir's statements of his own position were not entirely consistent. Near the end of the campaign, he warned that he might not resign from office if he lost. Technically, he claimed, a Prime Minister could make his own decision. Those who wished to remove him should move a vote of no confidence, in Parliament. He also stated that UMNO's tradition did not permit its leader to be challenged[37] – a theme he developed in the next decade to perpetuate his hold on the presidency of UMNO. He was now an advocate of incumbency.

It was not unreasonable for Team B to fear that Mahathir's regard for democracy, and the rules that have to be followed in order to sustain it, could not be relied on. Its members could never dispel their apprehension that he might declare a state of emergency, or might take advantage of some ethnic dispute (probably in a Chinese area), which could lead to widespread ethnic violence, thus validating authoritarian measures. Their fears were justified by the arrests of October 1987 (pp. 108–9).

It is hard to discern many clear-cut differences in policy between the teams.[38] The lack of success of some of Mahathir's projects – at least in cost–benefit terms – e.g., the Dayabumi building and the heavily subsidized Proton Saga car, provoked Team B's censure; it alleged that Mahathir was attracted by large-scale projects that verged on the grandiose, usually with a view to enhancing Malaysia's national image. They were also unhappy over the timing of these projects. Policy differences have been suggested concerning the role of government towards business and their implications for patronage. A promising line of political research would be to discover what kinds of capitalists were associated with the supporters of one team rather than the other.[39]

Once the lines of battle had been drawn, there were very few switches among, say, the top hundred or so UMNO politicians. There were noteworthy exceptions of people who were identified in the press as belonging to Team B, who ended up in Team A. Suggestively, no top Team A politicians switched to the other side. One, Badawi, a Team B member, was dismissed from the cabinet in Mahathir's "purge" of Team B supporters (p. 43), but later reappeared as Foreign Minister. One who switched sides was Datuk Najib Abdul Razak, son of the second Prime Minister, the Culture, Youth and Sports Minister. Two reasons were suggested for his move. He had been chosen as acting head of UMNO Youth, with good prospects of being confirmed as head; he was also said to have been motivated by personal pressures. The UMNO General Assembly elections were held on April 24, 1987; the contest between the teams produced a close result. For president, Mahathir defeated Razaleigh by 761 votes to 718, while Ghafar prevailed over Musa by 739 to 699. Team A also won about two-thirds of the supreme council elective seats and two of the three vice-presidential positions – the other was Badawi. Some believed that Team A's strength swelled towards the end of the campaign; in particular, on the Friday the long break for prayers during the process of voting was used by Team A to practise some high-powered lobbying.[40] Only a few days later, Mahathir removed seven ministers/deputy ministers from office.[41] In victory, no magnanimity had been shown – nor had it been expected. Razaleigh and one other minister had already resigned.

Team B now had recourse to the courts. A group of Team B supporters, known as the "UMNO Eleven," brought a suit to nullify the election in the General Assembly, because members of some branches who voted had not been properly registered, thus making their votes invalid. The High Court's ruling was a surprise. UMNO was declared an illegal organization. A rush began by each group to register a new party, and lay claim to UMNO's substantial assets, frozen until their ownership could be determined. After access to the assets was blocked, things were temporarily financially so bad for Team A that UMNO headquarters, according to the secretary-general, Tan Sri Sanusi Junid, had hardly enough money to buy paper for its operations.[42]

The power to rule on registration was exercised by the Registrar of Societies, who was under the control of Mahathir in his capacity as Minister of Home Affairs. The upshot was that the application of Mahathir to register was accepted, whereas the application of the two former prime ministers, Tunku and Hussein, was rejected on the grounds that the Registrar had not yet actually deregistered UMNO. Mahathir's party, after some delay, and after demonstrating that it had recruited most of the original UMNO's members, was able to gain control of the assets. It had been ruled that neither group could use the original name, "UMNO." The name chosen by Team A was "UMNO Baru," while Team B, their application to use the name "UMNO Malaysia" having been rejected, chose "Semangat '46" (the Spirit of '46), referring to UMNO's founding in 1946. The former soon dropped the "Baru," which of course helped to suggest that it was the rightful continuation of UMNO. In 1997, the Registrar of Companies told the party that, for it to use the name UMNO, the General Assembly had first to approve the change, which it did. Team B's hope of redress via the courts was blocked because the government took drastic action to render the judiciary subservient to its wishes (pp. 46–9). It was forced to continue the struggle in the political arena, where its chances were dimmer than before, because it had lost some of its original impetus and also the chance of acquiring UMNO's assets.

The government was in no hurry to call an election, because it believed, correctly, that time was on its side. In January 1988, Team B seized the opportunity to demonstrate its appeal to the public by entering with gusto into a series of by-elections. Not all the candidates put forward in these by-elections were actually members of the team, but they were widely recognized as supporting it. The small number of seats contested meant that the sample was not representative. In one instance a sitting member of Team B, Datuk Shahrir Ahmad, resigned his seat and fought as an Independent in the ensuing by-election. He won, but the Barisan Nasional candidates won some of the other by-elections. So, although the by-elections aroused excitement and enthusiasm, they gave no clear indication of what the result of a general election might have been.

A political economy approach

So far, the account of the struggle between Team A and Team B has been told in terms of personalities, political maneuvering, and, where discoverable, policies. The most important of these was probably Team B's opposition to the size and timing of Mahathir's large-scale, costly projects. However, another main factor was the effect of changes in the economy, both long term and short term. The former changes the parameters, for example in the composition of the electorate, by altering its occupational and class, as well as its ethnic, configuration. In the shorter term, the timing of elections has the effect of causing various groups of electors to vote differently at various phases of the economic cycle. Governments are known to hold elections when the economy is doing well. They also like to give the economy a boost by increasing expenditure and lowering taxation in the months preceding an election. All this is hackneyed, but indispensable, political lore.

The recession, which reached its lowest point in 1985, collided, so to speak, with a wave of rising expectations encouraged by the promise of the NEP. Politically, it produced frustration, engendering greater competition for the limited political rewards available, and, later, contributed to a split in UMNO. There was also a generational conflict. Mahathir stated the essence of the problem when he addressed the UMNO General Assembly in 1987. He referred to remarks of the late Dr. Ismail about the generation born after 1957:

> They did not experience the bitter struggle for independence. They tend to take independence and all its fruits for granted. In addition, they will have

high expectations. Because the younger generation had to be accommodated in UMNO, many members who joined UMNO much earlier would feel disappointed.[43]

By the mid-1980s, the long-term effect of changes in the economy had been to produce, through the NEP, a marked increase in the number of Malays in business and in their expectations. However, the recession of 1985, when Malaysia actually experienced negative growth, and the years immediately following, abruptly checked these expectations and the rise in bankruptcies was shocking. Consequently, support for the government declined. Team B, under the leadership of Razaleigh, acclaimed by Razak as a financial wizard, offered an attractive alternative.

If an election had been held in 1988, although the economy was already starting to improve, Team B would have had a reasonable chance of winning. However, Mahathir succeeded in delaying an election, and a political factor came into play. Power depended largely on patronage, and patronage required money. UMNO had a stock of capital, consisting of its assets, which were temporarily frozen, pending the decision of the courts. It also, through government activities (pp. 59–62), generated some income. Semangat '46 had only a *hope* of securing the assets, which was not fulfilled. It did not have any regular source of income except from its supporters, particularly Razaleigh himself.

The economy was in even better shape when Mahathir called the election of 1990 and won a clear victory. Between the 1987 Assembly vote and the 1990 election, UMNO Baru's superior financial resources enabled it to win back grass-roots supporters who had deserted it, and fortify its patronage networks, while Team B's network withered because of diminishing resources.[44]

Consolidation of power in UMNO

After Mahathir's victory at the 1987 General Assembly, he proceeded to reap the rewards. The Constitution of UMNO Baru was amended to increase the power of the president. He could nominate the heads of the Youth and Women's (Wanita) divisions, who previously had been elected by the General Assembly. The method of voting for the president and deputy president was altered so as to benefit incumbents at party elections. The system adopted gave weight, not only to the votes cast for these two posts, but also provided bonus votes for the number of *nominations* each candidate received.[45] The votes that could be gathered through nominations almost equalled the number obtainable from actual votes. Incumbents, usually better known than others, and with more power to influence others, were likely to attract more nominations. Considerable organization, courage, and money would be needed to make a dent in an incumbent's majority.[46]

The decline of Semangat '46

The weakness of Semangat's chances at the general election led Razaleigh to seek reinforcement. On the Malay side, he concluded alliances with PAS and some smaller parties, while on the non-Malay "flank" he formed an alliance with the DAP. Razaleigh had some difficulty in explaining these alliances with parties whose aims were so different from those of his own party – and even more different from each other. Earlier, Mahathir had referred to the Razaleigh–Musa alliance as one between "strange bedfellows;"[47] in the new arrangement they were even stranger.

Semangat's decline can be seen by making a very broad comparison with previous indications of support. At the 1987 General Assembly vote, Team B won almost half and in the January 1988 by-elections – not a representative sample – the two teams were running neck and neck. However, in the 1990 general election, Semangat won a much smaller proportion. Not all the 17.4 percent of the vote won by its candidates was cast by its own supporters; some of it came from PAS and DAP supporters who voted for it because it was allied with their parties. A more accurate estimate of its performance is given by looking at the UMNO losses in votes from the previous election, which were probably not much more than about 5 percent.[48] UMNO and the Barisan did quite well, though not as well as in 1986. They suffered one major blow – they lost all the parliamentary and state seats in Kelantan to a PAS–Semangat '46 coalition. They also came close to losing the state of Penang to the DAP.

Semangat performed even less well at the 1995 election. It ceased to exist in 1996, when its members, led by Razaleigh, joined UMNO *en masse*.

The judiciary

By far the most far-reaching and devastating attack by Mahathir on the "checks and balances" system in Malaysia was his destruction of the independence of the judiciary in 1987–8.

Malaysia's parliamentary political system was modeled after Britain, which would seem to indicate parliamentary supremacy. However, Article 4(1) of the Constitution proclaims that the Constitution is supreme and, borrowing from the US model, allocates certain powers, including judicial review, to the Malaysian courts, resulting in, at least notionally, a modified and fragile "separation of powers" system. Accordingly, the primary duty of the judiciary was to act as a sentinel for the Constitution, and to protect it from legislative and executive attack.[49] This doctrine of judicial review was also embedded as one of the five pillars of the national ideology, the *Rukunegara*: "The rule of law is ensured by the existence of an independent judiciary with powers to pronounce on the constitutionality and legality or otherwise of executive acts."

In response to expanding state control over political and civil rights and a decline in the avenues of recourse available, Malaysians in the 1980s increasingly turned to the courts for the redress of grievances. In 1986–7, a number of important decisions in High Court cases went against the government. In 1986, the High Court upheld a challenge to the government's expulsion order against a foreign journalist. In 1987 the government lost a citizenship case and had its prohibition against *Aliran Monthly* (a social action periodical) publishing in the national language successfully challenged. It also had an injunction issued against United Engineers Malaysia (*de facto* UMNO was the majority owner), preventing it (temporarily) from signing a huge government contract (p. 59). Also, in February, the government was unable to prevent the court from granting a writ of habeas corpus to an ISA detainee (a first in Malaysian legal history), a decision that was upheld by the Supreme Court in November.

These adverse decisions led to a sustained verbal attack by Mahathir against the courts and these stirrings of judicial activism. Whereas the Prime Minister encountered virtually no obstacles to his will in cabinet or in Parliament, he found his actions blocked at times by the courts. Since he seems to equate democracy with "majority rule," and views the power of the Prime Minister as being democratically mandated through elections, he interpreted the decisions of the courts as unwarranted infringements of executive power that thwarted the will of the majority.[50] In his frustration and anger, he accused the courts of trying to usurp power and run the country.[51] He also believed that the judges, lawyers, and the Bar Council were meddling in politics as a result of some of them, including two former lord presidents of the Supreme Court, having participated in a series of conferences which called for a review of the Constitution.

After UMNO had been declared illegal and Mahathir had successfully registered UMNO Baru, the ousted losers then filed an appeal to legalize the old UMNO. At stake were UMNO's vast assets. After this, Mahathir was preoccupied, if not obsessed, with the UMNO lawsuits,[52] and he moved quickly beyond verbal criticism to change the constitutional rules and conventions governing the judiciary.

First, the number of "ouster" or "finality clauses" attached to legislation, which exclude the supervisory powers of the courts, was dramatically increased. Then, in March, just one month after UMNO was declared illegal, Parliament quickly, and without much notice or press comment, passed the Federal Constitution (Amendment) Act 1988. By this Act, Articles 121(1) and 145 were amended. Henceforth, the powers of the judiciary would no longer be embedded in the Constitution; rather they would be conferred by Parliament through statutes.[53] Also, by this Act, the High Courts were stripped of the power of judicial review previously granted in the Constitution. Further, the attorney-general assumed control of instructing the courts on what cases to hear and which courts to use, and assumed responsibility for judicial assignments and transfers. Hence, virtually overnight, the modified separation of powers was terminated and the judiciary was stripped of much of its independence and power. The president of the Malaysian Bar Council was horrified by Mahathir's tone in Parliament: "His speech, which was full of venom, hate and spite," showed his ignorance of the role of the courts and the judicial process itself.[54]

Renowned former Lord President Tun Mohd. Suffian Hashim lamented that crushing the judiciary for doing its duty was like shooting the referee just because he interferes with the game by blowing his whistle.[55]

More blows were to follow. In early May 1988, the Lord President Tun Salleh Abas set the date for the Supreme Court to hear the crucial UMNO appeal. Because of the political ramifications, he noted later, he had decided it should be heard quickly and by a full bench (all nine judges). Soon after, on May 26, the Lord President was suspended for "gross misbehavior and misconduct" over some relatively minor breaches of protocol concerning a letter he had sent to the Agung, after discussing it with the other Supreme Court judges, nearly three months earlier (for example, there were breaches of protocol concerning the form and method of transmission of the letter).[56]

A tribunal was set up by the Prime Minister's Office in early June under the presidency of Tan Sri Abdul Hamid Omar, a school friend of Mahathir's and an "interested party," because he was the Deputy Lord President and obvious successor if Salleh were dismissed. Not only was Abdul Hamid in a conflict-of-interest situation, but also he had participated in discussions with the other judges earlier about writing a letter to the Agung. The Lord President objected to the composition of the tribunal, and refused to defend himself before it.

When the tribunal was about to submit its report to the Agung, the Supreme Court met in special session on July 2 and handed down a restraining order on the tribunal. Four days later the five Supreme Court judges involved were also suspended for "gross misbehavior." Soon after the reconstituted Supreme Court set aside the restraining order, the Agung dismissed Salleh, and Abdul Hamid was named as the new Lord President.[57] Tun Suffian summed up the situation in a nicely nuanced statement, saying that Salleh was dismissed simply because he was "a man of absolute integrity," whereas the Prime Minister "only wants judges in whom he has confidence."[58] Three days later, on August 9, the Supreme Court rejected the UMNO appeal, giving Mahathir his critical victory.[59]

The rapid shearing away of the powers and prestige of the judiciary, the ease with which its constitutional protection was stripped, coupled with the intimidating dismissals of judges and the enhanced powers given to the attorney-general, have largely succeeded in taming the courts. Observers were rather shocked that the whole judicial process was exposed as being so vulnerable and could be so readily and quickly altered. "We thought it was more difficult than that," said one Kuala Lumpur lawyer.[60]

Not unexpectedly, the situation concerning the rule of law in Malaysia has not improved, despite a reorganization of the courts. In 1995, the High Court was sent a controversial commercial case to hear, which was so unusual a move that the newly instituted Court of Appeal said it constituted abuse of the process of the High Court, since the implication was that those judges would be friendly to the plaintiff, thus raising questions about judicial impartiality. The Bar Council stated that it was deeply shocked, and its president wrote that something was very seriously wrong. Then the special rapporteur on the Independence of

Judges and Lawyers for the UN Commission on Human Rights complained that sending the matter to the Federal Court (formerly the Supreme Court) which subsequently heard the controversial case, was unconstitutional, because it illegally included a High Court judge.[61] However, the Malaysian judiciary, which can no longer constrain the vast power of the executive, is so subdued that it also no longer appears interested in making rulings even on legal technicalities.

The end of judicial independence in Malaysia was further ensured by a 1994 amendment to the Constitution. It amplified the grounds for removing a judge. The recommendation by the top judges to the Agung on this subject were to be prescribed in a written code of ethics formulated after consulting the Prime Minister. As the Bar Council pointed out, this provision would remove any separation between the judiciary and the Executive.[62]

Conclusion

The three episodes described in this chapter showed Mahathir in an aggressive role (against the Agung and the rulers), in a defensive role (in beating off an attack on his leadership of UMNO), and again in an offensive role (when he decided that the judiciary was the only remaining check to his exercise of absolute power). These different adversaries called for slightly different approaches. However, certain qualities were required in all three, and Mahathir was amply endowed with them. Two comments testify to Mahathir's determination. One concluded that no one strong enough and tough enough had emerged to challenge Mahathir.[63] The other was that too many people had said that he couldn't or wouldn't do this or that, but in fact he could and he did.[64]

3 The economy and development

Foundations for economic success: the New Economic Policy

Malaysia is now emerging from being a developing country. A 1993 study analyzed developments in Hong Kong, Singapore, Indonesia, Taiwan, Malaysia, and Thailand in order to discover what the secrets of their success were in having achieved, or almost achieved, the status of NIEs (newly industrializing economies). These countries have been distinguished by their high rates of economic growth, although in the late 1990s the *rate* of increase has somewhat slowed down, and there has been a major check to growth from the second half of 1997. The study found that three characteristics seemed to be essential for growth, in addition to natural resources and other "givens:" outward orientation especially concerning exports; stability; and investment through people.[1] Malaysia possessed these characteristics and also another feature that was auspicious for growth – a high rate of saving. In 1995 its rate of gross savings was 34 percent of Gross National Product, comparable with South Korea and higher than Japan.[2] Additionally, Malaysia, when it was still Malaya, started a series of development plans, enabling the government to check how closely implementation conformed to planning, making it easy to see what revisions had to be made in future plans.

Apart from these generalizations, there were other factors, not dependent on Malaysia's own policies, that affected performance. For example, it benefited from the administrative structure created by the British, and re-created by them after World War Two. Post-war, it also gained from the British decision that, in order for Malaya to recover from the Emergency, an adequate tax base had to be created.[3] Fortuitously, Malaysia was also a beneficiary from American expenditure in Asia in the course of the war with Korea.[4]

Such advantages placed Malaysia in the ranks of the three ASEAN NIEs, slightly behind Singapore but ahead of Thailand. Its rate of growth, like those of its neighbors', was checked by the recession of the mid-1980s, but later recovered to an annual rate of about 8 percent.

The four-year economic plans, which began in 1957, were not nearly as elaborate as those that were prepared in later years. Yet they reflected efforts to attempt diversification, by moving away from an economy that was mainly agricultural, and which concentrated on a few items. A manufacturing sector was developed for the domestic market, an early example being the production of wood and rattan furniture. New products also were introduced, for instance in printing and publishing and in chemicals. Some existing products were improved, or were produced more efficiently, for example by the use of higher-yielding clones in rubber.

A dividing line occurred in 1969, when the ethnic riots led to an attempt to satisfy Malay economic grievances through a "New Economic Policy." It emerged under the leadership of Razak, who was soon to become Prime Minister, and a group drawn from various sources: Ghazali Shafie (a civil servant soon to become a minister), other civil servants, party officials, and Just Faaland, a Scandinavian economist. The policy took an economic shape, but its declared objective was political – to produce national unity.[5]

There had been previous attempts to help the Malays, but they had not been comprehensive or determined. Their rationale was to be found in the Constitution itself, which in Article 153 made specific provision to improve the economic position of the Malays by giving them special access to certain jobs, licenses, etc. Some institutions were established, e.g., FLDA, later FELDA (the Federal Land Development Authority), MARA (Majlis Amanah Rakyat), a later version of RIDA (Rural and Industrial Development Authority), which provided finance and advice to Malays, as did Bank Bumiputra, which, as the name suggests, was more financially oriented. Institutions such as these were concerned principally with rural Malays. Firms that wished to qualify for "pioneer status," which entitled them to tax and other incentives, had to employ certain minimum percentages of Malays. The government was sometimes not too enthusiastic in providing help for Malays in business. On one occasion the (Chinese) Minister for Commerce and Industry, while indicating sympathy for such a request, emphasized that the existing rights of the non-Malays must be observed.[6]

The NEP was more explicit. This description applied both to the remarks used in presenting it and to the official plans when they were printed. To use a favorite phrase of Razak, things were no longer to be "swept under the carpet," they were to be spelled out. The plans abounded with targets and percentages. Saying that anything was part of the NEP legitimized it. The NEP, not the *Rukunegara*, was Malaysia's true ideology, at least for Malays.

One of the Second Malaysia Plan's two "prongs" was to reduce and eventually eliminate poverty for all Malaysians, irrespective of race. The other was directed at the ambitious task of restructuring society. Economic imbalances among the races were to be reduced and eventually eliminated, and race was no longer to be identified with economic function.[7] This entailed some modernization of rural life and the movement of Malays to the towns, which, it was hoped, would facilitate the growth of Malay commercial and industrial activity at all levels. No ethnic group was to feel any sense of deprivation. For this to be possible, given that the Malays would be making economic gains, the policy had to be predicated on economic growth.[8]

Some distinctive features of the NEP deserve brief consideration: incomes and poverty; employment; the ownership of capital. The average Malay family income was about only half the non-Malay one. So the problem of improving the economic lot of the Malays partly coincided with the problem of relieving poverty. However, within each ethnic group there were wide discrepancies in income. For example, in contrast to wealthy Malay landowners, or even civil servants, in many areas Malays were found in the most backward sectors – rubber smallholders, tenants in padi (rice) and rubber, inshore fishing, etc. The NEP was intended to help the poorer Malays, not only by making their lot better in their existing situation, but also by "leapfrogging" them from the traditional to the modern sectors of the economy.

The Malays were employed predominantly in the agricultural sector where output per worker was lowest, while the Chinese were more easily found in the manufacturing and commercial sectors, where it was highest. Employment targets for Malays were based on the premise that their proportion in agriculture should decrease, while the proportion in manufacturing and commerce should increase. In most employment sectors, however, the numbers (but not the proportion) of Chinese and Indians would not decrease.

The intention was that the Malays should occupy higher positions in the job hierarchy than before. Within one generation, Malays and other indigenous peoples (Bumiputera – sons of the soil) would own and manage at least 30 per-cent of all commercial and industrial activities of the economy in all categories and scales of operation.[9] Extensive training facilities would therefore be needed.

A main thrust of the NEP was to increase the numbers of Malay managers and entrepreneurs. (The two are not the same, although some government pronouncements on the question did not clarify this.) Entrepreneurs are distinctive – and comparatively rare – because, by definition, they have to take risks in business; if they are successful, they reap rewards, while, if unsuccessful, they suffer losses. Managers' rewards are not so closely linked to risk-taking. Their decisions are more closely guided by orders from above. Generally, managers predominate in government services and entrepreneurs in business. It is harder to find good managers than to find good entrepreneurs.[10] At the start of the NEP, the government decided, therefore, to encourage small business, by training and encouraging entrepreneurs of a corresponding calibre, but to train and employ managers in larger organizations, which would act "in trust for" Malays. Some time later (when Mahathir was Prime Minister), when more Malay entrepreneurs would evolve – some via functioning as managers – they would be competent to operate as entrepreneurs running larger businesses.

Some of the difficulty in producing Malay business people arose from Malay values. To be sure, the Malays available in the early 1970s were not the Malays portrayed by Mahathir in *The Malay Dilemma*. Yet neither were they the Malays envisioned by him as the "new Malays" of 2020 (p. 163). Exhortations were voiced by Razak and Razaleigh. The latter sounded a clarion call, but hardly offered a guarantee of success. He told them that under the NEP Malays had "a wonderful world of almost limitless opportunities," but that only the fittest survived and there was no charity in the world of business.[11]

Advice and financial help were available from organizations previously mentioned, such as MARA and Bank Bumiputra. Legislation enacted in accordance with the NEP also provided that a proportion of certain government contracts should be allocated to Malay firms. Another method of getting Malays into business was for them to form joint ventures with Chinese. An obstacle here was that, unless the Malays concerned already had some knowledge of business, it was likely that the relationship would be unequal. The Malay would produce the necessary license, available *because* he was a Malay, while a Chinese would actually operate the business, a common practice with taxis. The arrangement was known as "Ali-Baba," the Ali being the Malay and the Baba the Chinese.

The business environment was alien to most Malays. Even with all the assistance and training provided, they lacked the networks, including family networks, available to Chinese. Notions of what kind of business to go into or what scale of operations was feasible were vague. Initial expenditures tended to be spent on the showy non-essentials of business, such as lavishly furnished offices and impressive state-of-the-art equipment.

The Second Malaysia Plan (2MP) had a target, for 1990, of 30 percent for both Malay corporate ownership and Malay management. The target for non-Malays (mostly Chinese) was set at 40 percent, while the foreign share was to be 30 percent.[12] The problems of the Malays in attaining the target were huge, because they were starting from such a low level – 1.9 percent! The principal administrative instrument for achieving these goals was the Industrial Coordination Act 1975 (ICA). The overall percentages of ethnic owners was as listed above, but arrangements for particular firms depended on the nature of the business, the availability of technology, and the proportion of the product that was to be exported. Calculations were more intricate for joint ventures, in which the partners belonged to various ethnic categories. In practice, there were quite frequent "liberalizations," in order to encourage foreign investment, in many of which the broad decision was Mahathir's. Important liberalization measures, both for foreigners and non-Malays, were made during the mid-1980s recession. There were similar relaxations in some cases for employment targets.

Targets of various kinds had to be coordinated. Setting targets for Malays in employment categories was one reason that the intake of Malay university students had to be raised, especially where the existing intakes had been very small, as in science, medicine, and engineering. Additionally, to equip Malay students for university entry, the Malay language was made necessary for tertiary education.

Another aspect of the NEP was the direct transfer of wealth to Bumiputera in the form of shares. The main method used was via the Amanah Saham Nasional (National Trust Fund) which distributed capital from foreign and Chinese firms – originally many of these were derived from takeovers of British firms, such as Guthries, which had owned plantations. The government tried, not very successfully, to prevent shares being quickly resold by the Bumiputera beneficiaries to reap a quick profit.

Malay and non-Malay reactions to the NEP

Few Malays were opposed to the NEP; was it not intended to contribute to their economic advancement? On the other hand, many non-Malays were skeptical, and feared that it would be a zero-sum situation – the Malays' gain would be their loss. To those Malays who were in business, or wanted to be in business, the NEP was especially welcome. It became widely believed that money was to be made almost for the taking, and almost regardless of legal restrictions. Many welcomed the NEP, but went on to wonder why it did not promise them even more. Why should the Malay corporate ownership for 1990 be only 30 percent, when the proportion of the population was over 50 percent? (The need to have an allocation for foreigners was ignored.) Claims were also made, by UMNO Youth and Malay Chambers of Commerce, that Malays should be given allocations for tenders by governmental and semi-governmental bodies, that more natural resources should be reserved for exploitation for Malays only, and so on. There were some sources of Malay unhappiness. It was objected – not without reason – that the NEP would lay the foundations of a new Malay capitalist class. Another complaint was that the large organizations created by the NEP, such as Pernas (the state trading organization), actually competed with small Malay businesses. (This was incorrect. Pernas and the like were too large to compete with small business, whose potential rivals were more likely to be the smaller State Economic Development Corporations.)

Non-Malays who were in business had to contend with an accretion of irritations, although poor Chinese and other non-Malays could hope to derive some advantage from measures taken to reduce poverty. They were particularly frustrated by the controls imposed through the ICA. Except for very small firms, licenses would be required from the Ministry of Trade and Industry, and these could be revoked if a firm's operations conflicted with government requirements concerning the employment of Bumiputera.[13] There was room for some flexibility in the administration of the Act, but this was perhaps more likely to benefit foreigners, whose investments were recognized as vital to the health of the economy. Many Chinese business people could not predict exactly how the Act would be applied. Some smaller firms took advantage of a legal loophole by splitting a business among family members, so that the smaller units could escape having the ICA apply to them. At the other extreme for the Chinese was the strategy of seeking bigness rather than smallness. This did not constitute a way of avoiding the ambit of the ICA, but it offered the advantages enjoyed by some of the new semi-governmental organizations – large financial resources and the ability to make efficient use of managerial and technical human resources. This kind of thinking was behind the establishment of Multi-Purpose Holdings Berhad (MPHB) (pp. 92–3).[14]

Foreign investors were also concerned that the ICA should not be applied too rigidly – to their detriment. However, in the Third Malaysia Plan there was greater emphasis placed on the role of capital provided by the private sector than there had been previously, and foreign investors were given appropriate reassurances.

The "Look East" policy

Mahathir announced his "Look East" policy in 1981, soon after he became Prime Minister. The policy was not easy to understand. Some of his ministers had trouble in explaining it, and the *Asian Wall Street Journal* was also puzzled, as indicated by its headline, "Malaysia's Vague Campaign to Learn from Japan."[15] Elements of the policy had no doubt been in his mind for some time, and he summed these up in what he described as a slogan. His fuller account is too long to repeat. In essence, the idea stressed qualities that were worthy of emulation, such as diligence, discipline, loyalty, the promotion of group rather than individual interest, high quality and good management systems in business, etc. He was at pains to make it clear that the phrase did not mean buying all goods from the East or granting all contracts to the East. However, there was still an implication that economic activities would be carried on more extensively with the East.[16] Actually, the Japanese did rather well in gaining a large share of contracts.

To him "the East" apparently consisted of Japan and South Korea, the developed/rapidly developing countries that it might be most feasible for Malaysia to emulate. Taiwan and Singapore were not mentioned; the high proportion of Chinese in their populations might have made them confusing as examples. He also stressed that not everything in the East was wholly good, nor was everything in the West wholly bad.[17] The phrase was not intended to be anti-West, although he had recently verbally attacked Britain because of the London Stock Exchange's change of rules in reaction to the takeover of British firms in Malaysia and to Britain having raised the costs of university fees for foreign students.

Mahathir also mentioned two features which Malaysia proposed to adopt from the Japanese model. One was the concept of Malaysia Incorporated, intended to encourage business owners and workers in the public and private sectors to work together. Another was to create large companies based on the Japanese *sogo shoshas* (the large trading companies), although in Malaysia these were not developed as rapidly as the Prime Minister would have wished. Yet another feature deemed worthy of adoption, which was prevalent in Japan, was "in-house unions" which, as the term suggests, would have trade union "territory" delineated according to the place of work. This proposal was opposed by defenders of workers' rights, and the government did not press hard for its acceptance.

Some commentators perceived cultural problems in transferring some Japanese practices to Malaysia. One was that long office hours, resulting in employees working late, as in Japan, might meet with resistance from Malaysian wives. Also, educational training schemes, which would teach Japanese and Korean, were started but, given the predominance of English as a second language, did not make much headway. Neither did plans to make Japanese a widely taught optional language in secondary schools.

"Look East" was never explicitly abandoned as a policy. But it became clear that it was based on some premises that were not entirely appropriate. Habits of discipline, diligence, and so on cannot be inculcated in a short period. Furthermore, Japan was a developed capitalist state, while Malaysia (p. 50) was still a developing one, however close it was to becoming an NIE. It was difficult not to identify the relationship in terms of dependency. Japan was more developed industrially than Malaysia, which had a huge trade deficit with Japan in early 1984. Its exports to Japan were mostly primary products. Japan, it appeared, held "three cards" – trade, aid, and investment – while Malaysia held only one – trade – and even that was lower-ranking, because of Japanese restrictions on trade. Additionally, Japan was not very forthcoming in transferring technology. In August 1984, a Mahathir speech accused Japan of conducting a colonial relationship.[18]

It was a good idea that Malaysia should try to learn from the experience of Japan and South Korea. But the respective histories and capabilities of Japan and Malaysia had to be seen in context. It was unrealistic to believe that Japan would act towards Malaysia as if differences in their economic power did not exist, just because Malaysia admired Japan's achievements and desired to reproduce them. Malaysia could not replicate what Japan had done because Japan's continued successes presented a formidable obstacle to their replication.[19]

Privatization

Mahathir's privatization policy, announced in 1983,[20] reflected a world-wide trend, whose best-known exponent was probably the British Prime Minister, Margaret Thatcher. The policy appealed to Mahathir's own inclinations, which led him to believe that the profit-seeking private sector had an incentive to "deliver the goods," which was lacking in the government sector. He had demonstrated this view earlier when he made efforts to have the night-soil collection service privatized, while living in Alor Setar.[21]

There was another reason behind his support for privatization. It seemed an ideal vehicle for achieving the aims of the NEP, and correcting some of the evils that had resulted from previous policies. The NEP called for the employment of more Bumiputera in business, particularly as entrepreneurs (as well as adding to the assets held by Bumiputera). At first, the government tried to increase the supply in two main ways. One was to train Malays to start small businesses by providing training, credit, etc., for them, through organizations such as MARA. For training to undertake jobs in larger-scale business, Malays were to be employed in state organizations, such as Pernas (the state trading company) or UDA (the Urban Development Authority). The idea was that some of the managers produced by such training would develop entrepreneurial abilities and would be able to run risk-taking enterprises. Some training took place at state level through State Economic Development Coroporations. Unfortunately, not many of these were very efficiently run, and they tended to be "bloated" with excess human resources. These bodies at federal and state level, combined with the civil service, employed a staggering share of the workforce – roughly a quarter in 1983. They were a strain on finances, and their activities were neither well planned nor conducted with an eye for costs. Intended to solve one problem, they had created another.

Malaysia was fortunate, because the almost world-wide privatization "wave" had started, and was seized on by Mahathir as a better way to implement "the second phase of the NEP." It offered a way to develop Bumiputera entrepreneurship, while fulfilling Mahathir's belief in free enterprise. These were not the only prospective benefits. The proceeds from the sale of assets were US$10bn. up to 1995, and savings on capital expenditure were estimated at US$30bn. There were additional advantages from greater efficiency and productivity.[22] By the late 1990s, privatization in Malaysia had been applied to many of the activities that were candidates for conversion to private enterprise all over the world. Examples included airlines, airports, the generation of electricity, railroads, road construction, shipping, shipping containers, telecommunications, and so on. By 1995 about fifty entities were being privatized each year, either at federal or state level. Recent examples, completed or in progress, have included the Bakun hydro-electric dam in Sarawak, the Sabah Electricity Board, and the "second crossing" between Malaysia and Singapore. There have been two important examples of "corporatization," putting an enterprise on a more cost-accountable basis, perhaps with a view to its later privatization: the University of Malaya; and Bernama, the government agency for the distribution of foreign news.

The methods of privatization are too numerous to explore here. There were examples of partial privatization, with the government retaining some assets. In many cases, shares were issued to groups or individuals. This was a way of distributing benefits to employees, or of fulfilling the NEP goal of rewarding Bumiputera. It also helped to implement Mahathir's policy of building up a strong stock market in Kuala Lumpur. (He frequently used the performance of the stock market to gauge the health of the economy.) Joint ventures were common, and, when foreign firms were involved, they provided much of the necessary technological expertise.

Although by 1997 privatization was still proceeding, the government seemed to be considering alternative methods of achieving its benefits. One way was by improving the working of public enterprises without wholesale privatization. Thought was given to corporatizing organizations, without proceeding as far as privatization.[23]

Privatization clearly had great advantages, and solved many of the well-known defects of bureaucracy. Two broad categories of those affected by privatization (apart from the new owners of the enterprises concerned and the government itself), were labor and consumers. The former did rather better than expected, while some adverse effects on the latter were masked by the country's general prosperity. According to the Prime Minister, while, in many countries, employees who were deemed to be inefficient could have their services terminated, this was not so in Malaysia. Employees were given an assurance that their salaries would still increase. Alternatively, they had the choice of a new scheme, which would give them bonuses and the ability to buy shares.[24]

Consumers have faced increased charges for such items as road tolls and telephone rates. Sometimes, also, they are compelled to accept "improved" products, which they would not have chosen to pay for if they had been given the choice. This is happening with toll roads. When they were constructed, alternative (and free) routes still existed. But in 1997 Mahathir announced that sometimes there might not be any alternatives available.[25] Less well-off consumers are particularly hard hit. However, consumers have not often stridently objected. An important exception occurred just before the 1990 general election, when there were toll increases at Cheras on the North–South Highway.[26]

In privatizing, Malaysia, like other countries, had to make a decision: how much competition should be allowed? The dilemma is that if too many firms are allowed to compete, some advantages of large-scale enterprise may be lost. Yet, if too few are permitted, regulation of the charges, provided by the market, may be lost. Of course, there can be regulation by appointed regulators, but the system is not simple and regulators may be "captured" by interest groups. Mahathir pointed out that too much regulation might result in bankruptcy. "The government must ensure that existing competition…among companies involved in privatization projects would not be too intense."[27] Most privatization in Malaysia has conformed to this pattern. For example, the postal services, energy, and telecommunications have not been much exposed to market forces. Competition has been judged to be practicable in only a few instances, such as telecommunications equipment, or the use of containers in Port Kelang. Generally, public monopoly has been replaced by private monopoly.

What firms benefit from privatization contracts?

Criticisms of the allocation of privatization contracts are not based primarily on ethnicity. When interpreted, the provisions of the NEP and the ICA permit a Bumiputera share of at least 30 percent. As an example, the Bumiputera share for the construction of the Kuala Lumpur international airport in the mid-1990s was 40 percent of the total costs. However, many Chinese believe that, when sub-contracts are taken into account, they are not receiving as much as 30 percent. Statistics need careful handling. The value of the proportion received by Chinese originally is not the same as it is a year or two later. The Chinese and foreign share increases over time, while the Malay share falls. Many Malays, violating the intent of the NEP, do not hold their equity for long, but sell for the sake of a short-term capital gain.[28]

Allocations of contracts to Malays favored by the government are not restricted to privatization transactions. But, since privatization has become popular, it has formed an increasingly high proportion of such contracts.

Mahathir referred to the need for qualified people when he told UMNO members not to harbor ill feelings against Malays who had done well, especially those who had benefited from privatization. Before they were awarded projects, they had already proven their ability to run big operations. No doubt, this claim was correct in some cases, but sometimes, although a firm might have had experience in handling big projects, it might not have been the *same kind* of project. The North–South Highway project and the Bakun hydro-electric dam in Sarawak (pp. 59, 67) were examples. The highway project was the largest public works contract to date, and ran from close to the Thai border in the north to Johor Baru in the south. The contract was awarded to United Engineers (Malaysia) (UEM), a holding of Hatibudi (p. 60). It was vigorously attacked by Lim Kit Siang, the DAP leader, who alleged that UEM had been awarded the contract despite the fact that it was inexperienced in the field, insolvent, and was not quoting the lowest tender. This was only one example of open tendering not being enforced. There was a public outcry, and a court injunction imposed a halt to construction. This was only temporary, but the protest secured better terms for the public; government loans to UEM were to be reduced, and the period of toll collection was to be only twenty-five, as opposed to thirty, years.[29] The North–South Highway privatization was important in eliciting evidence of the links between privatization contracts and the operations of UMNO's corporate business operations (pp. 59–62).

UMNO in business

UMNO in business is a much less publicized topic than "money politics," which was touched upon in Chapter 1. It was observed there that money politics affected the party as far down as branch level. But UMNO's business activities are known to a much more limited number of people. They involve only a few persons at the apex of UMNO's organization,[30] plus a small number of people (formerly described as "proxies," nowadays known as "links") who manage firms whose operations provide finance for UMNO. It is probable that 99 percent of UMNO members know nothing about these arrangements, and the proportion of the employees of the firms in question who know may not be much different. This type of arrangement is rare in the world; quite possibly it is confined to Malaysia.

UMNO's entry into business did not occur until the early 1970s, and even then was initially only on a small scale. There seem to have been few formal mechanisms in UMNO in Tunku's time, although money was transferred to UMNO from the MCA.[31] Emergencies might be dealt with by Tunku's receiving help for the party from his Chinese friends. In the early 1970s there were three main motives for UMNO to try to raise money on a regular basis. One was to limit foreign control of the media. Another was to become independent of Chinese contributions. Another was to build up a fund for political use, and, in particular, to pay off the costs of UMNO's new headquarters building. The original estimate for the building was approximately US$48m, but eventually the figure turned out to be about three times as much. The building was elaborate, even opulent, in comparison with its predecessor, a building on Jalan Tuanku Abdul Rahman, which, literally, had a low profile. Its unostentatious exterior was matched by standard government-issue furniture. The elevator, often marked with scurrilous graffiti, was nasty, brutish, and slow.

In accord with the reasons for raising money stated earlier, UMNO's first significant business venture was Fleet Holdings which, under UMNO's Treasurer, Razaleigh, took over the Kuala Lumpur edition of the Singapore-based *Straits Times*, owned by Singapore and British interests.[32] Later, the holdings were extended, and passed into the hands of Mahathir's friend and Finance Minister, Tun Daim Zainuddin. It was under Daim that UMNO's corporate activities really took off, extending into television, manufacturing, mining, property, and so on. By 1990, the value of UMNO's corporate holdings was estimated at US$0.8bn. Before then, however, there were bewildering transformations of the structure of the holdings, some the consequence of takeovers, and others prompted by the wish to minimize damage to UMNO's assets from the court ruling in 1988 that UMNO was illegal (p. 43).

A new element on the UMNO corporate scene was Hatibudi Senderian Berhad, incorporated by a decision of the UMNO leadership in 1984. Its top personnel were linked to Fleet. One of its directors was Tan Sri Halim Saad, who was also appointed a director of UEM – a not very prosperous public company before it was acquired by Hatibudi. He was the best known of the "proxies," although others were prominent, such as Tan Sri Wan Azmi Wan Hamzah. Acting informally for UMNO and visible as directors, the proxies managed holding companies and executed takeovers to advance the party's business interests.

According to Daim, the story was simple. UMNO's response, financially, to having been declared illegal and having had its assets placed under the "official assignee," was to have Hatibudi, which controlled UEM, bought out by a new company, Hatibudi Nominees. Additionally, Fleet Holdings was acquired by unidentified parties, believed to be associated with Halim Saad. Fleet was taken over by a new company, Renong; the proceeds of the transaction went towards reducing Fleet's debts. These transactions were intended to meet two objectives. They were meant to centralize all UMNO's assets. At the same time, the aim was to sever all direct links between the party and the companies it controlled. According to Daim: "After Renong takes over, I have no more say. It's purely a private company."[33] Mahathir was technically correct in telling Parliament that UMNO was not involved in any business.[34]

Daim's story is not simple, unless a key is provided. The key is the use of proxies, principally Halim Saad, but also others, such as Wan Azmi. Halim, Azmi, and others were paid glowing tributes by Daim. They were intelligent, financially astute and hardworking. They had a long association with Daim, dating from the time when he was a director of Peremba, the commercial and construction arm of UDA.[35] Halim had a reputation as a philanthropist, well known for his donations for the building of schools and mosques. In 1995 Mahathir commended the activities of Halim and others like him. In so doing, he provided a useful summary of the highlights of the proxy system and its benefits.

> I think we should share the happiness of their success. These individuals have not forgotten UMNO. They make all sorts of contributions to society, but they prefer to maintain a low profile. But it's a fact that they help build schools, provide scholarships, and undertake many other projects. Part of their success was made possible through the government's privatization programme. Before these individuals were awarded projects under the programme, they had already proven their ability to run big operations.[36]

The "insulation" of UMNO's business activities from public view had several advantages. To have public discussions on the topic could limit the freedom of action of those in UMNO now concerned with the business side. Some of the UMNO rank-and-file might be appalled at the size of the rewards reaped by the proxies. Halim Saad was reputed to be already a billionaire several years before 1990; such wealth would buy several UMNO buildings, even at current prices. Proxies are also said to be close to some UMNO leaders with whom they have financial connections. Another reason has been mentioned, but it would apply only during a period of UMNO instability, such as the late 1980s. At such a time, it would be better for party leaders not to have official party assets, which could not be freely spent if a court order were successfully brought against the party. Informal arrangements, such as proxies, may, in retrospect, have their disadvantages. If, for example, a proxy dies suddenly, UMNO may be unable to recoup any assets which, informally, he was holding for the party.[37]

Seldom mentioned are UMNO's corporate business activities at divisional level. In 1995, there were about sixteen thousand companies set up by UMNO divisions, branches, and individuals. Many of these were established principally in order to receive and allocate shares allotted to Bumiputera companies. In 1995 Mahathir deplored the practice by which these organizations sold them for short-term profits, instead of being allocated to those who genuinely wanted to go into business. Future applications for shares, he said, should be submitted to the UMNO supreme council, to ensure that they were not linked to party divisions or branches.

Contracts continue to be awarded to Renong and the other companies with which it is associated. It is hard to think of fields into which it has *not* expanded. Recent instances of its activities include the privatization of electricity in Sabah and the new bridge, the "second crossing," between Malaysia and Singapore (1997). UMNO's corporate arrangements were not immune from the economic crisis of August 1997, although they were aided with public money. In November 1997, the cash-rich UEM bailed out Renong, UMNO's chief financial arm, the cost being RM2.4bn. The effect was to benefit major shareholders at the expense of the minority shareholders. An overall loss of investors' confidence was reflected in a fall of the ringgit.[38]

In this transaction, there were, so to speak, wheels within wheels. Some of the bailout money, allegedly, was taken by the government from the Employees Provident Fund (EPF), without having consulted with the contributors. (For a similar, earlier, government use of the EPF, see p. 70.)

It should be added that UMNO's funds are not entirely derived through the arrangements just described. Some come from donations, not all of which are from UMNO members; many well-off Chinese think that they will get better returns from contributions to UMNO, in preference to giving to the MCA.

A chief objection to the Malaysian government's entry into business on a large scale is that, although the government is a supporter of capitalism, it does not practise the free-market policies that offer the best prospects of achieving an optimum allocation of resources, because of the business activities of the political party with which it is so closely associated. As things are, a limited number of not necessarily meritorious beneficiaries enjoy "rents" at the expense of a large number of consumers. Why should the beneficiaries of government policies not support political parties through campaign contributions, instead of the government imposing what is in effect a tax on the public? The present "system" seems to have grown up as an *ad hoc* effort to meet UMNO's financial problems, without thought being given to the wider implications.

The New Economic Policy and the Malay middle classes

Information about the Malaysian class system should help to explain the patterns and evolution of politics in the country. It may be of use in identifying the sources of power and their shifts, and in providing clues about possible changes in the attitudes of government, for example towards greater openness or democracy.

Unfortunately, there are obstacles to such endeavors. Classes are elusive and ambiguous, as are terms such as "the middle class," or even "the middle classes." Data must be considered in their social context, and developments in western Europe or North America may not have parallels in Asia, including Malaysia. In Malaysia, particularly, class interpretations, even as they chronicle class developments, have to pay regard to the constraining effects of a pervasive ethnic framework.

One account of class, written in the mid-1980s, made no mention of business people, propelled upward by the NEP, as constituting part of the "hegemonic fraction" of the ruling class.[39]

Since the effects of the NEP have become clearer, attempts have been made to speculate on the changing composition and behavior of the Malay middle class or classes. Between 1970 and 1993, the Malay middle class rose from 13 percent to 28 percent of the population. The working class tripled from 7.8 percent, while the agricultural population fell from 65.2 percent to 33.5 percent – it was cut almost in half.[40]

Another calculation, covering almost the same period (1957–99), found that the Bumiputera numbers in the middle class rose at a higher rate than their Chinese or Indian counterparts. A more refined version of this research split the "middle class" into four groups – professional and technical, administrative and managerial, clerical, and sales. All four grew substantially, 1957–1990.[41] Even without direct benefits from the NEP, and even though some of them were unhappy about "discrimination," non-Malays, especially the Chinese, also experienced a rise in the proportion of those engaged in middle-class occupations. Although the NEP was intended primarily to improve the condition of the Malays, there was a "spillover," by way of economic growth, to the advantage of other ethnic groups. Had this not occurred, non-Malay discontent might have been hard to contain. The NEP was predicated on growth, and, fortunately, for about fifteen years this assumption held good.

Relying mainly on the analogy of western Europe, it is sometimes said that the rise of a middle class leads to a growing number of people being in favor of increasing democratic tendencies in government. There is a degree of plausibility for this view, as applied to Malaysia. Those who are members of interest groups, particularly those that have a political approach, such as Aliran, the Consumers' Associations, etc., tend to be middle class, as do professional associations, such as the Bar Council. However, members of such groups, apart from some eminent exceptions, tend to be idealists rather than activists. Moreover, the focus of their efforts seems to be to assert human rights rather than to promote democracy. The impact of such groups is lessened by government restrictions (p. 110–11). The government has also been successful in persuading many people that Malaysia is already essentially a democratic country, because relatively free and fair elections give the government, the winner of elections, a mandate to act according to its convictions.

Arguments, based on European experience, about the behavior of the middle classes are misconceived.[42] There are few Asian counterparts of some European institutions that have a high degree of autonomy, such as universities and a non-government-controlled press. Those who believe that economic development will lead to democracy underrate the fact that the process of economic development in Southeast Asia was more state directed than in Europe. In Malaysia, the government has the ability to dispense favors. So, one consequence of greater material prosperity may not be to strengthen claims for more democracy, but to intensify demands for whatever additional benefits can be extracted from government.

The success of the NEP in nurturing, and consolidating, a Malay middle class – and upper class – is undeniable. The consequences, however, do not – at least so far – seem to have had all that much to do with promoting democratization. Rather, the NEP has raised expectations of further material success. Furthermore, the exclusive "club" to which Bumiputera were given access by the NEP, may soon have new "membership rules" when "Vision 2020" comes into force (pp. 165–7) if it really does have the effect of obliterating distinctions between Bumiputera and non-Bumiputera. Future governments have to be aware of possible pressures for more democracy. However, they should also be prepared to cope with ethnic tensions which may actually be exacerbated because expectations about the withering away of ethnicity may have been too optimistic.

Beyond the NEP's declared purposes lay the attractive political possibility that it might make a substantial number of Bumiputera so grateful that they would support UMNO for many years to come. A 1997 government measure to help the economic prospects of Bumiputera, while in conformity with the initial thrust of the NEP, may also be attractive to Bumiputera electors. It is intended to fill a gap in the training of Bumiputera who fall between the extremes of middle- or upper-class business people and those in low income brackets. Those judged to be qualified would be trained for moving into service industries, trading, and franchises.[43] Politically, the new scheme might derive partly from a perception that, at the 1995 election, the behavior of the urban middle class may have been a key element.[44]

The heavy industries policy

Until the 1980s, manufacturing in Malaysia had concentrated on processing imported raw materials, food, and chemicals, and assembling imported components, such as of electronics and of vehicles. The domestically added value of such items was quite low, technological transfer was minimal, and the contribution to developing a skilled labor force was limited.

Mahathir did not think that this was a pattern conducive to industrialization and economic progress. He therefore launched a "heavy industries" policy in 1980 when he was Minister of Trade and Industry. HICOM (the Heavy Industry Corporation of Malaysia), later renamed HICOM Holdings, was established to plan, identify, initiate, invest in, and manage such projects.

Heavy industries have been defined as having at least some of the following characteristics: requiring large investments to match their large scale; possessing long periods of gestation; yielding initial rates of return that are low by purely commercial criteria. The sting is in the tail. Leaders who embark on such projects have to believe deeply in the worth of the long-term benefits to nurture them devotedly in the early stages. Mahathir possessed such a belief, trusting that a heavy industries policy would bring spin-offs and encourage links among industries. He saw joint ventures with foreign firms as a way for Malaysia to acquire know-how. His strategy was to inspire management with his own dedication. He sought to dramatize the new products. For instance, he drove a model of the Proton Saga car (an early product of the policy) over the new Penang bridge in September 1985, six months before it was open to the public. A photograph shows him framed by two testimonials to his commitment to modernization – the car and the bridge.

Mahathir continued to have jurisdiction over HICOM when he became Prime Minister in 1981. Looking beyond the immediate economic effects, he thought that such activities were an expression of nationalism and would show that Malays could advance beyond the economic limits portrayed in the early Malaysia Plans.[45]

In the mid-1980s, when Malaysia was undergoing a recession and its commodity exports' earnings were declining, he claimed that setting up heavy industries would reduce Malaysia's dependence on world commodity markets. The costs of promoting heavy industries were met largely from loans from abroad. These could be incurred with some confidence because of the rapid increase in revenues from petroleum sales. However, to estimate the costs of the Proton, it is not enough to count the actual monetary costs to consumers and others. The inclusive costs must also allow for "opportunity costs" – the costs of giving up making other things that could have been made, if the Proton had not been manufactured.[46]

HICOM set up companies in accordance with its mandate, which were incorporated in an Industrial Development Master Plan, drawn up by a group of United Nations development experts. The two best known – the Proton Saga (Perusahaan Otomobil Nasional) national car project and Perwaja Trengganu, a steel mill – are described below. The others included a gas processing plant, a pulp and paper project, a small engine project (for motorcycles), cement plants, etc. Not all the projects were undertaken by HICOM. Others were initiated by the state petroleum company, Petronas, or by one of the State Economic Development Corporations. Foreign participation, via a joint venture, with an injection of technical know-how, was an essential component in the projects.

The Proton was launched without much consultation, either outside or inside Malaysia. While still Minister of Trade and Industry, Mahathir contacted Mitsubishi, apparently without sounding out any other possible Japanese partners, and reached agreement with Mitsubishi. Only a narrow circle of Malaysians was engaged in the negotiations.[47] Decision-making on heavy industries, and on some related topics, seems to have been centralized in the Prime Minister's Department.[48] A council of economic advisers had been set up, but apparently did not last long, the reason being, reputedly, that it was not very supportive of Mahathir's insistence on the importance of heavy industry, including the Proton.[49] There seems to have been reluctance to make use of knowledgeable Chinese in the Proton project. However, on marketing and selling, the government relied on existing Chinese firms. There was some truth in comments that the Proton was not really a Malaysian car, but a Japanese car with a Malaysian "chop" (name). In 1994 Mahathir accepted this, admitting that Malaysia would not have the know-how to produce a fully fledged car for ten to fifteen years.[50]

Some basic difficulties were encountered by the car project. One, which was seemingly almost inescapable, was how to sell enough cars to reach an optimum, or even viable, scale of production. One possibility was to widen the "domestic" market. A previous attempt to agree on the production of an "ASEAN" car had failed. So did talks with Indonesia (1985) to cooperate in producing a car. (Actually, Indonesia started to produce its own car in the 1990s.) Malaysia, beginning with a production rate of 80,000 cars annually, saw two ways of expanding its production and selling it, and tried both of them. (A third possibility, of increasing Malaysia's population to 70,000,000 by the year 2100,[51] was floated by Mahathir, but was not very helpful in the near future.) One was to place a high tax on imported cars, which was done. By 1996, duties on imports ranged from 145 to 300 percent. The remaining strategy was to develop an export market, beginning with promotion campaigns in Britain and the Far East, and by 1996 a fifth of the Protons produced were being exported.

After years of losses, it was decided that structural adjustments were needed. A team of consultants was recruited from Mitsubishi to replace the existing directors, which was not replaced by Malaysians until 1993.[52] With better management, and having reached the 60 percent local content necessary for entry into Western markets, the Proton has been making profits (taking no account of subsidies) since 1990.

The Proton was privatized in 1995, when the bulk of the government's controlling share in HICOM, which owned 27.4 percent of Proton, was sold.[53] The buyer was a Malay businessman, close to Mahathir, who died shortly afterwards in an accident. Proton is now cooperating with firms, some of them Japanese, other than Mitsubishi, which was not perceived as having transmitted technology very rapidly.

Other cars (including other "national cars") have appeared on the scene, or are scheduled to appear. There are different versions, including vans and sports cars. The Proton pattern is followed, through a consortium of a local firm(s) and a foreign firm(s).

A problem will soon face the Malaysian car industry. Malaysia's membership of the World Trade Organization will compel it, in 2002, to give up the benefit it enjoys from its protective duties. The Proton is widely regarded as a success, especially in Malaysia. While the benefits may be judged to have exceeded the costs, critics believe that Malaysia's essential dependence on Japanese auto firms has not diminished.

The story of Perwaja Terengganu, originally a joint venture between the Trengganu State Economic Development Corporation and the Nippon Steel Corporation, is one of almost unrelieved gloom.[54] In effect, the tragedy was in two acts, separated by what is now (1998) seen to have been a temporary remission. Like the Proton, the "venture" was based on a subsidy. Perwaja attempted to convert imported ore into "sponge iron" through the use of gas from offshore oilfields. Unfortunately, the process had not been tested commercially. The costs exceeded those of the imported product, even though they were heavily subsidized by cheaper gas and electricity prices. The local product was just not good enough to be acceptable. Luckily, the project was less important for the economy than was the Proton venture. Nevertheless, the consequences were bad enough. Compensation paid by Nippon Steel was not sufficient to make the project viable, and in 1988 Perwaja was removed from HICOM's jurisdiction and put under the management of Tan Sri Eric Chia, who had been in charge of Proton's domestic marketing. Chia resigned in 1995, and the new managing director ordered management changes and an investigation. It appeared that there had been production problems, and possibly bad management, and financial losses, which are being investigated by the Anti-Corruption Agency. Perwaja's "recovery" under Chia was an illusion. The government had to write off the losses,[55] which amounted to over US$1bn.

The Bakun dam in Sarawak is a heavy industry project that aroused international criticism and demonstrations from people who were due to be resettled (pp. 119–20). In August 1997, in view of the plunge in stock market prices in Malaysia and the drop in the value of the ringgit, the government announced that dates for the completion of the Bakun dam and some other heavy industry projects would have to be postponed. Soon afterward, in late November 1997, Ekran, a vital component in building the dam, stated that it was no longer interested. The government announced that it would rescue the operation, which gave rise to fears that it might do the same for other projects, thus damaging government finances even more, and undermining investment confidence. The value of the ringgit fell to a record low.

Mahathir's buildings and architecture

Mahathir has been a builder, but some of his constructions were designed not just to be serviceable or to meet economic needs, but to impress, or even embody some aesthetic aspirations. He was defensive about charges that he was building too many "competitive" monuments. In his opinion, people could, and should, be proud of monuments or towers, but not of him. Building high was justified, because in the towns land was scarce. In fact, some projects were highly visible, and public interest was stimulated by those that competed with each other to be noted, however briefly, in the record books. The twin Petronas Towers in the centre of the capital were a good example, visible from well beyond Kuala Lumpur's boundaries, unless obscured by the haze caused by Indonesia's forest fires (p. 120). For a time, they were the highest in the world, although there were definitional conflicts with the claims of the Sears Tower in Chicago. Both will be surpassed in 1998 by similar towers in China and elsewhere. Record-seeking seems to be infectious. It was claimed for Malaysia that, in constructing the towers, another world record had been set – for the continuous pouring of concrete.

A good deal of care has been devoted to planning new building projects in Malaysia. For instance, the new city center for Kuala Lumpur was chosen by a committee representing the investors in the project, the city, and the government. The result was intended to project the national vision and to be in harmony with Malaysia's heritage, as well as to constitute a prime example of building excellence, including the New City Tower – the spectacular Menara Kuala Lumpur.

> Dr. Mahathir said that he had visited nearly every country in the world and it was his view that this was the most beautiful tower ever built. Noting that there were people who likened it to a child's rattle, he said "These comments only show that they are envious."[56]

It was hardly convincing for Ghafar to defend Mahathir's projects by saying that they were not lavish and were only in the interests of the economy.[57] They were surely *intended* to astonish, rather than to be practical or utilititarian – that was meant to be the essence of their beauty.

Nevertheless, to the politically aware, aesthetic reactions were sometimes overpowered by symbolism. The Dayabumi Complex, completed in 1984, was for a time the highest structure in Kuala Lumpur. It was completed ahead of schedule by a Japanese consortium, but cost millions of dollars more than a tender submitted by a local firm. At the building's completion, Mahathir observed that it "held the attention of many not only because of its beauty but also because a group out to defeat the Look East policy has made it a symbol."[58]

Apparently, not only did the Prime Minister identify himself with his new projects, political considerations may affect the aesthetic judgments of others – at least until the origins of the buildings have been forgotten.

Crashes and controversies

This section is concerned with financial disasters which involved politicians or government officials in the main during Mahathir's tenure. They were of various kinds. Some had to do with the misuse of public funds, others concerned individuals who misused their official positions or official information. In the mid-1980s such scandals reached almost endemic proportions, so much so that they prompted the question: were they not at least partly the consequence of a get-rich-quick mentality, encouraged by a policy of encouraging Bumiputera in business, which led to the pursuit of wealth, untempered by ethics, or even by fear of the law?

The outstanding Malaysian financial disaster of the 1980s occurred when Bumiputra Malaysia Finance (BMF), a subsidiary of Bank Bumiputra, which operated in Hong Kong, collapsed with losses of about US$1bn in 1983. What is relevant to the theme of this book is not the precise financial details but, rather, the lack of Malaysian direction of the organization's activities, and the absence of sufficient checks on those employees who contrived to extract personal benefits from it. The former can be easily summarized.[59] Bank Bumiputra stood at the apex of those organizations created to improve the economic condition of the Malays and other indigenous peoples. Its functions were to train Bumiputera in business methods and to advise and support their business ventures financially. It betrayed that endeavor. Unfortunately, not enough attention was given to allowing for the inexperience of those employed, many of them young Malay graduates. In Hong Kong, the financial atmosphere was hectic because of the recent escalation of property values. BMF worked in the property market, especially through the Carrian group, and became the greatest source of its loans. Although, apparently, BMF had not been intended to operate in the property market in Hong Kong, to the uninitiated the prospects of gain seemed just too tempting. Not only were BMF's transactions with Carrian inept, they were also corrupt. Carrian made improper payments to BMF officials, in the form of "consulting fees," etc. In exchange, BMF extended unauthorized loans to Carrian. It was unaware of the imminent fall in prices, and when Carrian, as a consequence, went bankrupt, BMF was unable to recover most of its losses. Operating in Hong Kong was intended to be part of a learning process for BMF personnel, so the stakes should have been smaller. Hong Kong Chinese, maybe correctly, pride themselves on being financially smarter than Southeast Asian Chinese; to expose BMF personnel to their dealings was to plunge them into more competition than they would have faced at home.

The losses suffered were equivalent to about 3 percent of Malaysia's national income. After the crash, most of them were taken over by Petronas, the state oil company. However, this device failed to conceal that there *had* been a loss – a real loss, not just a "paper loss." The money had been diverted from objectives that had a higher priority than supporting unsuccessful speculators. The Malaysian economy, then suffering from a recession, a large budget deficit, and balance-of-payments problems, could ill afford it.

There was consternation in Bank Bumiputra and in Bank Negara (the Central Bank), which denied that it was responsible for Bank Bumiputra, and in the government. Neither the Prime Minister, nor anyone else at cabinet level, admitted to knowing about BMF operations. In October 1993 the Prime Minister denounced BMF officials who had, in effect, awarded themselves consulting fees. Three resigned, and one had already resigned. Later, a committee of inquiry named those people and others as having received improper payments from Carrian. No criminal charges were brought against anyone by the Malaysian authorities.[60] This seemed to accord with Mahathir's view that, although a "heinous crime" had been committed, and those concerned were morally wrong, it was within the law and we could not take them to court.[61] In Hong Kong arrests were made, and extradition proceedings were begun against BMF officials in Britain, one of whom was extradited, tried, convicted and sentenced.[62]

The principle of ministerial responsibility did not operate. Names of people at the highest levels of government were mentioned, but no action followed. It seemed to be a government policy not to take any responsibility. The operations of the bodies concerned seemed to be impenetrable. Lim Kit Siang denounced the government for failing to take responsibility. A few prominent Malays, including Hussein and Anwar, then Minister of Agriculture and head of UMNO Youth, called for further inquiry, but without any response. Members of the government were rumored to have been involved, from the top down. No action was taken against them. However, action was taken *by* one of them – Razaleigh. In 1996 the London *Sunday Times* apologized to him and agreed to pay damages for allegations about a "corrupt connection" to a banking fraud in Hong Kong.[63]

The majority of Malay politicians were not just defending themselves. They wished to preserve the reputations of the NEP and those, including employees of BMF, who were now occupied in helping to implement it. They did not want further enquiries. This was the position of the Finance Minister, Daim, in 1984: the unpleasant episode of the BMF scandal was now a thing of the past.[64]

A previous banking controversy had been on a smaller scale, and had some points of difference from the BMF case. Harun, chairman of the Bank Rakyat, and Menteri Besar of Selangor, was convicted of various charges, including criminal breach of trust, in 1976 and 1977 (p. 6). He had shown his entrepreneurial spirit by promoting a Muhammad Ali–Joe Bugner fight in Kuala Lumpur in 1975. If there had been a profit, it would have benefited the bank and also a UMNO Youth complex. The fight was successful in obtaining great publicity, but financially it was a loss. To recoup, Harun had recourse to using the bank's funds.[65] The comparison with BMF was not very close. The loss was only US$3m. There were also extenuating features: Harun claimed that his actions had been sanctioned, unofficially, by Prime Minister Razak. Another obvious difference was that Harun was actually sent to jail where he was placed in charge of the prison library. The larger BMF crime went unpunished, as far as the principal figures were concerned. Those who *were* punished were convicted, not in Malaysia, but elsewhere.

Other controversies during the period involved the use of government funds or the stock market, and involved Daim, the Finance Minister.

A minor, and not very widely publicized, breach of propriety concerned the government's handling of funds in the EPF (Employees Provident Fund). It used some of the EPF money to make investments designed to stimulate the economy. The transactions were not illegal. However, the government did not explain the issue clearly enough to prevent DAP charges of "share speculation" seeming plausible.[66]

Two other incidents were more serious. The first concerned a risky and unsuccessful government policy. The second had to do with Daim's private fortunes. As regards the former, the government decided to try to establish a tin cartel through a company, MAMINCO. However, despite the government's support of tin, prices collapsed and the treasury suffered a loss of about US$200m.[67] It is hard to say who was responsible for the failed policy – Mahathir, the Prime Minister, or Daim, the Finance Minister. Whatever the constitutional niceties, their personal relations were so close that on many occasions they acted as one. They were born in the same *kampong* (village) in Kedah, but, unlike Mahathir, Daim studied law in London, joined the government legal service, and then worked for a private law firm. In the early 1970s he specialized in property development, and built his own fortune on the basis of a gift of land in Selangor from the Menteri Besar, Harun. After studying urban planning at Berkeley, he entered politics, and in 1984 accepted Mahathir's invitation to become Finance Minister. He was active in UMNO's corporate activities. Even after Anwar succeeded him as Finance Minister, Daim continued to be financial adviser to the government. His power has been based on his competence in finance, and on his close relations with the Prime Minister. He lacks a secure base inside UMNO, and is not a credible successor to Mahathir. He has not shrunk from power, but has wanted to exercise it where his own capabilities would be most effective. He probably would not have been averse to accepting a really senior post in an important international body.

Relations between Daim and Mahathir have been so close that they exchange telephone calls every day. They have worked well together, not only because of their long association, but also because Mahathir is convinced that, unlike any of his other colleagues, Daim could never be his political rival. One feature of their relationship may indicate that either Daim was even tougher than was generally supposed, or that Mahathir was less tough. Daim, apparently, was less tolerant of inefficient management. For instance, it is said that he, rather than Mahathir, was mainly responsible for firing some unsuccessful senior executives in heavy industry projects.[68]

Daim was the leading figure in a major scandal, which was unravelled by professional journalism at its most persistent. In September 1986, the *Asian Wall Street Journal* suggested that Daim had benefited from the sale of shares in the United Malayan Banking Corporation to Pernas, the state trading organization, and that he had acquired the shares shortly before becoming Finance Minister. The key issue concerning Daim's transactions was whether he transferred his shares before or after he joined the cabinet. Mahathir declared that the transfer came first, but the *Asian Wall Street Journal* maintained the contrary.[69] The conflict of views provoked fierce reactions from the government, leading to temporary bans on the *Journal*.[70]

Journalists, in search of words to characterize Daim, have had recourse to terms such as "quiet," "shy," "reluctant," and the like. To write a flamboyant headline on him would have constituted a real challenge. It would be an understatement to say that he was at his best in working behind the scenes. He amassed money in a quiet way. His publicly listed and private holdings were valued at about US$250m. in 1984, just before the question of his wealth became a matter of public discussion. They must be much higher now (1998).[71] In spite of his association with some of the scandals and "incidents" referred to above, his performance as Finance Minister was favorably judged. He was well suited to be in the post at the time of the mid-1980s recession, and was adept at implementing the downsizing that it entailed. When Mahathir was outside Malaysia for two months in 1997, Daim's opinion on economic issues was widely quoted, though not as much as Anwar's. In the economic crisis of 1997, he helped to moderate Mahathir's inappropriate initial reactions (pp. 75–6).

The cases referred to above were concentrated within a few years. It was not farfetched for a Supreme Court judge to say, in 1987, that in his opinion they were a by-product of the NEP. He asserted that many Malaysians in both the private and public sectors had lost their sense of values and had lived beyond their means.[72] He added that increasing dishonesty among financial institutions was attributable to the current economic downturn.

In looking for parallels in the 1990s, some similarities and differences are apparent.[73] Bank Negara's 1993 loss of about US$2bn. through speculating in foreign exchange is reminiscent of "the tin caper" (p. 70). There are also dissimilarities. There has been nothing quite comparable, as far as financial institutions are concerned, to the examples of Bank Rakyat and also Bumiputra Malaysia Finance. Nowadays there are perhaps more examples of "mismanagement" which, however, may include acting on behalf of self-interest, rather than the public interest, such as in Perwaja steel and the Bakun dam (pp. 66–7). Deficiencies in the banking system were revealed during the economic crisis, 1997 and after (pp. 175, 178). Comparisons are made more difficult by lack of data. An opposition politician believes that financial scandals may not be less common nowadays, but that reporting of such items would be checked by the government's use of the Official Secrets Act, etc. He doubts if a 1990s equivalent of, say, the North–South Highway scandal could safely be reported with the same amount of detail.[74] There seems to be no reason to attribute such scandals to any new source. The "get-rich-quick" mentality still operates in a context of corruption, which started to impinge seriously on the public consciousness only in mid-1997.

The National Development Policy: the *Second Outline Perspective Plan*

As 1990 approached, the terminus of the NEP, speculation intensified about what would replace it. Some major NEP targets, among them the much-publicized target for Malay corporate ownership, had not been reached, according to the government's statistics. Should the preferences for Malays be extended, and, if so, for how long? Given that the Malays had made some economic gains, was it now time to review the claims of non-Malays? Fortunately, by the late 1980s the recession was practically over. If reconsideration of the NEP had been due a year or two earlier, the debate would have been more acrimonious. If it was now becoming almost a cliché to say that the NEP was dependent on growth, it would also seem to be true that fruitful *discussion* of the NEP's future was dependent on the perception of existing growth.

In 1988, to ensure that these issues were discussed, Mahathir (possibly prompted by the MCA) set up a National Economic Consultative Council (NECC) to consider possible changes.[75] The Council contained equal numbers of Bumiputera and non-Bumiputera, covering a wide range of views, but did not include top decision-makers. However, it was clear that the government was already pursuing its own course. The Economic Planning Unit, in the Prime Minister's Department, was currently working on the relevant sections of the *Sixth Malaysian Plan* and the *Second Outline Perspective Plan* (*OPP2*).

A 1988 Mahathir speech in Singapore was illuminating. The NECC was participating in shaping policy, he said, but it was unlikely that its members would agree, and he thought that eventually they would hand over the task of formulating changes in the NEP to the government. This was a correct estimate of the extent of the NECC's influence, and also sounded like a self-fulfilling prophecy. After many vicissitudes, it did indeed submit a report. Some of its recommendations were included in *OPP2*, which contains the best summary of the National Development Policy (NDP), the NEP's successor.[76] The NDP restated some of the NEP's aims, such as promoting balanced development and optimizing growth, as well as eliminating social and economic inequalities. However, in some respects there was an evident shift in approach. There was to be more emphasis on quality than on quantity. This was to be achieved through more stringent selection of participants when training Bumiputera for important business positions, and setting higher standards of products and services. This was done, for example, by the states cooperating in identifying business people who could be groomed into middle-class Bumiputera entrepreneurs. The new emphasis was less on the transfer of wealth and more on the rapid development of an active Bumiputera commercial and industrial community, and the expansion of capacities to generate income and wealth. More attention would be paid to strengthening the capacities of Bumiputera to retain and manage their wealth effectively.

As regards ethnic implications, the lack of attention paid to the NECC's recommendations seemed ominous to non-Malays. No dates were set for the attainment of the NEP's targets, nor were assurances given that quotas would be set for non-Malays that were close to their proportion in the population. However, the non-Bumiputera actually did better than that – mention of quotas and targets was simply avoided. The relaxations of the NEP, which were introduced during the mid-1980s recession for both Chinese and foreign investors, were continued.

OPP2 concluded that the NEP had been partly successful, but that it had failed to meet some of the targets set, particularly those for greater Bumiputera ownership of corporate wealth. Also, whatever increase there had been was due more to holdings acquired and kept in trust for Bumiputera than to shares held directly by Bumiputera investors.[77] As contemplated in previous plans, Malay gains in representation in the higher levels of the economy were mostly in sectors where previously they had been most *under*-represented; for example, the percentage of Bumiputera in the professions has risen steeply.

To supplement the findings of *OPP2*, it should be added that a change was noticeable in the attitude of the Chinese and other non-Bumiputera.[78] In the early years of the NEP, non-Bumiputera business people fought against the state-controlled policies of the government. However, later many tended to cooperate with Bumiputera partners, who were more active than if the arrangement had been an "Ali-Baba" one (p. 53). Some Chinese adapted to the NEP by forging links close to centers of Malay power, thus achieving more success than those who remained within Chinese business circles.

An obvious question, to which there is no easy answer, is: did the NEP retard growth? *OPP2* asks the question, and makes some pertinent observations. It asserts that, over a period of twenty years, Malaysia had not only achieved growth, but had also effectively addressed the problems of poverty and of economic imbalance. It added that, in the opinion of some, it had retarded growth, because, other things being equal, it had interfered with the free play of market forces. But other things were not equal. The NEP provided an atmosphere of peace and stability that was conducive to growth and to reducing poverty and inequalities. So the case against the NEP was not proven.[79]

The findings of *OPP2* on poverty were reassuring. Such policies, especially those aimed at hard-core poverty, had been successful up to 1995. This was due partly to the expansion of the economy and to the work of unpaid people, as well as of government officials. Increased employment opportunities in urban areas helped to diminish poverty because they attracted people from rural areas – where incomes were lower. The incidence of poverty had fallen to about 9 percent by 1995. Hard-core poverty had been tackled in various ways, including the promotion of income-producing projects and the provision of free loans. Inequalities in incomes were reduced, for example differences between the highest 20 percent and the lowest 40 percent groups had narrowed. [80]

Bumiputera at various times have been given opportunities to buy shares at favorable terms. This privilege has been abused in two principal ways. The recipients of shares have tended to be already at an advantage, through being, for example, related to royal families or connected with UMNO leaders. Second, the shares, once received, are often quickly sold, often to non-Bumiputera, thus making a welcome profit, but defeating the purpose of the scheme – to enable Bumiputera to acquire and *retain* wealth. Names of individuals and firms have not been released but the value of such transfers, 1992–5, was over US$1m.[81] Even if these defects were eliminated there would still be a conflict with one of the main objectives of the NDP – to encourage the Malays' capacity to generate income (p. 73).

So far, the NDP has been much less controversial than the NEP. It has been harder to attack, because it does not present identifiable targets to aim at. Also, up to August 1997, Malaysia had a period of continued prosperity. Policy has also been more accommodating to non-Bumiputera than before, thus helping to moderate ethnic tensions.

The economy: successes and problems

Until August 1997, economic prospects seemed bright. GDP growth reached 9.5 percent and 8.2 percent in 1995 and 1996 respectively, although the rate of increase was expected to decline. Investment continued to increase, having reached a record high in 1996. There has been full employment since 1992; indeed the labor market is tight, in spite of the presence of about a million foreign workers. It was only in August 1997 that the ringgit weakened, following the fall in some other ASEAN currencies, particularly the baht. The stock market also fell. The government's perception that the situation was indeed serious was shown by the end of the year by its contingency plans to slow down, or even postpone indefinitely, the completion of even some of the Prime Minister's favorite projects, such as the Bakun dam.

Looking ahead, two relatively neglected issues claim attention.[82] The Federation of Malaysian Manufacturers has proposed that tax concessions should be granted for research and development. The 1996 amount was only 0.17 percent of GDP, the fortieth position in the world rankings. The other item that has to be tackled is increasing productivity, and the government has committed itself to doing this. It seems less willing to move on R&D; however, in 1997, R&D grants were announced for firms in the Multimedia Super Corridor.

Mahathir and economic policy

In conducting economic policy, the government relies on the services of an established bureaucracy, principally the Economic Planning Unit (EPU). Among ministers, the Minister of Finance and the Minister of Trade and Industry have the main economic (and arguably also political) roles. Under Mahathir, the economic adviser, Daim, is also a key figure. The EPU is in the Prime Minister's Department. Mahathir has more to do with it than his predecessors had, because many of his main interests are focussed on construction, for which careful preparation is essential. There has also been a special section in the EPU concerned with privatization, a special concern of Mahathir's.

After he assumed control of the Ministry of Trade and Industry in 1977, Mahathir became the main director of economic policy. Even with Daim playing a part, Mahathir has had the last word. He also has a number of fixed ideas, on which orthodox economic theories make little impact. Mahathir did not help to formulate the NEP, but in interpreting it, he quickly liberalized it to encourage foreign and non-Bumiputera investment,[83] and is now in the process, it seems, of de-ethnicizing it, through the NDP and, eventually, "Vision 2020." Other policies were also given Mahathir's individual stamp, or sometimes had it withdrawn. The "Look East" policy lived on in name, long after it had ceased to be a potent influence. As an illustration, although there is a Japanese component in the Multimedia Super Corridor, it is not strong by comparison with the US contribution to the project.

The crisis of 1997

In August 1997 Mahathir's command of the economy was severely shaken, so much so that his continuance in office became questionable, although the odds were that he would weather the storm at least for a year or two. There were preliminary signs of trouble which could be inferred from his own statements. Investment was welcome, but local investors should dominate the scene. The economy was not overheated, nor was the government spending beyond its means; growth had been planned, the government contended. The crisis came when the fall in the value of the Thai baht spread to the Philippines, Indonesia, and also Malaysia. The ringgit dropped to a four-year low – in early 1998 it traded at nearly five to the dollar – and the share index fell by 40 percent. Mahathir estimated that per capita income had fallen from about US$5,000 per head to about US$4,000.

External analysts attributed the initial trouble to the combination of an exchange rate that was pegged to the US dollar and a widening trade gap, which gave speculators a good target to aim at. The problems were intensified by government policies. Initially, it tried to shore up the value of the ringgit, through a 60bn. ringgit fund, and also placed a ban on "short-selling," which caused investors to feel trapped. The result was that they sold as much as they could as soon as they could. Many domestic investors also sold. Mahathir had failed to control the market; it was not amenable to the power of his will. Apparently Anwar nudged Mahathir into a reversal in early September 1997 by cutting down expenditure on projects and introducing measures to reduce the deficit, as well as by making it easier for investors to sell shares.[84] Mahathir regained the initiative in 1998, and followed a policy of expanding the economy (see pp. 176–7). The crisis revealed insufficient central control of the banking system, as shown on previous occasions (pp. 68–70).

Economic measures were accompanied by holding demonstrations. Representatives of political parties – even from the opposition – were induced to rally in his favor, as were members of a bank employees' union. The technique was reminiscent of North Korea. Mahathir was not trying to convince foreigners. Evidence of foreign opposition, for instance by foreign magazines, was useful in *stimulating* internal support. While some foreign opinion, for example *The Nation* (Bangkok), called for his resignation, he was resolute in believing in his own analysis of what had gone wrong. He attributed his problems to the rogue speculative activities of George Soros. He, and some other Jews, were said to resent any progress that was made by Muslims. Speculation, he believes, should be banned by international agreement. He was financially innocent. He did not believe that an "invisible hand" was at work. He thought that a visible hand was there and that it was part of a conspiracy. He saw globalization as infringing on his control of Malaysia, yet the foreign investment, which he saw as essential for Malaysia's development, was a manifestation of that same globalization.

These, and subsequent, stormy reactions by Mahathir to the crises are used (p. 174–8) to try to interpret his behavior in adverse situations.

The Multimedia Super Corridor

The Prime Minister's latest and, until now, greatest project is the Multimedia Super Corridor (MSC). It was conceived in 1994 as part of the final phase of the country's industrialization program; however, details are still vague in some respects. At present (1998), its scale is so vast, and the risks and rewards so great, that it has captured attention not only in Malaysia but also in the remainder of Southeast Asia and beyond.

The MSC is multipurpose.[85] As well as being part of Mahathir's industrialization policy, it is also meant to streamline the work of the government by making it eventually "paperless."[86] It is also intended to represent a step beyond even heavy industry. Malaysia's labor costs have become higher than those of most of its neighbors, and its oil reserves may be limited. The aim is to move Malaysia into an information-based economy, as trade barriers are lowered. The MSC, as a potential money-maker, is also seen as a possible help against the effects of a recession.

The MSC is a zone extending to the south of the present capital, Kuala Lumpur (measuring 15km by 50km), which is scheduled to provide an environment for companies seeking to create, distribute, and employ multimedia products and services. It is, broadly speaking, a planned, concentrated, and government-directed variation on the theme of Silicon Valley. It contains three elements. One is a high-capacity global communications and logistics infrastructure and a new large international airport, which critics say will be under-utilized for some time. The second consists of new policies and "cyberlaws," to facilitate the development of multimedia applications and to make Malaysia a leader in the protection of intellectual property. The third aim is to create an attractive, environmentally friendly area for living. There will be no skyscrapers, and 30 percent of the area will consist of green space.

Although the concept seems almost ethereal, compared, say, with factories or dams, the physical development of 7,000 hectares will lead to the creation of massive structures. It would not have been possible to locate anything so extensive within the cramped confines of the existing capital, even with possible extensions. As well as a new airport, Sepang, there will be a new high-tech city, Cyberjaya (still little more than a blueprint in 1998), the nucleus of the corridor, which will extend from the heart of Kuala Lumpur to Sepang.[87] Also near Sepang will be the new administrative capital, Putrajaya, whose site was chosen in 1993. Its population is estimated to exceed 75,000 by the year 2000. Not all government departments will move there; the Ministry of Foreign Affairs will remain in Kuala Lumpur. However, the Prime Minister's Office will be the first to go there, in 1998. All these estimates, of course, are subject to changes in timing occasioned by the financial crisis of August 1997. As well, some states – for instance, Penang – are already preparing to complement the MSC's functions. Construction on the corridor is being carried out by a joint venture, headed by a company comprising the well-known Renong group.

Because of the intricacy of the MSC's operations, a good deal of coordination will be required. Two committees are involved. The higher one, which is mainly consultative and supervisory, is composed of people from both the private and the public sectors. The implementation committee includes two ministers, the Minister for Energy, Telecommunications and Posts, and the Minister for Education, as well as Anwar until 1998. Mahathir is chairman of both committees. It is widely believed that he alone knows enough about the project to be able to coordinate it effectively.[88]

No matter how well structured or innovative the MSC may be, it cannot succeed unless it attracts the best talent. One facet of this is to persuade the most deservedly prestigious firms to participate. In order to do this, the MSC offers a definite area of operations, defined policies, and a government friendly to the investing companies.[89] Two other prerequisites are closely linked. The government must demonstrate its friendliness by providing appropriate incentives. It must provide generous tax concessions and also relax regulations about employment for non-Bumiputera and for foreigners. On the other hand, if the monetary incentives are *too* generous, the overall profitability of the MSC will be reduced. Both of these have been promised.[90] The MSC policy on employment provides an elite version of what all Malaysia may look like after the implementation of "Vision 2020." Cyberlaws are also being drafted, designed to facilitate electronic commercial transactions. Among other things, they license and oversee transactions, and impose fines for infractions such as hacking, implanting viruses, and divulging secret passwords. Other laws are being drafted to penalize the infringement of intellectual property. By October 1997, sixty-six high-tech companies had met the strict criteria demanded for acceptance as having "Super Corridor" status. About half are Malaysian controlled. Foreign companies willing and qualified to participate included, to name only a few: Siemens, Mitsubishi, Oracle MSC, DHL International Limited, and the Nippon Telegraph and Telephone Corporation.[91] The United States was strongly represented because of Malaysia's decision that, although in the past Japan and Korea had been a model for Malaysia (as in the "Look East" policy), the most appropriate (adapted) model would be Silicon Valley. Recruiting prestigious companies is not enough to provide a good chance of success. Local talent must also be obtained. Malaysia is short of high-tech professionals, and efforts are being made to attract qualified Malaysians living abroad, particularly in the Silicon Valley.

Two examples may illustrate the government's determination that the MSC is a top priority. In April 1997 Mahathir gave instructions to the states that they should give MSC projects top priority.[92] Also, in Parliament, bills concerning the MSC should be given preference over other bills (they were also drafted in very broad terms so as to be adaptable to rapid technological change).[93]

Plans for the MSC have difficulties to contend with. Some are particular to Malaysia. The shortage of professionals has been mentioned. Steps have been taken to remedy it by setting up two technological universities in the area. Also, in 1997 the country was suffering from frequent interruptions of electric power. The target is to reduce these by about 40 percent by 2000. The electricity industry is to be reorganized, and charges raised to make more revenue available.

Other problems arise because the future of information technology is uncertain. In a field where rapidly changing technological know-how can be decisive, how can a country be assured that it has committed resources to employing the most appropriate techniques and technology? Malaysia has attempted to be as well informed as possible. It has assembled an impressive international panel of advisers which the Prime Minister and the government can consult on the whole range of relevant issues. The list reads like a *Who's Who* of the world of information technology. Among the names are Bill Gates of Microsoft, James Barksdale of Netscape, Lewis Platt of Hewlett Packard, etc.[94]

Mahathir has devoted much effort to mastering the technological aspects of the MSC, and shows great proficiency in the use of technical language, which impresses long-time experts. Curiously, Lim Kit Siang, the Leader of the Opposition, is also well versed in the subject. If Malaysian politicians are asked which political figure should rival Mahathir's knowledge of the field (expecting a Barisan member to be named), the answer is quite likely to be "Lim Kit Siang."

Lim Kit Siang commends Mahathir for having secured the services of accomplished advisers, but he differs from him on a broader issue. He thinks that the publicity accorded to the MSC has overshadowed previous plans for information technology. He does not want to see a division in the population between the "information poor" and the "information rich."[95] An even more critical comment is that greater information priorities exist than the MSC – that there is a more pressing need to provide electricity to schools that are without it, particularly in Sarawak and Sabah.

One of the closest rivals to Malaysia in the field of information technology is Singapore. Singapore has no specifically designated MSC. It did not need to do this, because it is a small country – the corridor is larger! It has adopted an approach similar to Lim Kit Siang's through an "intelligent island" program, to be completed by 2000. By that date, half the households and practically every business will be connected to a high-speed cable network, providing links to cable television, Internet services, and government offices. This will be extended to banks, libraries, and so on. The similarity is in the determination and political will expressed by the leaders of the two countries. These qualities of Mahathir are evident. Correspondingly, Prime Minister Goh Chok Tong "has taken personal charge of the project and runs it as others would a war effort."[96]

Mahathir takes all his projects with great seriousness, but he is perhaps more immersed in the MSC than in any previous undertaking. The possible fierce competition, the risks, and the uncertainty of the market, have only steeled his resolution. Not only has he mastered its technology; he also devoted his two months' "leave" from Malaysia in 1997 to tirelessly "selling" it to people whose knowledge is perhaps exceeded only by their hardheadedness.

Despite Mahathir's dedication to the Corridor and the construction that will surround it, the timing will almost certainly be slowed down by the crisis that began in 1997.

4 Containing ethnic discontent

The art of governing, in an ethnically diverse society such as Malaysia, consists in ruling so that the interests and feelings of various ethnic groups are not unduly wounded. Unless the government is watchful, resentment may accumulate and be expressed in a larger opposition vote at the next election, or worse, in violence. In the early days of independence, because of the salient and controversial nature of "the bargain," the focus in Malaysia was mainly on the Chinese and, to a lesser extent, the Indians. Possible sources of discontent were augmented in 1963 with the addition of Sarawak and Sabah, about whose inhabitants the federal government knew little.

There were sources of discontent among Malays; PAS represented a major center of dissent which might outbid UMNO on its greater devotion to Islam or its stronger commitment to Malay nationalism. Until the late 1970s, the policy lines between UMNO and PAS had been quite clearly indicated. About that time, however, there emerged an Islamic "resurgence," which transformed the picture. Groups were formed, which added to the complexity of the Islamic trends with which the government would have to deal, and both PAS and UMNO received recruits from these new effervescent sources, who, in turn, influenced their own policies. What measures, or combinations of measures, could UMNO employ in the face of a challenge that was not entirely unexpected, but which was conducted with surprising and disturbing intensity?

The first section of the chapter is devoted to this issue. The second is concerned with the government's relationships with the Chinese and the Indians. The third deals with the government's attempts to control, and promote development among, the diverse inhabitants of Sarawak and Sabah.

The "Islamic resurgence" and the government's response

There is no abrupt break between government policies on this issue before and after Mahathir; nevertheless he put his own distinctive stamp on the government's policy. He felt strongly on the matter, and the full force of his personality was summoned to ensure the implementation of his beliefs. In the late 1960s, Gordon Means observed that government policies had inhibited doctrinal diversification within Islam, and had tended to check some dynamic and modernist trends.[1] The Islamic resurgence, a few years later, burst through the barriers of government policies, although not much of it represented modernizing influences. Perhaps modernization was best typified by the government's *reactions* to the resurgence.

The nature of the resurgence

Unquestionably, the roots of the resurgence lay in a new intensity of feeling about the place of Islam in people's personal and political lives.[2] The resurgence was aimed at making Muslims *better* Muslims, not at converting non-Muslims. It was motivated partly by a desire to assert one's Malay identity. The resurgence was particularly attractive to the young, and originated among students at the University of Malaya in the late 1970s, who had been affected by the events of May 13, 1969 and its aftermath. There was a connection between the reactions of such people towards the problems of the time – such as Malay poverty, Malay language and education, and corruption – and a search for what the teachings of Islam could suggest for solving these problems.[3]

The extent of the resurgence was hard to miss, visually, in its areas of concentration, urban centers in general, and in and near the University of Malaya, in particular. It was obvious in attire, most often in women's headgear, where different versions of the veil conveyed to the initiated the degree of religious fervor in the wearer. Such variations in dress, etc., were sometimes referred to by a near-synonym for the resurgence – *dakwah* (a call to believe in Islam). Less obviously, there were distinctive dietary rules, not only about what could be eaten, but also about how it was prepared and who prepared it. Personal choices on eating had deep social effects. Those with religious views on diet tended to eat together, leading to less collegiality between Malays and non-Malays and even among Malays themselves. Additionally, some of the resurgent groups encouraged, or even stipulated, segregation between the sexes in many aspects of living.

There was no single impetus for the resurgence, which perhaps helps to account for the different forms it took in the various groups involved. There was influence from abroad, e.g., from Libya and Iran, although some Malays found it was disillusioning to visit and experience the ways things worked in some of these countries. Internal influences were certainly strong. It has been argued that the NEP, with the increased opportunities it afforded to Malays, was a potent factor. These greater opportunities increased the confidence of Malays who were able to take advantage of the new policy. However, socially, the "beneficiaries" were often placed in situations where they felt ill at ease, and they sought the security and solidarity that a supportive religious group could provide. Support was all the more necessary for young people who were studying aboard, in Britain or elsewhere, and had to cope with different mores and only partly familiar languages.[4] It was observed that the appeal of the resurgence organizations was attractive initially because it helped personally, but that this was sometimes followed by an interest in Islamic ways of thinking on social and political issues.[5]

In spite of the distinctive nature of the organizations in question, they had some basic tenets in common, which may be briefly summarized. Islam was not only a guide to religion, but also *the* key for understanding the state, politics, law, and society. This precept had sometimes been neglected by Muslim countries that followed Western values, and the organizations believed that Muslims should return to studying the Koran and the teachings of the Prophet Muhammad. Islamic law had to replace Western-inspired civil law. Science and technology should be accepted, but only if they were subordinated to Islam.[6]

The two most powerful Malay political parties in the 1970s, UMNO and PAS, held opposing views on Islamic law and the Islamic state. UMNO looked on itself as *the* party of the Malays, who were Muslims. Consequently, it was an upholder of Islam and Islamic values, but was seldom militant about it. Beyond the purely religious perspective, UMNO did not see Islam as a source of trouble or a threat to economic development policies. Except for irritating dissenting views, emanating mainly from PAS, Islam was viewed as a source of stability, especially in the 1950s and 1960s when it seemed to be a necessary bulwark against the spread of communism.

PAS's religious stance was more forthright than UMNO's. From its inception, it had supported the idea of an Islamic state. At the same time, it had a good deal of common ground with UMNO. It reacted to the events of May 13, 1969 and afterwards in rather the same way as UMNO, namely as a threat to Malay supremacy, and this attitude contributed to its willingness to join the Barisan National in 1974. However, the accord did not last, and it was expelled from the Barisan in 1977. The federal government, acting for "political" reasons, then declared a state of emergency in Kelantan, and, after a split in PAS, UMNO, with the aid of one of the resulting factions, took over the state government of Kelantan after winning a state election in 1978.[7]

Actually, PAS's commitment to Islam was not unalloyed. Its concern about the 1969 riots and the damage to the Malays was a reminder that the party had a strong Malay nationalist strain. Indeed this followed from its origins. One of the organizations that came together to form it in 1951 was a Malay nationalist party, as indicated in its title, Partai Kebangsaan Melayu.[8]

It was not until 1982 that the Islamic component became paramount. In that year a group described (without much originality) as the "Young Turks" took over the direction of the party from the "Old Guard,"[9] and in the mid-1980s conducted a campaign against "ethnic chauvinism." The new policy was exemplified in the creation of a Chinese Consultative Committee, and in a condemnation of the NEP as ethnically based. It is not certain that Malay nationalist influences have been completely eradicated – they are so easily linked with support for Islam. However, the official change in policy provided an additional reason that members of Islamic resurgence groups would choose to become members of, and sometimes electoral candidates for, PAS.

Understanding of PAS has been obscured by claims that it was completely opposed to economic development – rather than making the point that development should be subordinate to Islamic principles. What did seem to be true was that PAS often found it difficult to *implement* policies based on the application of Islamic beliefs to any given situation.

Components of the resurgence

The non-party components of the Islamic resurgence subscribed broadly to the Islamic beliefs as summarized above (pp. 80–2). Yet the four examples cited here showed divergences in their immediate objectives and their spheres of operation.[10] Curiously, it was a "non-political" group, Darul Arqam, that was most ruthlessly dealt with by the government in the 1990s.

The first group, Jaamat Tabligh (often referred to as Tabligh) may be described very briefly. Deriving from an organization based in New Delhi, and exclusively male, it had a missionary function. It gave the government little trouble. The second group, Darul Arqam, was founded by Ustaz Ashaari Mohammad; it had about 10,000 supporters, and manufactured about sixty products, including chili sauce and soap. It aimed at putting into operation an Islamic lifestyle, based on a high degree of self-sufficiency. The life was communal, although the sexes were largely segregated. Polygamy was practised, and women were not treated equally. It had its own markets, schools, clinics, and hospitals. It wished to deepen its knowledge of Islam and to spread the Islamic message, particularly to Muslim students. Because it believed that the influence of Islam should originate first through the individual and then through communities, it appeared that activity at a national level, if indeed it was an objective, would be contemplated only in the very long term.

The Islamic Republic Group (IRG) (whose name indicates its objective) was an offshoot of ABIM (Angkatan Belia Islam Malaysia – Malaysian Islamic Youth Movement), which took over control of the student unions from ABIM in the early 1980s. It planned to found a religious party, but its application to do so was rejected by the Registrar of Societies. Some of its members joined PAS when the Young Turks took over in 1982, and several of them later attained high office in the party.

Unlike the IRG, ABIM was not political, although, through its discussions and experience of promoting social issues, it provided useful training for future politicians. It was the intellectual powerhouse of the Islamic resurgence. Its thirst for knowledge led it to emphasize the importance of education and the need to upgrade the quality of training for Islamic groups. By 1997, ABIM was running 300 kindergartens, three primary and three secondary schools, and some study centers. Ritual was a secondary consideration. At its inauguration in 1971 it had only 153 members, but by 1974 this had risen to 17,000. However, its importance lay not in the number of its members, but in their quality. Some of its members became PAS candidates in the 1978 elections.[11] It was seen as a threat by UMNO. Its leader, Anwar, seasoned in the 1969 campaign against Tunku, by struggles against the authorities at the University of Malaya, and as the spokesperson for the societies affected by the proposed amendments to the Societies Act in the early 1970s, was well qualified to enter national politics. He was reputed by some to favor PAS, although he himself denied this, which he confirmed by standing for election as a UMNO candidate in 1982.

Mahathir's views on Islam

Mahathir's views on Islam were quite decided. He did not aspire to be a theologian, or to offer a comprehensive view of the relation between government and religion. But, as a politician, he believed that he could distinguish between courses of action that he thought were unworkable and those that had a good prospect of being successful in Malaysia. He had beliefs which applied not only to religion, but also had a wider reference. He repudiated the "either/or" approach. He called for a balance between this world and the next.[12] He was quick to discern, in any religious injunction, what was the relevant substance and what was the inconsequential form, originally chosen to suit the circumstances in which it was delivered but currently perhaps not so relevant.[13]

Mahathir was particularly indignant about proposals for *hudud* which the PAS government in Kelantan wished to establish there. It was deterred by threats from the federal government – which originally had not made clear pronouncements on the issue, that it would intervene by declaring a state of emergency (1996). *Hudud* was an Islamic criminal code which stipulated punishments, including whipping and stoning, for offences such as theft, robbery, unlawful carnal intercourse, drinking alcohol, etc. He claimed that it was unfair that such laws should apply to Muslims alone. (On the other hand, non-Muslims all over Malaysia, not convinced by federal government assurances, feared that some day such laws might be applied to them.) Mahathir singled out for criticism the requirement in these proposals that, to prove rape, four witnesses were required, claiming that such testimony would be extremely difficult to obtain.[14]

Mahathir questioned the worth of forced conversion to Islam. What was wanted, he thought, was that Muslims truly adhere to Islamic values, and non-Muslims should adhere to noble values that certainly did not conflict with Muslim values to be able to live in peaceful harmony, progress, and happiness. Similarly, he believed that to institute Islamic laws would result only in outwardly true Muslims.[15]

He was not an admirer of the *ulama* (Islamic scholars), asserting that the decline of Islam was due largely to their arrogant rejection of secular knowledge. In the context of the present day, he preferred his views to theirs. As a final argument, he pointed to the ethnic composition of Malaysia, and contended that the large proportion of non-Muslims constituted a bar to a government adopting Islamic law.[16]

The government's response to the resurgence

These are examples of Mahathir's *intellectual* reactions to the beliefs of Islamic resurgence. His *political* reactions, to deal with the resurgence, were drawn from a standard repertoire: cooption, competitive institution-building, and the use of force.

Mahathir's strategies: cooption, institution-building, coercion

Mahathir made use of some well-known strategies, but there were some striking features in their implementation. The new institutions, particularly the Islamic Bank and the International Islamic University, had both a practical and a symbolic value. The cooption of Anwar into UMNO was a masterstroke. Outside the political parties, he was currently the most influential thinker on religion and politics – and later revealed himself as able to compete successfully in the top league of professional politicians. Cooption afforded a double benefit – it represented an asset gained by UMNO and, simultaneously, a potential, perhaps even probable, asset lost by PAS. This was not the only surprise about the cooption. It was known that Anwar's father had been a UMNO Member of Parliament. It was not at all well known that, some time earlier, his mother had had the forethought to take out a UMNO membership in her son's name. Many in ABIM were sorry to see Anwar leave. On a non-personal level, obviously ABIM would now have greater access to government, but it would lose, or appear to lose, some of its independence. Some in UMNO asked who was using whom, and wondered whether the process should be considered as cooption or infiltration. In retrospect, the answer was that it was both. Anwar was asked to become active in UMNO, and he did. One of the reasons he was asked to do so was that he might contribute ideas and followers that might be useful in shaping UMNO's policy. He did, and they were.

The institutions with an "Islamic" aspect set under Mahathir were not the first of their kind to be established. Since UMNO had been the government, it had supported, both emotionally and financially, a number of causes, as it thought proper in a country where Islam was the state religion. Among these was the building and maintenance of mosques and the like, Koran-reading competitions, and assisting Muslims to go on the *haj*, the pilgrimage to Mecca. Since Tunku had founded (1960), and continued to take a deep interest in, Perkim (Pertubuhan Kebajikan Islam Malaysia), which helped converts to Islam to adjust during the process of their conversion, it had been government assisted. Indeed, the official status of Perkim was shown by its possession of the sole right to issue a conversion certificate to new converts.

By the late 1970s, the Islamic resurgence was being perceived as increasingly radical, and some government bodies dating from that time, between, say, 1977 and Mahathir becoming Prime Minister in 1981, appeared to be in response to this perception. Perhaps the most important was *Pusat Islam*, established in 1980, which was in effect a government-sponsored *dakwah* group intended to compete with other *dakwah* groups and to report on their activities. It was fully funded by the government, and was placed under a cabinet minister inside the Prime Minister's Department. Other innovations might also be considered to be responses. As early as 1977 there was an Islamic Research Center in the Prime Minister's Office. There was also an Islamic Training and *Dakwah* Institute in that office. In December 1978 a "*dakwah* month" was launched. In rural areas, state governments set up educational foundations which could compete with institutions established by ABIM. Without disparaging previous efforts, it was only after Mahathir became Prime Minister that calculated and coordinated government responses were made.

A major larger-scale institution set up by Mahathir, the Islamic Bank, was a "brainchild" of Anwar. Before proceeding with the creation of the Bank, the relevant experience of other countries was considered. The Bank was not intended to be the basis of a new parallel system competing with the existing one. Changing the basis of bank earnings from interest to profits – to conform to Islamic principles – did not entail incompatibility. It did not prevent it becoming part of the existing banking system. According to Bank Islam's director, it fitted quite well into the system, and relations with other bankers were good.[17] The bank provided services for some Malays, mostly rural, who were unhappy with the concept of interest. Such people were reassured by the existence of a religious supervisory council, working jointly with the bank's board.

The International Islamic University, which started teaching in 1983, aspired to be the counterpart, in modern times, of the renowned Egyptian Al Azhar University, where many Malay nationalists had been educated. Although the new university was situated in Malaysia and sponsored by its government, it was co-sponsored by the Organization of Islamic Conference, and was international in the composition of its faculty and students. These did not need to be Muslims if they accepted the concept of the university. Clearly, it intends to be an elite institution, distinguished from other such institutions by a primary commitment to learning more about Islam and its relation to the modern world.[18]

Another new institution was the restructured Islamic Economic Foundation (1984), intended to collect contributions to charity (mostly from inside Malaysia) from Islamic sources, such as the Tabung Haji, which existed to help intending pilgrims to save towards the cost of their undertaking the *haj*. A less benevolent body was created in 1994 – a committee of religious experts, administrators, etc., chosen to prepare a program for dealing with "deviationist" organizations that had been identified as such.

Two other new institutions were directly engaged in promoting the government's policy on Islam.[19] One was the well-funded Institute of Policy Development, which was founded by Anwar in 1985. It was intended to carry out human development training for student leaders, youth activists, junior managers, and public servants. The second, 1992, was the Institute of Islamic Understanding (IKIM), with a twofold task – to channel the challenge of the Islamic resurgence along state-defined lines, and to establish a dialogue with non-Muslims both inside and outside Malaysia. External relations were important: Mahathir wished to project to the world that Malaysia's interpretation of Islam was progressive rather than backward. Unlike some of the other newly created institutions, whose functions to promote government policy were mainly symbolic or peripheral, the plainly stated purposes of the two just mentioned sprang from the very core of government policy towards Islam. Indeed, the first task of the Institute succinctly expressed the Islamic impact on Malaysia according to his wishes. Another institution, to be completed by 1999, was an "Islamic hospital." In it, only women doctors will attend women, and prayer will precede diagnosis and treatment.

The weapon of last resort for Mahathir was coercion. If parties or groups resorted to violence or crossed the dividing line between dissent and "deviationism," he was ready to use force. PAS was one of the government's targets. As a prelude to its (successful) plan to take control of Kelantan, a state of emergency was declared in November 1978. Three members of PAS were detained under the ISA for incitement to violence and other unlawful means, in order to achieve their aims. In another case, PAS was alleged to have supported Ibrahim Mahmud – also known as Ibrahim Libya – who used violence which culminated in a struggle between his followers and the police. Fourteen civilians (including Ibrahim) and four police were killed. In 1985 the community he had created in Memali (Kedah) had acquired arms and provoked local disturbances. The local police were unable to cope with his followers' tactics. The government used too little force at the start, and probably excessive force later, when its troops stormed Ibrahim's house, where his supporters were concentrated.[20] The attack contributed to deteriorating relations between Mahathir and Musa, and eventually to Musa leaving the government in 1986. Mahathir had left the country just before the attack on Ibrahim's men occurred. According to Musa, Mahathir was critical of him because the operation had not been more carefully planned. Musa, however, asserted that the responsibility was his, as his deputy, and that he had left the details of the attack to the police.[21]

Mahathir's repression of Darul Arqam was, apparently, not primarily a response to violence. Repression was used, allegedly because of the group's deviationism, although the government also said that the organization was training armed warriors. Finance for this might have come from the movement's extensive commercial activities. Apart from doctrinal differences, credibility was given to the government's charges by its allegation that Ashaari had claimed that he was a prophet and had had visions of the Prophet Muhammad. The group was disbanded in 1994, when action was taken under the ISA. After Ashaari and some of his followers were arrested, they made confessions which were carried on television. Two years later, after they had been released, there were arrests of eighteen of the former members who were charged with attempting to revive the movement.

Reasons have been advanced that the government's attitude to Darul Arqam, which had earlier been rather tolerant, had become so intransigent. Was not the movement eccentric and idealistic rather than "political" and dangerous? The most plausible explanation is that originally its objective of setting up autonomous institutions did not appear to threaten the government. Nevertheless, as the scope of the movement's activities expanded, the implications of its "autonomy" became ominous. It seemed to be attracting numbers of upwardly mobile adherents. Its claims, originally limited, now increasingly resembled those of a state. So the actual state, to preserve its sovereignty, thought it wise to remove a competitor.[22] The method was so sudden and severe that it resembled a "surgical strike." An alternative, or additional, explanation was that Darul Arqam constituted a challenge to the government's rural development programs, which had improved the conditions of many Malay supporters. Darul Arqam rejected these programs as incompatible with Islamic principles, so they constituted a threat to a major source of support for the government.[23]

Evaluation of UMNO policy

The summary (p. 84) of Mahathir's religious beliefs was intended partly to explain the foundations of his policies. Beyond that, his speeches were part of a campaign to define relations between the government and Islam in terms of his own views. They reached a wide audience, because they were given prominence in the media. He made a point of choosing Islam as a major theme in several of his annual speeches to the UMNO General Assembly, his principal forum for influencing opinion. The themes chosen most often for delivery at the UMNO General Assembly were those closest to his heart.

As UMNO's Islamic credentials grew, some of its leaders were led to make bold claims; Sanusi asserted that UMNO was the world's third largest Muslim political party,[24] which seemed quite plausible and could not readily be challenged – while a claim that it was the first or second largest might have been easier to disprove.

In 1997, overlapping with the two months when Anwar was Acting Prime Minister, during Mahathir's absence abroad, questions were raised about the applicability of religious officials' decisions. One incident in Selangor, in July, was the arrest of participants in a beauty competition. The other in Sarawak, in August, was a ban on a male body-building contest. Mahathir denounced the arrests, and the Chief Minister of Sarawak, Datuk Patinggi Amar Taib Mahmud, was "surprised" (unfavorably) by the ban.[25]

Although Mahathir's approach to the Islamic resurgence, through cooption and competing with the resurgence by institution-building, now appears to have been vindicated, there were some apprehensions in the early 1980s. Two of Khoo's observations may usefully be considered together.[26] On the one hand, some Muslims thought that the resurgence had shown that Islam should have a larger role in the personal lives of Muslims and in the conduct of public affairs. On the other hand, the familiar comparison of Mahathir's policy to an exercise in "tiger-riding" might have had some validity. The question was: who would end up in control? A UMNO minister was seriously worried that Mahathir had gone too far with Islamization, and would not be able to stop where he wanted to.[27]

From the perspective of the late 1990s, Mahathir's methods for controlling the development of the Islamic resurgence in Malaysia seem to have been largely successful. The worst fears of the early 1980s, that concession would be followed by concession, were unwarranted. To be sure, some thought that the various

Islamic projects he sponsored made the government part of the resurgence. This may have been true, but some of the "participation" had taken the form, not of following trends, but of participating in order to try to influence them. Mahathir drew a line, and would not go beyond it. He was prepared to back up his eminently reasonable and tirelessly repeated thoughts on the role of Islam by force, if necessary. The resurgence has spread knowledge about Islam, much of which has been accepted. To an extent, therefore, there has been an "interpenetration" between resurgence views and government (Mahathir) views. But this has not resulted in anything approaching the adoption of Islamic law or the Islamic state. The resurgence may not have run its course, but it has been substantially domesticated and demystified.

A question remains: what is ABIM's future role? Undoubtedly, UMNO gained by the transfusion of people and ideas accompanying Anwar's cooption, but was this a zero-sum game? Did ABIM lose by the transaction? Probably not. ABIM can surely play a necessary role, largely detached from government. Among other things, it can continue to reflect on the broad issues of how an Islamic approach can be useful in suggesting solutions to social problems. In 1997 the new president of ABIM, Ahmed Azam Abdul Rahman, said that "explicitly" it was leaning toward UMNO, but it guarded its non-partisanship. "Neither PAS nor UMNO trusts us 100 percent."[28]

PAS remains the main political stronghold of Islamic beliefs. However, its current prospects are not very bright. Except in Kelantan, where it is still dominant, and possibly in the other northern states of Terengganu and Kedah, it does not have much prospect of improving its vote. Nor, since the takeover of the "Young Turks" in 1982, does the party seem to have produced any new vision of where an Islamic state would lead.[29]

Non-Malays' grievances

Most of this section concerns the Chinese, who make up about three-quarters of the non-Malays in Peninsular Malaysia. However, first of all, it should be said that in many ways other non-Malays share the problems of the Chinese. Like them, they were cut off from the special treatment accorded to Malays and other indigenous peoples by the Constitution and by other legislation, including that which spelled out the working of the NEP. They also suffered from the implementation of policies in ways that were disadvantageous to them. For instance, non-Malays sometimes complained that development plans did not provide for a sufficient number of places of worship to meet their needs. Many non-Malays, including Chinese, feared that, at least in Kelantan, they might be subject to the penalties of Islamic law which had been proposed by the PAS government of Kelantan (p. 82). Many were also fearful of the Islamic resurgence, and even thought that it was deliberately aimed at confirming the "second-class status" of the non-Malays.[30] The non-Malays were gratified at the modification of a measure that they had resisted in its original form. In June 1997, it was announced that there would be a compulsory "Islamic Civilization" course for institutions of higher learning. (Previously it had been taught only in some.) After heated objections by non-Muslims, the title was altered to "Islamic and Asian Civilizations."[31]

However, the Chinese seemed to be especially vociferous on language and educational issues where they were attacked on two fronts – from the government's sponsorship of Malay, as well as by global influences, via the increasing use of English. They also resisted what they saw as the erosion of Chinese customs and neglect of temples and burial grounds.

The Chinese: the MCA, Gerakan, and the DAP

The Chinese, especially those in the MCA, have suffered from delusions about power. To be sure, they constituted the second largest ethnic group. They might also have been proud – if they had known about it – that the MCA was the third largest Chinese party in the world, after the Chinese Communist Party in China and the Kuomintang Party in Taiwan. In reality, this was not an important consideration, compared with their number-two ranking in Malaysia, where the party was the junior partner of a dominant Malay party. As number two, it could try harder, but there was no prospect that it could ever be number one.

Originally, the MCA had high status as the co-founder of the Alliance, along with UMNO. But the Alliance was founded in 1953 before the implications of the "bargain" (p. 18) were either recognized in the Constitution or had become evident from the way in which the Alliance was operating. The power of the MCA was further weakened by the dilution of the influence of the original Alliance parties, when the Barisan was formed, by the inclusion of a rival for the Chinese vote, Gerakan, in the Barisan. There have been further fluctuations in the fortunes of the party, including several splits and one choice of a leader which turned out to be disastrous. Beyond these troubles, however, there were several "basic" reasons for the decline.

First, demographic projections indicate that the proportion of Chinese in the population is declining. Most of the Chinese in Malaysia have acquired citizenship, but some estimates claim that the Chinese percentage – a third in 1990 – will fall to something between 13 and 24 percent by the year 2100.[32] Emigration is one reason for this decline. Statistics are hard to obtain, but a high proportion of the emigrants from Malaysia is Chinese. A common strategy for Chinese contemplating emigration is to try to have children educated abroad and become established in the country concerned, even if, at least for a time, the parents have to remain in Malaysia.

Second, before 1969 the MCA was the recipient of more Chinese votes than any other party. There were few competing parties, ethnically, and some were subjected to harassment by the police, because of suspicions that, during the Emergency, they had been infiltrated by Communists. In 1964, when the Emergency was over, the MCA received almost half of the Chinese vote. However, in the late 1960s, two parties were formed which were competitors because, although they aspired to be multiracial, each drew votes mainly from

Chinese. One of them was the successor of the (Singapore) PAP, which had contested nine seats at the 1964 elections. It was registered in 1966 as the Democratic Action Party (DAP). The other party, Gerakan, founded in 1968, had its origins in the MCA split of 1959 (pp. 91–2). Lim Chong Eu, after he was compelled to resign the MCA presidency, started the United Democratic Party, and subsequently Gerakan. He attracted some members of the Labour Party and a few Malay intellectuals to it, as well as Chinese.

Subsequently the fortunes of the three "Chinese" parties fluctuated. Estimates of which votes came from where are hard to discern. In the case of the MCA, many Chinese candidates are returned in seats that have a Malay majority of votes, which complicates calculations. Both the MCA and the DAP attract a larger vote than Gerakan, but Gerakan had two circumstances in its favor. It has benefited from MCA splits, after which MCA defectors often joined it, wishing to belong to a party that was also in the Barisan. Also, Gerakan is based largely in Penang, where in state elections the DAP has a chance of winning control of the state government. The Barisan has decided that the choice of a Chinese from Gerakan as Chief Minister offers the best chance of defeating the DAP and retaining control of the state government.

Another sign of MCA decline is that the weight of the party has diminished, as judged by its allocation of seats in the cabinet. The proportion has dropped from 29 percent in 1962 to 23 percent in April 1996. Even more distressing is the decrease in importance of the posts that were allocated in the 1980s and 1990s. In 1957 both the portfolios of Finance and of Trade and Industry were given to Chinese. The former was a key ministry, because the minister draws up the budget which sets the parameters for economic policy for the coming year. The latter also conferred power, because the minister had, virtually in their gift, the ability to distribute eagerly sought licences, etc., which, under the NEP, assumed even greater significance than previously. However, the Trade and Industry post was soon "lost" by the MCA, while the Finance Ministry, the last bastion of Chinese strength in the cabinet, was lost in 1974.

It was generally accepted that a Chinese would never be Prime Minister. In 1973, Tan Siew Sin asked that he be appointed as a second Deputy Prime Minister, but Razak refused the request.[33] It is difficult to imagine anyone with stronger credentials than Tan, yet it now seemed that no Chinese could ever be even a Deputy Prime Minister. Nietzsche was Tan's favorite philosopher,[34] but his insistence on the primacy of power had not quite prepared Tan to accept the rebuff with composure.

It has been mentioned (pp. 24–5) that the formation of the Barisan increased the power of the Prime Minister. The MCA also played a lesser part than previously. There were now more party leaders than before to compete for his attention.

Splits in the MCA

There were three major splits in the MCA. The first came to a head in 1959. The original point at issue concerned a government education bill. The newly elected MCA president, Lim Chong Eu, representing "reformers" in the party, wanted the bill to include equal treatment for Chinese, and also proposed that, at the coming general election, the MCA should be allocated candidates for 40 out of the 104 seats. Lim had the support of Chinese schools' and teachers' associations. However, the majority in the MCA supported Tunku, who refused to accept Lim's demands and required that the chauvinists be purged. Many of the reformers then quit and, soon after, Lim, under pressure, resigned as president.

The MCA had been torn in two directions. If it had supported Lim, its relationship – and even its political links – with UMNO might have been imperilled. As it was, it paid a penalty. Criticisms of Tan Siew Sin gained force because it was alleged that he had opposed Lim; it was believed that he was not sufficiently "pro-Chinese" (he was a Straits Chinese, who did not speak Chinese, and who held his seat through Malay votes).[35] In his favor, it could be argued that he was actually defending Chinese interests, although they were financial interests, not educational ones. His closeness to Tunku added to his clout on financial matters, which he could use to the MCA's advantage. According to him, before 1969, when he was consulted as Finance Minister about introducing measures that would have produced policies resembling those of the subsequent NEP, he simply refused to consider the idea, and the matter was dropped.[36]

The MCA suffered not only through the loss of Lim and other leaders. It had also alienated the leaders of Chinese educational associations, who had supported Lim. A second split occurred in the early 1970s. In 1971, Prime Minister Razak, in order to help the MCA recover from its "post-1969 depression," appointed one of its Perak leaders, Dr. Lim Keng Yaik, as head of a Perak Task Force to mobilize grass-roots support for the party. Lim was also made a minister.[37] Similar bodies were set up in other states. However, in Perak there was heavy opposition from some established leaders, and Lim and some of his associates were forced out of the party. He joined Gerakan, and, like his predecessor Lim Chong Eu, later became its head.

The third major split in the MCA took a different course. The actual split was protracted and divisive, but the main damage came later. Tan Siew Sin's successor (1974) was Datuk Lee San Choon, who had been challenged for the presidency by Datuk Michael Chen, much esteemed by Razak. The bid failed, and Chen duly joined Gerakan. When Lee resigned in 1983 there were two main contenders visible. Unfortunately, Lee did not give decisive support to a successor. One was Datuk Neo Yee Pan, who combined a science doctorate with a non-flamboyant personality. His opponent, Tan Koon Swan, provided a vivid contrast. Widely regarded as a financial wizard, he joined the MCA in 1977 and was made managing director of the MCA's investment arm, Multi-Purpose Holdings Berhad (MPHB). This was a huge enterprise, and many Chinese had invested in it, hoping that it could provide for the Chinese equivalent benefits to those received by Malays through investment bodies set up as part of the NEP. Neo had been appointed acting deputy president in 1982, but the preliminary stages of the contest between him and Tan were marked by polls to see who would prevail and by allegations that "phantom voters" (those voters listed who lacked legal residence requirements) might influence the result. After two years of acrimony and dissention, in a general assembly meeting vote in November 1985, Tan was the victor, although Neo contested the result through litigation. A few days later, one of Tan's companies, Pan-Electric Holdings, collapsed, hopelessly in debt. On a visit to Singapore, Tan was arrested for criminal breach of trust. Apart from other failing ventures, MPHB was reputed to have lost $US60m. in 1985.[38] Tan resigned from his post, and was sentenced to two years' imprisonment. He was succeeded as MCA president by Datuk Seri Dr. Ling Liong Sik, who still (1998) holds that position.

These splits contributed to the MCA's decline but, even though one must take into account their cumulative effects, they were haunted by a basic problem. How could the party, on the one hand, satisfy its members and potentially supporting organizations such as the schools' and teachers' associations, and, on the other, maintain its link with the UMNO leaders? Yet, if that link were to be severed, all the perquisites which the followers of a government party enjoy would be forfeited. The other two "Chinese" parties have also had leadership problems, though not nearly as serious as the MCA's. A challenge to the Gerakan leadership in September 1996 failed. The leadership of the DAP has been in the hands of Lim Kit Siang ever since the party was founded. He still displays resiliency in spite of the time and effort he has contributed to the party, with few material rewards. When he does retire, there may be some difference of opinion about whether or not his son, Lim Guan Eng, will fall heir to the leader's position.

Relations between "Chinese" parties

The policies of the three parties are directed largely at Chinese electors, but apart from the difference between the MCA, which has an exclusively Chinese membership, and the other two parties, which must also cater for other ethnic groups, the parties also differ in some other respects. For example, in economic policy the class interests of the party members have some influence. In the MCA the appeal is more to middle-class and higher-income electors than in the DAP, and possibly also Gerakan. However, the DAP has attracted some support from professionals. The DAP manifesto for the 1995 election mentioned several non-Malay (including Chinese) policies, some of which the DAP claimed credit for having helped to promote. These included democratization, e.g., in the functioning of Parliament and in restoring elections in local government, and the independence of the judiciary. The DAP is encouraged to keep on going because it is able to expose wrongs, and has been able to resist the assimilationist policies of the government.[39] In 1997 Lim Kit Siang attributed some DAP losses of votes to professionals who formerly voted for the party, now having become more interested in making money.[40]

Gerakan attracts recruits from a variety of sources. The party shows considerable concern for human values – it has sometimes been called the "conscience" of the Barisan. An example relates to the Official Secrets Act, which Gerakan has denounced although the Barisan required that Gerakan members must vote for it in Parliament.[41]

Not only is the MCA ethnically based, it is also tied to another party – UMNO – which is also ethnically based and is the dominant party in the Barisan. The MCA cannot make its own policy, and is circumscribed in its criticism of UMNO policies, including the more provocative forays of UMNO Youth.

Despite these differences the three "Chinese" parties have a good deal in common, as is shown by movements of individuals from one party to another. Such movements are perhaps most usual – especially at higher levels – from MCA to Gerakan. In 1997, however, two state assembly members in Negri Sembilan moved from the DAP to MCA. Occasionally, members of different parties get together, for demonstrations or consultation, to show the depth of their feelings on some issues. This occurred at a demonstration to affirm Chinese unity in 1971. However, it had been organized by a newly formed committee, which was denounced as a usurpation of MCA authority. At the low-key end of the scale, in April 1987, when ethnic tensions were high, Dr. Ling, the new president of the MCA, and Lim, the secretary-general of the DAP, met to talk for the first time in several years. Also, in 1988–90, all three parties were involved in trying to influence decisions on the future of the NEP (in public and in the NECC). They all questioned the government's statistics.

Mahathir's influence on "Chinese" parties' leaders

There have been at least three occasions on which Mahathir may have had an effect on the fortunes of the two "Chinese" parties in the Barisan and their leaders. The most clear-cut example consisted of Mahathir's decision to continue the practice of backing the choice of the Gerakan state leader to head the Barisan-held Penang state government. Moreover, to derive the maximum advantage from the decision, it had to be announced well in advance of the next election – which Mahathir did. Second, it has been said that Lee San Choon's resignation as MCA president was occasioned by his wish not to continue working with Mahathir.[42] Third, in the Neo–Tan contest for MCA president (pp. 92–3), Mahathir dropped two of Tan's key supporters from their posts as deputy ministers.[43]

Types of Chinese grievances: government responses

What are the main Chinese grievances? Which are unlikely to be remedied? Which have recently been (partly) met? These questions are not as simple as they look. The ISA, for example, has affected some Chinese, but did not always affect them *as* Chinese. Also, what constitutes redress? If there is a complaint that Chinese are under-represented in a particular segment of the public service, has there been redress if the proportion is increased, even if it does not reach the percentage of Chinese in the population as a whole? Grievances are unlikely to be redressed with a fanfare of publicity. This was true about the improved university entry quotas for non-Malays (p. 95). The government's idea is to try to avoid adverse reactions from other ethnic groups – in that instance the Malays. However, sometimes a party cannot refrain from advertising its successes. The MCA did that at the 1986 election by issuing (in Chinese) a supplement to its manifesto, providing a list of the concessions it had achieved.[44] After the operation of the NEP was reviewed in the early 1990s, no clear-cut announcement of changes was made by the government.

There are two main types of Chinese grievances. Some are based on the principle that Chinese should be hired in the public service, armed forces, etc., in accordance with their proportion in the population. The principle of proportionality has been regarded as desirable for the issue of permits, licenses, etc., to operate a business. Chinese are prepared to see Malays and other indigenous peoples receive more benefits as a temporary measure; hiring could be more than proportionate to Malays until the numbers are proportionate. Chinese would also urge that disparities in the population of electoral constituencies should be reduced. (Actually, since independence they have increased.)

Positive responses to Chinese (and other non-Malay) voiced grievances were few until the 1990s. One such response occurred in 1978, when Hussein was Prime Minister and Musa was Minister of Education. After complaints that the university entrance quotas for Chinese and other non-Malays were too low, the quotas were gradually raised over a period. The MCA, until recently, has not found it easy to obtain concessions. Mahathir is reputed to have assured the party that, while opposition parties would gain nothing by shouting, an MCA leader would need only to whisper in his ear. However, although whispers may imply access, they seldom led to action. Yet, some high positions were opened to non-Malays in 1997, according to a deputy minister, although the details were vague. The positions included armed forces chief of staff, police chief, and state government secretary.[45] Significantly, the effects of the NEP led the Chinese, including the MCA, to issue publications containing statistics that showed that the Chinese were obtaining less than a proportionate share of various benefits. However, the last important publication of this kind was in 1988.[46] After that, the theme was much less publicized.

The second type of grievance concerns language, education, culture, and customs. Questions of where Chinese is permissible in schools and universities have been mostly determined by now. Proportionality is harder to measure here. Contention remains on some issues, which might be regarded as relatively trivial, except that the symbols are not just symbolic, because they stand for deeper cultural issues. Respect is demanded for Mandarin. In 1987 there was widespread resentment against headmasters' appointments that were being made in Chinese schools. The point at issue was not that those appointed were not Chinese – they were: the grievance was that they were not trained in Mandarin. The observed type of grievance is based on what are perceived as attempts to thrust other cultures (in however indirect a way) upon Chinese. An example was to try to compel Chinese, and other non-Muslims, to wear songkoks (a variety of Malay headgear).[47] Another example was a directive from a (Malay) chief education officer that students, irrespective of ethnicity, should be required to recite what seemed to them to be Islamic prayers. Other Chinese cultural grievances are immediately recognizable as serious. Burial grounds are a case in point. One of the author's initial political interviews in Malaysia (1964) provided an example. During the first five minutes of an interview with half a dozen state leaders from the MCA, the question of burial grounds came up. One of the MCA representatives observed that the government would not even let Chinese die properly in Malaysia.[48] (In 1997, Dr. Ling recommended that Chinese should adopt the practice of cremation.) There was a 1980 dispute over a threat to the ancient temple on the Bukit Cina site in Malacca town. The temple was threatened by development proposals, but the outcry was such that the plans were revised so that the temple could be saved.[49] Now, in the 1990s, lion dances which had long been discouraged were performed in the Prime Minister's presence and with his approval.

Reflective of its defensive posture, the MCA was determined to preserve what remained of the Chinese cultural component in the education system – particularly the continuing status of Chinese (and Tamil) primary schools. Assurances of their retention have long been requested and were authoritatively given by Mahathir. He added that, to help national integration, these schools would be located on the same campus as the national schools. In 1994 extra funds were provided by the government for Chinese private secondary schools.[50]

One explanation of the government's growing willingness to accommodate the Chinese, is that it wished to recoup a loss in Chinese votes at the 1990 election. Then, when it tried a "softer" approach at the 1995 election, it was so pleased at its success that it continued the new policy. There has been a greater change in government sensitivity towards the Chinese since the mid-1990s. Briefly, there appears to have been an attempt to "encourage dialogue." Since 1994 or 1995, speeches by Anwar and others – including those made at the 1995 election – seemed to include themes that addressed the feelings and fears of the Chinese. All this may represent a move towards multiculturalism, and to be related to some thoughts expressed in Mahathir's "Vision 2020," on establishing a "united Malaysian nation" (p. 166). [51] Needless to say, many Chinese welcome the government's more conciliatory mood. The MCA president, Dr. Ling, no doubt sees it as a vindication of his "step-by-step" approach. There were other examples of government accommodation to the feelings of non-Malays in 1997. For the first time, non-Islamic religions were given time on state radio and television. They could not actually propagate religion, but could promote good values.[52]

The MIC

The Malaysian Indian Congress (MIC) is a small but useful component of the Barisan. Economically, the Indians are the poorest of the three ethnic groups that formed the core of the Alliance. They made the least progress of the three toward attaining the intended target that the NEP set for them for 1990. In the decline of the agricultural sector of the economy, they have suffered the greatest dislocation geographically, because the plantation component of economic activity (in which they used to be well represented) now offers less employment. Two circumstances have made Indians less unhappy than they might be, as the year 2000 approaches. Until 1997, the general health of the economy was good. Also, those Indians who are members of the MIC enjoy the benefits of belonging to the ruling party, although their share is reputed to be less than proportional to their 9 percent share of the population. Membership of the party is officially estimated at 500,000 but may be as low as 200,000[53]. The party does not have a majority in any parliamentary seat, but is strong enough to have been allocated seven seats in 1995, all of which it won.

Since its inception, the party has been faction-ridden. An editorial in an Indian newspaper in 1973 affirmed that at that time there was no difference between an MIC meeting and a clash between gangsters.[54] However, one faction has been dominant since the present leader and president, Datuk Seri S. Samy Vellu, was elected in 1979. There is no credible and determined challenger. Also, it is believed that the Prime Minister may tolerate the situation, because it is useful to have a leader who can keep the party under control. The system is perhaps best described as "forced consensus," in which his deputy, Datuk S. Subramaniam, forbore from challenging him at the 1997 party elections. In 1997 Samy Vellu appealed for the party's support, so that he could continue with his projects for another seven years or so. He has launched a succession of schemes to raise money to help Indians with business, education, and so on. Possible contributors may have been somewhat disillusioned by the leadership's handling of telecommunications shares offered by the Ministry of Finance in 1990. The allocation of the shares was apparently concentrated on benefiting relatively few people.[55]

Developing and controlling Sarawak and Sabah

To conclude this chapter, a word should be said about Sarawak and Sabah, territories that joined Malaya (along with Singapore, temporarily) to form Malaysia in 1963.[56] In them, the federal government intended to promote development through plans modeled on those that had succeeded in Malaya. An additional need was to exercise control over the populations in each, some of whom appeared to Malayans to be quite primitive. There was still an active Communist insurgency in Sarawak. Elections were a novelty, and originally were accompanied by rampant bribery and violence, or the threat of violence. A complication, both for politics and business, was the huge rewards to be gained by exploiting natural resources and the environment, initially mainly timber. A vicious circle was soon in operation – government contracts, money, government contracts, and so on.

Mahathir's preoccupation with development found scope for action when he became Prime Minister in 1981, when there was still a pressing need to provide infrastructure for development in Sarawak and Sabah, especially in the form of communications and energy. At times his drive to clear away and construct seemed to be ruthless, and not sufficiently solicitous of the personal and environ- mental effects. A much-publicized example was the M$1.5bn. Bakun Dam (p. 67). He had little sympathy with those, like the Penans in Sarawak, who were resistant to progress, intent only on preserving their traditional patterns of living (pp. 117–19).

Changing party allegiance was frequent, and in the early days of Malaysia there were several parties in each of these states. One Sarawak politician of the second rank was reputed to have been a member of five parties in succession. Most parties were basically ethnic, but there was nothing as simple as the tripar- tite division in Malaya. Ethnic groups were themselves still in the process of formation and ethnic boundaries were fluid. It was difficult to decide whether the Iban in Sarawak should be considered as a single ethnic group or several groups, as a result of differences arising from their location and history. Also, were the Iban more properly seen as a component of a wider group, Dayaks, which would include other components, such as Bidayuh (Land Dayaks)? In Sabah were those who proclaimed themselves as Kadazans really different from the wider category of "Dusuns"? More ethnic components were recognized than in Malaya, and the number of possible combinations was consequently greater. Chinese, who in 1965 constituted about 30 percent of the population in Sarawak and about 25 percent in Sabah, further enriched, but also confused, the ethnic pattern. Ethnic groupings along religious lines were also possible in both states, and, if Chinese were not included, Muslims and non-Muslims were roughly equal in numbers.

Sarawak

In Sarawak, in 1965, Chief Minister Datuk Stephen Kalong Ningkan, a feisty Iban from the second division, put together a coalition, but it was unstable and a rival coalition, led by a Muslim party, with links to Kuala Lumpur, threatened to replace it by moving a vote of no confidence in the legislature. After the dispute was taken to the courts, a state of emergency was declared, which the federal government "justified" by exaggerating the dangers of violence. After Ningkan had been removed, the resulting ruling coalition, from 1970, was Muslim domi- nated. This type of coalition has governed Sarawak since, under only two chief ministers.

Since the early 1980s the term "Dayakism" has been used to indicate Dayak aspirations. Socially and economically, it expressed dissatisfaction that the Dayaks were less developed than the Malays/Melanaus or the Chinese. Politically, it led to the conclusion that Dayaks could not exert their rightful share of influence, unless one Dayak party was formed, which commanded the alle- giance of nearly all of them. The PBDS (Parti Bangsa Dayak Sarawak – Party of the Dayak Peoples of Sarawak), founded in 1983, was meant to embody this ambition, but some Dayaks still supported other parties, particularly the Sarawak

National Party, of which PBDS was an offshoot. The PBDS bore some resemblance to the Parti Bersatu Sabah (PBS; United Sabah Party) in Sabah, but for at least two reasons it was less successful. It lacked the mystique and the deeply rooted cohesive cultural base of the PBS. Also, by the time that Dayakism was gaining support, the number of constituencies in the state had been enlarged in such a way that the Dayaks could no longer win a majority if votes were cast on an ethnic basis.[57]

A change of Chief Minister took place in 1981 when Datuk Haji Abdul Rahman Yakub was succeeded by his only slightly younger nephew, Taib. Rahman Yakub was named as Governor. The elevation was in formal status but not in power. Earlier, they had worked together politically, but later the relationship turned sour. Taib made extensive use of timber concessions and other favors, as Yakub had done before him, to fend off attempts by his uncle to get him to resign. Simultaneously, in response to non-Muslim pressures, the government's approach became more multi-ethnic. This change of leadership was apparently approved by the federal government, now under Mahathir.[58]

At the 1996 state elections, the government, which had held all the seats, lost three to the DAP, and two to independents. Incumbents can attract votes by using large sums of money allocated to them for development projects, similar to the practice in Peninsular Malaysia. Moreover, quite small areas that vote for opposition candidates can be pinpointed and punished by having government development expenditure in their areas reduced.[59]

Taib is acceptable to both the federal government and to many of the people in Sarawak. The former is happy when it contrasts the political restiveness in Sabah with the relative lack of trouble in Sarawak. Taib is acceptable ethnically to many local ethnic groups. He is a Muslim who is also a Melanau, a small group which contains some Christians as well as Muslims. For the present, UMNO has decided not to take part in Sarawak politics, although one advantage of doing so would be to secure representation from Sarawak at UMNO General Assemblies.

Sabah

Political developments in Sabah were less predictable. At first, there were two main parties, one mainly Muslim and the other mainly non-Muslim. The leader of the former, Tun Mustapha bin Datu Harun, backed by the federal government, was born in the southern Philippines; he began his career in Sabah as a houseboy, and had little education. He would not have been entirely out of place in a Joseph Conrad novel, although his doings would still have put some strain on the reader's credulity. He amassed great wealth which he used in many ways, including buying a restaurant in London where, reputedly, he was known as Mr. Brown. Mustapha was detested by nearly all non-Muslims, but warmly supported by many UMNO leaders, especially Tunku, who were impressed by his dedication to Islam. The costs of his palatial residence and of several state-of-the-art jets were paid for out of government funds. He was utterly ruthless. At one election he so terrorized opposition candidates that nearly all of them were prevented from campaigning. He had tens of thousands of non-Muslims converted to Islam, following the reverse pattern of Spanish conversions to Christianity in the Philippines four hundred years previously. Reputedly, he helped channel arms from Libya to separatist Muslim rebels in the southern Philippines. Eventually his dreams became so grandiose that he planned to have Sabah secede from Malaysia, and to found a new state consisting of Sabah and part of the southern Philippines. This was going too far, and the federal government had him replaced.

The new state government, supported by the federal government, was formed by a party, Berjaya, headed by a rival of Mustapha, Tun Fuad – Donald before his conversion to Islam – Stephens. He re-entered politics as head of Berjaya, and then, after an election, became Chief Minister. Unfortunately, in 1976 he died in a plane crash along with several of his closest political associates. He was succeeded by Datuk Harris Salleh, whose tenuous local roots made him depend largely on federal support.

Some aspects of Harris's rule were uncomfortably reminiscent of Mustapha's, for instance his campaigns for conversions to Islam. There was also increased immigration, mainly of Muslims from the southern Philippines, and many of the immigrants became citizens with the power to vote. However, inside Sabah, part of Harris's support base was non-Muslim. Reactions against such policies assumed at first a cultural form and later were also expressed politically.[60]

Kadazans, who were mostly Christians, were, on some calculations, the largest ethnic group in Sabah. Their assertiveness had coincided with the debate on the conditions for entering Malaysia in the mid-1960s, when their views were voiced by Donald Stephens and embodied in a demand that the "Twenty Points" stipulated by his party when Malaysia was formed, should be accepted.[61] In the 1970s it became plain that some of these conditions had not been observed under the Mustapha and Harris governments. There was high economic growth, but it was not greatly benefiting Kadazans and other non-Muslims. They were not securing anything like a fair share of civil service positions, and Mustapha had violated the Twenty Points by declaring that the state religion was Islam.

Kadazan consciousness of these, and other, infringements of the Twenty Points was fostered by the formation of the Kadazan Cultural Association in 1963 which contributed to a cultural renaissance, climaxing each year in a harvest festival. Significantly, the next person to be acclaimed as Huguan Siou (Paramount Leader) since Donald Stephens was Joseph Pairin, who gave these cultural feelings a political voice. Pairin, a lawyer who was a third-generation Sabahan, had been in Harris's cabinet, but had split off and formed a new party, PBS, which contested and won a by-election in 1984. When Harris called a general election, the PBS won on a states' rights platform which was based on the Twenty Points. The PBS won an absolute majority.

However, Mustapha and Harris thought up a ploy which did not fall short of Mustapha's earlier standards of crudity. (He had made a previous attempt to grab power from Berjaya in 1976.) Harris and Mustapha phoned the Deputy Prime Minister, Musa, and asked his approval for forming a government. (Mahathir was officially out of the country.) If permission had been granted, the Mustapha–Harris coalition could then have nominated sufficient appointed members to obtain a majority. Musa refused. It is not known how Mahathir would have reacted if the decision had been his. However, Mustapha and Harris gained access to the Governor, and persuaded him to swear in Mustapha to head the new government. Pairin's attempts to see the Governor had been unsuccessful, but, after hearing Musa's radio statement that he supported Pairin, the Governor revoked Mustapha's appointment and Pairin was finally sworn in. The government took no action against Mustapha or Harris.[62]

In response to federal pressures, the PBS became part of the Barisan in 1986, but the federal government was unhappy that it maintained its strong states' rights stance. The PBS then decided on an action, which replaced UMNO suspicions by an irreparable breach. In the context of the 1990 general election struggle between UMNO and Semangat '46, PBS disassociated itself from UMNO, and pledged its support for Razaleigh's party. UMNO won decisively, except in Kelantan. UMNO then announced that it would go into Sabah politics, where it would directly challenge PBS. (In Sarawak, on the other hand, UMNO decided not to enter politics in the state. The decisive factor, no doubt, was that in Sarawak the federal government had a state government that was willing and capable of furthering its interests without alienating the federal government, which seemed not be the case in Sabah.) The federal government harassed the PBS through arrests of its members, and Pairin himself was detained for a short period.[63]

The 1994 Sabah state election was marked by lavish spending by Pairin's opponents. The result was a narrow victory for the PBS; both Pairin's party and the opposition parties sequestered their supporters to ward off their being wooed to defect. The Governor took some time to announce that it was Pairin who would be sworn in as Chief Minister; Mahathir was angered, and threatened that police action might have to be taken if politicians were detained against their will. Pairin's government did not last long. Carrot and stick were used to obtain the few defections necessary for the government to be toppled, and a new UMNO-led government took office.[64]

In his fashion, however, Mahathir demonstrated his regard for ethnic equity two years later. He had decided that the office of Chief Minister in the new government should rotate among the three categories: indigenous Muslim, indigenous non-Muslim, and Chinese. When the indigenous Muslim holding the office was slow to relinquish it, Mahathir compelled him to give way to the person whose turn was next, a Chinese.

Two things stand out in the rise and fall of the PBS. One was the degree of support Pairin was able to attract, which far transcended the votes of indigenous non-Muslim electors, let alone the numbers who, like him, were Kadazans. To be sure, some of his support may have been due to a perception that he would be the winner. His victories, also, were achieved in spite of the votes of those

Muslim immigrants who had become citizens. (There may actually have been some "backlash" among indigenous Muslims.) The other impressive feature was the tenacity of Mahathir in dislodging Pairin, especially after he had been "betrayed" in the general election of 1990.

Conclusion

It is difficult to generalize about Mahathir's handling of ethnic grievances and discontent in Sarawak and Sabah. The states are separated from Peninsular Malaysia by water and by the absence of a shared history. Fears and suspicions aroused by the conditions for becoming part of Malaysia have not entirely disappeared, as shown by the Kadazan revival. In Sarawak, they have been partly dissipated, because the federal government has been wise enough to avoid a heavy-handed approach – except for Mahathir's insistence on possibly too rapid development – and has left much to the state government, which is more sensitive to local conditions and sentiments.

Mahathir's views on balancing ethnic demands are realistic:

> In order to satisfy everyone, we must actually dissatisfy everyone. Each shall be deprived of his wants and needs to a degree that brings about a sense of being equally deprived and dissatisfied.... The moment we find that one race is totally satisfied, we can rest assured that the government is being unfair and is giving more for one than for the other.[65]

5   Human rights

The contemporary emphasis on human rights provides a stark contrast to society in pre-colonial Malaya, say, roughly, in the seventeenth century. The relationship between rulers and ruled in that feudal period was very different. The paramount concern was unquestionable loyalty to the ruler who, in return, provided protection to the ruled. The politics of the feudal epoch was based on this cardinal factor.[1]

The traits typical of "feudal" Malaya have left their mark on current Malaysian political institutions and behavior. They are to be found in the Constitution, in the sections that refer to the rulers, and in the creation of the Agung. Chapter 2 demonstrated that the feudal remnants embodied in the Constitution did not fit all that easily with the modern notion of constitutional monarchy. Nor were the feudal elements totally congruent with the reality of a strong party, confident of its mandate from the people. Feudal elements were still found in politicians until quite recently. On one occasion Tunku referred to Dato Onn as feudal, paused, and then added, engagingly, that he supposed he himself was too.[2] A prominent UMNO politician arrived at a compromise between feudalism and the role of a party politician. He thought that you should not choose your leader blindly, but that once you had chosen him, you should give him your blind loyalty.[3]

The ideal of human rights derived from the thinking of eighteenth-century Western philosophers and the post-revolutionary constitutions of France and the United States. However, the topic was not prominent on a global scale, or among the many as opposed to the few, until after the Second World War. The newly founded United Nations promoted human rights by distributing information, by encouraging discussion, and by inviting countries to pledge themselves to take action to promote human rights by signing covenants, protocols, and so on, which some countries signed, others signed with reservations, and some others signed and even complied with. These efforts were supplemented by the work of organizations which operated at world or continental level, such as Amnesty International or Asia Watch. Non-governmental organizations (NGOs) were established in developed countries, and then spread to developing countries. Sometimes a national human rights association was set up by a government.

The ideas of such groups have been spread in three main ways. One was the

United Nations conference in Vienna in 1993, which was attended by representatives of over 90 percent of the world's governments, and members of over a thousand NGOs, from all over the world. It publicized many important issues, particularly about the extent to which human rights might be universally applicable, although a lack of consensus on this was evident in the carefully calculated text.

The second way in which the human rights "message" was transmitted was through the increasing reach of television and camrecorders, which made it possible for millions to use the screen to bring vivid images of violence before their eyes. Two notable examples in Southeast Asia were the shootings of civilians by the military in Dili, East Timor, Indonesia in 1991, and similar horrifying scenes in Bangkok, Thailand in the appropriately named "Bloody May," in 1992. The third way was through Western governments, particularly the United States. These governments took up human rights as a "cause," in the United States almost as a "crusade." Their advocacy often equated human rights with democracy, although analytically the two concepts are quite different. Western countries did not merely advocate the observance of human rights, they also tried to pressurize countries, including Malaysia, to observe human rights by imposing "conditionality," economic sanctions, through the use, or threat, of limiting aid or trade (pp. 139–40).

The scope claimed for human rights nowadays would astonish the eighteenth-century advocates of rights. Until a few years ago, it was customary to classify human rights into: civil and political; and economic, social, and cultural. The former concerned bodily security and integrity, and the freedom to function politically, respectively. The meaning of the latter is almost self-evident, although some claim that they are really "entitlements," claims that may be hard for some governments to satisfy, because their resources may be limited. Ideally, such "rights" should be enforceable, but this may provide little consolation to those who do not actually receive any benefit. Two other categories of rights have been accepted by many. One has been named "solidarity rights," which includes environmental rights and the attractive-sounding "right to development." The other, sometimes called "group rights," refers to the rights of ethnic minorities to use their group's language, practise its religion, and so on. Some supporters of human rights still remain skeptical about the way in which their scope has been so widely extended, so that anything that is good or highly regarded has been transformed into a human right.[4]

Human rights in Malaysia

Attempts to rate countries numerically on human rights have not been entirely successful. During the last few years, an annual publication has tried to do this through an index on political rights and one on civil liberties.[5] On the former, it generally ranks Malaysia slightly higher than Singapore, but slightly lower than Thailand and the Philippines. On the latter, it is generally ranked equally with Singapore and Thailand, but slightly below the Philippines. In 1994–5, on both indices it was, unflatteringly, given the same ranking as Cambodia. Malaysian protests were one reason that the United Nations Development Programme dropped its "Human Freedom Index" in 1992 and replaced it by a Political Freedom Index. Among other things, the previous index took into account the personal right of homosexuality between consenting adults. Malaysia had been given the same rating as Iraq and almost all the former members of the Eastern European Communist bloc.

It may be more useful to give the main strengths and weaknesses of Malaysia on human rights, compared to other ASEAN states in non-numerical form.[6] Malaysia performs quite well. Unlike Indonesia, in Malaysia the military is under the control of the center. There is a complete contrast with the Philippines regarding law and order. In that country, until very recently, the government has simply not had much control of certain areas. This is not just because of the Communist rebellions or the "Moro" (Muslim) rebellions in the South. The rest of the country (including places fewer than 50 miles from Manila) is subject to the activities of private armies and vigilantes which practise violence. Their ranks have been swelled by police while they are off duty. There is nothing that resembles the violence that sometimes erupts in Thailand. Annual reports on the civil rights situation in Malaysia list no entries under "Political and Other Extrajudicial Killing" nor are there reports in the sinister category of "politically motivated disappearances."

The general impression about Malaysia is that breaches of civil rights do not arise from a lack of government control of law and order, or because the state is not the sole body able to exercise force. The explanation is rather that the government, including the Prime Minister, does not set a really high priority on civil rights. Its main priorities are economic development and stability. Indeed, the government thinks that human rights activists, often encouraged by some foreign countries and organizations, are a hindrance to economic development by endangering "stability."

Concern for political rights in Malaysia is not high. Political competition is not as great as it is, in different ways, in Thailand or the Philippines. Many of the formal prerequisites for fair and free elections are observed. Physical force is not exerted against opponents (except in the form of the "political" arrests of some opposition leaders), nor are ballot boxes "stuffed." But the government has many advantages just by virtue of *being* the government. In addition, the government parties own much of the media, and the media are under government control. The difficulty is that, without some transformation of the political scene such as might possibly have occurred between 1987 and 1990, the Barisan type of formula seems to be the only feasible one for maintaining Malay supremacy yet tempering it so as to be acceptable to minorities. So some imperfections in the system are overlooked because of the need to preserve stability and an appreciable degree of consensus.

Constraints on civil rights in Malaysia

State of emergency

Many of the instruments that constrain human rights in Malaysia have their legal basis in the declaration of a state of emergency. After the declaration, the executive is given wide legislative powers which suspend most constitutional rights.[7] There is no recourse to constitutional or judicial remedies. The only means by which a state of emergency could be revoked, and decrees based on it invalidated, would be through a vote in Parliament. Realistically, this is unlikely to happen, because the ruling party (the Alliance and then the Barisan), which exercises party discipline, is likely to be strong enough to prevent defeat. Nor is it conceivable that the existing law validating a state of emergency could be revoked. There would be an even greater hurdle to surmount – the need to obtain a two-thirds parliamentary majority. Many of the restrictions on human rights mentioned in this chapter derive from powers granted under previous states of emergency. This does not apply to the best-known declaration, that of 1948, intended to deal with the Communists. When the "Emergency" ended, most of the powers conferred it were transferred to new acts, for example, the Sedition Act. There were four other emergency declarations, which, technically at least, are still law. One is also well known: the declaration made after the 1969 riots. Another was made during confrontation with Indonesia (1964). Two were essentially "political" – being directed at opposition parties that were causing difficulties for the ruling party.[8] The first was in Sarawak, intended to remove the Sarawak National Party (SNAP) from power in 1965, and the second, 1977, was aimed at PAS in Kelantan.

Civil rights: respect for the person

The following headings are adapted and abbreviated from those used by the US Department of State in its annual reports to Congress.

The most serious challenge to civil rights in Malaysia is through arbitrary arrest, or detention. Suspects can be detained without any charges being filed and without judicial review. The grounds for arrest are having acted in a manner prejudicial to the security of Malaysia. The statistics of arrests and releases, which are provided from time to time by the authorities, are not presented in a manner that makes research easy. The Internal Security Act (ISA) is used not just for security, in a strict sense. In 1996 the majority of ISA detainees were forgers, who worked for criminal syndicates. "Political" detainees may have numbered about two hundred. There are also persons detained under the Dangerous Drugs Act and its amendments: in 1996 there were about 8,500 persons detained in this category. Immigration laws may also be used to detain possible illegal aliens.

Original periods of detention may be renewed. There is the right of appeal to an advisory board,[9] but the power is only advisory and the government is not obliged to accept the advice. An example of this occurred in the case of Datuk

James Wong, a former Deputy Chief Minister of Sarawak, originally detained under two other ordinances, but later put under the ISA. He appeared before an advisory board, which apparently recommended his release. However, the government did not accept this advice.[10] He had, it seems, some powerful political enemies.

Detainees in all the categories mentioned have, allegedly, sometimes been subjected to torture or other cruel, inhumane, or degrading treatment or punishment. It is government policy to punish police and others who abuse their power, or who deal violently with prisoners, and there seems to be a trend towards implementing this policy more thoroughly.

Some former detainees have written about their time in prison after they have been released. Naturally, those who do this are likely to be among the more literate. A university professor, Dr. S. Husin Ali, an expert on Malay culture who did so, said that, apart from his physical ill treatment, what seemed to be depressing to him, as an intellectual, was rigorous interrogation, psychological pressures, and the cumulative effect of "minor" items, such as the absence of spectacles, toothbrush, comb, shaving kit, and so on.[11]

After the Emergency was over (1960), detention was still used against a wide range of persons including political opponents. It is sometimes not easy to remember that, originally, it was used mainly against armed Communist rebels, and those who helped them. Detention was employed against opposition leaders, top leaders in the DAP, including Lim Kit Siang, the secretary-general, and local-level leaders in PAS. James Wong, referred to above, was detained not as a political opponent, but for allegedly having supported Brunei's claim to take over the Limbang area of Sarawak. Among the academics was Husin Ali. Perhaps the detentions that had the strongest claim to be headline material took place in 1976. Two prominent Malay journalists were arrested, one of whom, Samad Ismail, had been an adviser to, and a confidant of, the late Prime Minister, Razak. Two deputy ministers were also arrested, one of whom, Datuk Abdullah Ahmad, was Razak's own Deputy Minister. By virtue of his closeness to Razak, both officially and through his being in Razak's "clique," he wielded considerable power. A complete account of just what happened has not been made public.[12] The story would have to include information on links with Singapore journalists, confessions on television, and rumors of contacts with the Soviet authorities in Kuala Lumpur. If only because of the connections with Razak, a factional interpretation of these surprising events would seem to be warranted.

The arrests of 1987; later arrests; conclusions

One might have thought there was too much else going on politically in 1987 (in the form of contests inside UMNO) for Malaysia also to be embroiled in ethnic violence that threatened to become almost as bad as in 1969. The Malays had divided into two major, opposed factions. There was still an economic recession.[13] Government scandals, in particular the one concerning Bumiputra Malaysia Finance (pp. 68–70), were also a fascinating topic of conversation. But a number of ethnic disputes, mostly between Chinese and Malays, many in themselves not of great consequence, proved to have a cumulative impact. Even Mahathir became embroiled in making assertions and refutations, and UMNO Youth, perhaps because its acting head, Najib, wished to be seen as suitable for continuing in his role, lived up to its usual standards of combativeness.

The contentious issues were not surprising and were typical of what everyday ethnic disputes are about. Educational changes which provided for greater use of the Malay language provoked adverse reactions from Chinese (see pp. 95–6). So did the continuing issue of use of Chinese characters on certain signboards. Allegations were also made that Malays were being subjected to Christian proselytizing. All these reactions were deeply felt and also ominously recurrent.

However, the immediate precipitating issue was the appointment by the Education Ministry of non-Mandarin-speaking Chinese to administrative posts in Chinese-medium primary schools. Appeals to reason, and for order, by the leaders of the component parties of the Barisan went unheeded.[14] Tensions became heightened and resulted in invocations of ethnic solidarity and in planning to hold larger meetings. Party barriers were overrun by ethnicity. The MCA collaborated on some occasions, not only with Gerakan but also with the DAP. Consociationalism was breaking down. Followers no longer followed, but felt driven to assert their ethnicity. UMNO Youth staged a mass rally in support of Education Ministry actions and to defend the honor of the Malays against "Chinese insults." UMNO proposed to follow this rally with an even bigger one, planned apparently by Mahathir himself, with an expected turnout of half a million, timed to commemorate the fortieth anniversary of the party's founding and intended to be a show of support for Mahathir and UMNO unity and strength. Mahathir, faced with a repetition of May 13, took two decisions which had a certain air of impartiality. He banned all rallies – actually only UMNO had planned a big one. Also, starting on October 27, over several weeks, a total of about 120 arrests were made.[15] In launching Operation Lalang (long coarse grass, or weed), Mahathir stressed the need to avoid another May 13, and claimed that the police had recommended the arrests. (Actually, it is doubtful that they would have made recommendations about some of the non-political persons detained.) A month later, he said that two main things were to blame for the tension. One was his own liberal attitude over the last few years;[16] the other was that the press's playing up of racial issues had escalated.

Mahathir did show that he had learned from the experience of 1969. An immediate reason for the outbreak of violence then was that processions were permitted, and resulted in violent incidents. Rallies do not offer the same danger of marchers coming into contact with onlookers, but they were dangerous for another reason. Any large number of persons collected together and sharing strong ethnic feelings is liable to be inflamed by oratory. Possible trouble, arising from a ban on meetings, was probably less dangerous than trying to restrain members of a mass rally once they had been aroused.

Although those arrested were not "representative," in that they were not selected by some form of sampling technique, they represented members of all kinds of parties and organizations. In some cases, they were from organizations alleged to have been infiltrated by Communists. A good guide to Mahathir's choices was that they were people who, in his opinion, constituted a danger – or a threat, or a nuisance. Lim Kit Siang, apart from being the DAP leader, had delivered a damning indictment of the government's favoritism in the allocation of contracts for the North–South Highway project (pp. 58–9). Another target was leaders of prominent NGOs who had obtained a court injunction against UEM, indirectly partly owned by UMNO, and who had exposed government favoritism, mismanagement, etc. Dr. Chandra Muzaffar, founder of the outspoken NGO Aliran, came into this category. Some opponents of logging in Sarawak were also arrested. The number and range of detentions, especially of opposition MPs, represented a major extension of the use of the ISA. About half of those detained in Operation Lalang were released by the end of 1987, but others, including Lim Kit Siang and his fellow MP Karpal Singh, were held for two years.[17]

The use of the ISA in October 1987 was only six months after Team A's victory over Team B at the UMNO General Assembly elections. Apparently there was no direct connection between the arrests and the struggle inside UMNO. However, in making the arrests, UMNO's internal struggle must have been very much in Mahathir's mind. Means suggests, though somewhat cryptically, that there may have been some connection: Mahathir acted to enhance his political position and power. Many of the detainees had been only minimally involved. Others (presumably including organizers of rallies), who could have been arrested, were not.[18] Khoo's analysis is more direct. He suggests that the arrests may have constituted a "trade-off;"[19] in return for having to accept the ban of the UMNO rally, UMNO militants were given a favorable "balance" in the arrests. While some in the top echelons of the DAP were detained, the only three UMNO politicians detained were from the Youth Executive Council, and all of them were from Team B.

The most noteworthy example of the political use of the ISA after 1987 arose from the strained relations between the federal government and the Sabah party PBS (Parti Bersatu Sabah). Between May 18 and July 7, 1990, seven party members were arrested. The most prominent was Jeffrey Kitingan, brother of the Sabah Chief Minister. He was alleged to have been planning secession from Malaysia. In the 1990s members of the Islamic movement Darul Arqam were detained (pp. 87–8). During the economic crisis of 1997, some members of a religious group were detained under the ISA. It was said that they should have been tried by a religious court or under the Sedition Act. In 1998 the former Deputy Prime Minister, Anwar Ibrahim, was detained under the ISA for three weeks without being charged (see p. 157).

Less well known than the ISA is the Emergency Ordinance of 1960. Detention can be ordered for up to two years to protect public order for the suppression of violence or for the protection against crimes involving violence. There were fifty-six persons in detention under this order in 1996.[20]

In 1962 the original draftsman of the ISA, Professor H.R. Hickling, said he hoped that detention without trial should not be regarded as permanent. Former minister Datuk Dr. Rais Yatim amplified this by pointing to the original aim of dealing with communism and controlling terrorism, the former now not a threat.[21] Its continuance can become an excuse for the authorities to administer the country on an emergency basis. Mahathir maintains that the Act is still needed to deal with racial riots and general strikes. He still feels that Malaysia needs to have the power to prevent irresponsible actions.[22] For some years the government has said that there should be amendments to the ISA but only to permit more flexibility in the present mandatory period of two years. However, no substantial change in the law has yet been achieved.

Political rights

This section is concerned not with the liberty of the person from damage or imprisonment, but with the freedom of the person to associate with others. Specifically, the topics are: freedom of religion; freedom of assembly and of association; universities; worker rights; freedom of speech and of the press and the other media.

Freedom of religion

Islam is an important component of the Malay way of life, and it benefits from government funding. Islamic programs are regularly transmitted on government television and radio stations. Islam is the state religion, but its claims must be reconciled with preserving the religious freedom of other groups. There are limits to this freedom in some respects. Circulation of translations of the Bible in Malay is discouraged. Conversions of Muslims to other religions occur, but the proselytizing of Muslims by Christians and other religions is prohibited by some state governments. Most Malaysians understand, and practise, the spirit of accommodation that is needed. With the exercise of care, it is only very occasionally that unpleasant incidents occur.

The government and associations

Government policy on associations is stated in the Societies Act of 1948 and its amendments. Any association with more than seven members must register with the government as a society. The government may refuse the application, or may register it only subject to certain conditions. For some time after an application is made, it may be hard to determine if the delay in granting it is just "bureaucratic," or whether it indicates that there are difficulties ahead. There were about 14,000 registered societies in 1982.

The Act became a contentious issue in the early 1980s, just before Mahathir became Prime Minister. Amendments had been proposed, advocating that a distinction should be drawn between societies that were "political" and those that were not.[23] The Registrar of Societies would be given complete discretionary powers and could declare any society "political." Apparently the aim was to target societies that were likely to engage in political activity, such as Aliran (Aliran Kesedaran Negara),[24] the Consumers Association of Penang, and ABIM. Unlike ABIM, most of the groups that were inclined to be "political" had a membership that was mainly non-Malay and middle class. Their memberships were small, but the government was nevertheless sensitive about the issues they might publicize.

Rights of assembly and association: interest groups

By the Constitution, these rights may be limited in the interests of safety or public order. The Police Act of 1967 requires that permits are needed for all public meetings, with the exception of workers on picket lines. There are two aspects of such rights that are relevant politically. One has to do with political rallies and campaigning (pp. 115–16). The other involves government policy towards NGOs and universities. A related term is "interest groups," although this directs attention to the more self-serving activities of groups, while many associations and NGOs profess to be operating in the *public* interest. In most Western countries, interest groups are accepted as "a fact of life," as an unavoidable component in the political process. Some groups, however, are liable to arouse suspicion. Militant trade unions are not liked by right-wingers, because they may hinder economic development, while some think that big business may wield too much financial power to be compatible with democracy. In the United States, PACs (political action committees) have been criticized as supporting single issues, and so threatening the more general objectives of political parties. In many developing countries, and certainly in Malaysia, and in Mahathir's estimation, groups are regarded as intruders. They seek to come between the government and the people who elected it. Only the government has a mandate and the knowledge to govern. Government antipathy is intensified if a group has foreign connections, because it is possible that it may be acting, at least partly, to promote foreign interests.

The issue of how the government should handle societies was complicated by the impact of changes in appointments and roles. The Home Minister, Ghazali Shafie, was replaced by the more liberal Musa in mid-1982. Also, the leader of the societies' negotiating committee, Anwar, was now a rising star in UMNO. A new set of amendments was adopted in 1983. The "political" distinction was discarded, but, in spite of Anwar's extra clout, some features repugnant to the societies were included, such as the Registrar's power to order a society's premises to be searched.

Ironically, a 1988 amendment to the Societies Act had little direct connection with rights or freedoms, although it had everything to do with where power would reside. It was made simply to avoid a repetition of the court decision in 1987 that UMNO was illegal. The law now stated that, if a registered society established a branch without the approval of the Registrar, the branch, but not the society itself, would be unlawful.[25]

Universities

Universities are not usually classified as interest groups, and, as private universities have been set up only recently, until the 1990s they were certainly not NGOs, but, because universities have certain claims to autonomy, a word about them may be in order here.

Some students and staff were politically active after the May 13 incidents. Anwar, who was a student at that time, and Mahathir met and talked with many students about the current implications of Malay nationalism. During the 1970s, Mahathir was in contact with people at the University of Malaya when he was Minister of Education. Some students had become interested in social issues, as shown by their 1974 demonstrations supporting peasants in Baling, Kedah, opposing inflation, and against the falling price of rubber, poverty, and corruption. Students also demonstrated in support of squatters in Johor Baru in 1974. In 1979, after a large demonstration, many students were arrested, some of whom were detained. An amended Universities and Colleges Act, introduced in Parliament by Mahathir as the Minister of Education, sought to make students less "political" by limiting their political activities and preventing them from joining or supporting any political party, trade union or similar organization without written permission. Mahathir was said to have taken a hard line.[26] Now that he was in the government, he had to deal with student dissatisfaction.

Workers' rights: the right to organize and bargain collectively

Most workers, except defense workers, managerial and executive, etc., personnel, have the right to join trade unions. However, unions are weak, and contain only about 10 percent of the workforce. The government is not very favorably inclined towards them. Some legislation prohibits interference with a worker's right to engage in lawful trade union activities, but also restricts a worker to representing only those in a particular establishment, trade, occupation, or industry, or in a "similar" establishment, etc. National unions are prohibited in the electronics industry, a symptom of its important role in the economy.

Unions are not affiliated to political parties, but individual union members may belong to them, and, as opposition members, have sat in Parliament. There might be adverse government reactions if an opposition party were able to mobilize substantial union support, but this has not yet happened. The government's probable course of action, if challenged, may be indicated by the events of 1989, when Mahathir threatened to set up a rival to the Malaysian Trades Union Congress (MTUC) when it seemed to be getting too close to Semangat '46.[27]

Mahathir believes that workers need constant reminders of the economic facts of life. To ensure a favorable economic climate, they should not be choosy about their jobs. They must stop giving the impression that they are creating problems for their employers. In March 1996, he repeated the message to the MTUC, when its leaders protested at a cut in the Employees' Provident Fund dividend, claiming that, without it, Malaysia would be on the verge of bankruptcy.[28]

Freedom of speech: the media

The Constitution provides for freedom of speech and of the media, but also stipulates that this freedom may be restricted by legislation in the interests of security or public order. The principal instrument used is the Sedition Act, which prohibits public comment on issues defined as sensitive.

The rest of this section is concerned with the media, mainly the press, rather than with the spoken word. Mahathir is not enamored of the press. Soon after taking office, he proclaimed that the narrow interests of the press as an institution faded into insignificance if we think of our country and our people.[29] As Mahathir said, nobody elected the press, but there was no such guarantee of continuity for elected people. Sometimes, if people perceived that you were wrong, they could reject you at the next election. Newspapers had their own opinions. What they reported was their views, not news. During the war, Goebbels had control of information so he was able to change a very highly cultured race, the Germans, into beasts.[30]

The degree of press control on Malaysia, through a variety of methods, is consonant with Mahathir's views. A Chinese editor commented that a week was enough for a foreigner to understand the Malaysian press, asking, rhetorically, where one would ever see an article critical of the government.[31] This is an exaggeration, but it expresses a common perception. Mahathir's mistrust of the Malaysian press is exceeded only by his detestation of the foreign press (p. 71).

Given these opinions, it is not surprising that, in controlling the press, Mahathir "improved on" the work of his predecessors. In 1987 the Sedition Act was once more amended, and toughened in several important respects. Also in 1987, the Printing Presses and Publication Act 1984 was amended. The publication of "malicious news" was prohibited, and the government's power to ban or restrict publications was expanded. The suspension or revocation of permits to publish could no longer be challenged in a court.[32] Also in 1987, in conjunction with the large-scale arrests, three newspapers – *The Star*, *Sin Chew Jit Poh*, and *Watan* (a weekly) – were banned. The ban was lifted six months later. There were no conditions attached, but *The Star* was required to make editorial rearrangements.[33]

The Official Secrets Act of 1972 can also be used to restrict press freedom. The original scope, which was very broad, was limited by a 1986 amendment, which, however, provided for a mandatory jail term for those found guilty.

There is a general impression that the Chinese, and possibly the Indian, press is less strictly controlled than the English and Malay press, possibly because the scope of its circulation is more circumscribed. However, in 1995 the Home Minister warned the *Nanyang Siang Pow*, the *Sin Chew Jit Poh*, and the *China Press* that their permits would be revoked if they did not stop publishing articles that criticized the government's efforts to create a multiracial society.[34] The timing was significant. Several Chinese papers had been criticized for favoring the Opposition at the 1990 election, and the next general election was due before the end of 1995.

Control of the press through legislation has been reinforced by ownership, which is now almost entirely in the hands of the government or of pro-government organizations.[35] The English press and the Malay press are now almost exclusively government owned. The main English-language newspaper group is the New Straits Times Press, owned by Fleet Holdings, an investment arm of UMNO. The politicians in control of this group were, successively, Razaleigh, Daim Zainuddin, and Anwar until his dismissal in 1998 (a succession of finance ministers). Four senior newspaper executives were later put in control, including the group editor, all close to Anwar. There were also changes (within the UMNO inner circle) in the control of the Malay language *Utusan Melayu* group.

The second newspaper in the English medium, *The Star*, has had a more varied career, passing from the control of the unpredictable Tun Mustapha, a former Chief Minister of Sabah and close friend of Tunku, to the MCA – the paper appealed to many Chinese readers. The Tunku fearlessly used his column, "As I See It," to tell the government where he thought it was going wrong, which was quite often. In 1987 *The Star*'s license was suspended for some months, and apparently a condition for its restoration was that the Tunku should no longer write his column. He then resigned his chairmanship of the paper's board.[36] The Chinese press and the Tamil press are now controlled largely by pro-government groups. Access to party publications was limited in 1993. PAS's *Harakan* and the DAP's *The Rocket* were no longer supposed to be available to people who were not members of the respective parties.

The government's instruments of control already mentioned were also used to censor books, pamphlets, etc., as well as newspapers. Curiously, the ban on Mahathir's *The Malay Dilemma* was not lifted until he became Prime Minister. In the press, the effect of control plus ownership is so strong that it makes investigative journalism difficult. What is particularly inhibiting is that it may lead to self-censorship, because of the fear that something one writes may be regarded as too sensitive to the authorities, which can lead a journalist to "play safe." The Sedition Act may be used "politically," just as the ISA has been used to endanger the freedom of the person. In a recent case, a DAP MP, Lim Guan Eng, was charged because of his comments about a statutory rape case which involved the former Chief Minister of the state of Malacca. Lim alleged that the charge was politically motivated, but he was nevertheless convicted. When his appeal was heard (1998), his sentence was actually increased, which led to vehement protests against such a violation of human rights.

During the economic crisis (1997–) informal restrictions were used to limit press comment.

The government has a monopoly of the ownership of radio and television stations,[37] except for "TV3," established in 1985, and for some stations that are joint enterprises in which government has a share. Even TV3 did not lack UMNO credentials – it was owned largely by the UMNO-controlled Fleet group. In all countries, governments tend to obtain greater coverage on radio and television stations, because what they do is more important news than what opposition parties only *propose* to do. However, even this consideration does not entirely justify the overwhelming preponderance enjoyed by reports on government activities in the press. Apparently, since the mid-1990s there has been some tendency towards a more liberal approach to television and radio. Chandra Muzaffar, Husin Ali, and others have been appearing regularly on television talk shows. However, a show on the possibly contentious topic of divorce was replaced at short notice by a program on nation-building.[38]

The Malaysian government had two satellites launched in 1996. Datuk A. Kadir Jasin, the group editor of the New Straits Times group, commented that the press must learn to live in a freer and more competitive environment and must learn to limit self-censorship to what was absolutely necessary.[39]

Elections

In 1990, the crushing defeat of Semangat '46 everywhere except Kelantan gave the government ample reason for confidence. Yet, at the even more decisive election victory in 1995, and since then, the Prime Minister has been determined not to take anything for granted.

The government's conduct of the 1995 elections, and the implications for human rights, may be looked at under three headings. They are: the constitutional setting for the elections, including the delineation of constituency boundaries; the rules for the conduct of the elections; and reports on the elections in the press. A fourth aspect is more difficult to describe succinctly. It refers to the spectrum of tactics employed by the Barisan, ranging from what could be termed "taking advantage of the law for the party's advantage" to the use of "dirty tricks." This is not to say that opposition parties are purer in their approach, but they have less money and they lack the advantage of being a "government" party, so their repertoire is more limited. Criticisms of the electoral process should be seen in context: elections are held regularly, and the ballot is secret (but see p. 97).

The parameters of the 1995 election were determined not just by the Malays' superiority in numbers over the non-Malays, but by the Election Commission's use of "rural weightage." A rural vote counts for more than a non-rural vote, because, on the whole, rural constituencies contain fewer electors. Furthermore, there are more rural Malays than rural non-Malays. Some opposition leaders made representations to the Commission, but they did not create much of an impression. The allocation of seats to Sarawak and Sabah also gave greater weight to these states than to the rest of Malaysia. Because the discrepancies just mentioned are so obvious (and have important ethnic implications), another feature shared with many other countries is sometimes overlooked. In a two-party system – even in the attenuated form that it assumes in Malaysia – the difference in votes between the parties is magnified when "translated" into seats. This is an arithmetical consequence, not a political contrivance.

In the conduct of the campaign, there were restrictions that affected government parties less than opposition parties. Rallies and large meetings were forbidden, although *ceramahs* – meetings held in a house and/or garden – were permissible during the campaign period. However, as the US State Department tartly remarked, the government parties held several large-scale events that very much resembled rallies.[40] Permits were required for *ceramahs*, and opposition parties had more difficulty in obtaining these promptly than had government parties. The press, television and radio were as uneven in their coverage of the parties as they were in non-campaign periods. However, parties were allowed a small number of radio talks free – government parties were given more talks because they had entered more candidates. The talks were recorded and had to be submitted in advance.

Government tactics were said to include payments, some taking the form of "minor projects," such as the construction of bridges, roads, etc. The services of government employees, for example from the Information Ministry, were sometimes available at no cost to Barisan parties. Information for the government about grass-roots political sentiments may be gleaned from community development bodies such as Kemas (Kemajuan Mesyarakat). In seats where the majority at the previous election had been small, individuals were sometimes encouraged, and assisted, to move from one constituency to another. Sometimes it was party employees who had the task of "moving" the electors' hearts and minds. In 1990 young people working for UMNO were billeted in the homes of electors, providing their living expenses in order to conduct an intensive conversion and reinforcement course.[41]

Finally, misleading "news" was reproduced in the press, which was almost impossible to remove from people's minds once the message had been planted. During the 1990 campaign, pictures appeared in *Utusan Melayu*, and were run for three days, which showed Razaleigh wearing a curious hat, on which there was a cross. The implication, of course, was that Razaleigh's devotion to his religion was less than absolute. In fact the cross was a Kadazan, not a Christian, symbol, and members of Team A had previously worn a similar hat in public without eliciting comment.[42]

Taken together, two changes in election procedures gave cause for concern. Ballot papers now had numbers printed on the counterfoils, and votes were now counted separately at each polling station, and not gathered together for the whole constituency before counting took place. The new system could make it possible to estimate where groups of opposition electors were located, thus possibly facilitating retaliation by the government downgrading the services they received.

The formal process of voting was quite closely observed. Yet political rights were infringed upon, because, both during election campaigns and between them, the playing field was far from level.

Discrimination: women; the Penans

Two groups in Malaysia merit discussion, because they are subject to decided, but different, forms of discrimination. Muslim women have to reconcile their aspirations to rights with the status of Islam as the state religion. They enjoy support from Mahathir's wife, Datin Seri Dr. Siti Hasmah, and also from Mahathir himself. The Penans, a small, underdeveloped group in Sarawak, unwilling to give up their ancestors' ways abruptly, have found little sympathy from the modernizing Mahathir.

Discrimination against women is practised in a number of ways. Groups concerned about women's issues have focussed upon: violence against women, including domestic violence; trafficking in women and young girls; lack of an opportunity to work with equal pay; the need for greater participation in higher education and in attaining high-ranking positions. Action has been taken on some aspects of the first of these issues through the 1994 Domestic Violence Act, which gave powers to the courts to protect victims and provide compensation and counselling for them. However, there were allegations three years later that it was sometimes hard to get the police to act on allegations of domestic violence. There has also been a drive to improve the position of Muslim women, especially as regards polygamy. Individual states have been asked to standardize the rules on polygamy by the National Council for Women. The Council was not officially against polygamy, as it is allowed under Islamic law, but urged that stringent measures should be taken to ensure that the practice was not abused. Dr. Siti spoke out strongly against a Selangor state government ruling that married Muslim men could lawfully wed another wife without the consent of the first wife.[43] The advances made in women's opportunities have been extremely uneven, and they have been more advanced in the educational, than in the occupational, sphere. In the scientific and medical fields, women now constitute more than half of university graduates, while only about 1.5 percent of women hold what are described as "decision-making posts." As a modernizer, Mahathir sees an improvement in the position of women as important, particularly in regard to their possible status under Islamic law.

Discrimination has been alleged against the *orang asli* (aboriginals) in Peninsular Malaysia and natives in Sabah and Sarawak, but the example that reveals Mahathir's views most clearly concerns the Penans of Sarawak. There are only about 10,000 in this group; some are nomadic, although the majority, described as "semi-settled," are based in longhouses. Their immediate problem in the 1980s was that their ancestral areas of food-growing and food-gathering to which they were emotionally attached, were being encroached upon by extremely profitable logging operations.[44] Logging was subject to much dispute. Supporters claimed that the operations were conducted with due regard to the environment, and that greater damage was done by the unorganized "slash-and-burn" practices of the natives. The Penans wished their old ways could continue, and, although some were willing to work for logging companies, many wished to continue as before, rather than enter the cash economy. To deter what they regarded as a danger to their way of life, they attempted to block the loggers by erecting barricades, for which many were arrested and some were detained.

Mahathir became officially involved at an international level when the question of the Penans came up at a 1992 press conference held after a meeting in Rio de Janeiro. He had previously conducted a brief correspondence with a Swiss activist, Bruno Manser, who had taken up the cause of the Penans and had lived with them for six years.

A letter that Mahathir wrote to Manser, dated March 5, 1992, indicates his very decided reactions:

> If any policeman gets killed or wounded in the course of restoring law and order in Sarawak, you will have to take the blame. It's you and your kind who instigated the Penans to take the law into their own hands and to use poison darts, bows, arrows and parangs [knives]…
>
> It is fine for you to spend a short holiday tasting the Penans' way of life and then returning to the heated comfort of your Swiss chalet. But do you really expect the Penans to subsist on monkeys until the year 2500 or 3000 or forever? Have they no right to a better way of life? What right have you to condemn them to primitive life forever?
>
> The Penans may tell you that their primitive life is what they like. That is because they are not able to live a better life like the other tribes in Sarawak. Those of the Penans who have left the jungle are educated and are earning a better living have no wish to return to their primitive ways. You are trying to deny them their chance for a better life, so that you can enjoy studying primitive peoples the way you study animals. Penans are people and they should be respected as people. If you had a chance to be educated and live a better life, they too deserve that chance.
>
> Stop being arrogant and thinking that it is the white man's burden to decide the fate of the peoples of the world. Malaysians, the Penans included, are an independent people and are quite capable of looking after themselves. Swiss imperialism is as disgusting as other European imperialism. It is about time that you stop your arrogance and your intolerable European superiority. You are no better than the Penans. If you have a right to decide for yourself, why can't you leave the Penans to decide for themselves after they have been given a chance to improve their living standards.[45]

At the Rio press conference Mahathir supplemented the views contained in his letter.[46] He claimed that the Penans had a right to development, and they should be exposed to education and development, so that they could choose their preferred way of life. His opinions on the Penans expressed three themes close to his heart: his belief in modernization, his skepticism about adulation of the "noble savage," and his abhorrence of sentimental and would-be superior Westerners. He also turned the tables on the West by invoking the Penans' "rights," claiming that they should have freedom to choose their way of life. One wonders whether Mahathir's mind might have speculated on the opportunities open to the Penans compared with those available to the Malays forty years earlier.

Human rights organizations

NGOs are not regarded with much favor by the Malaysian government. It is sensitive to criticisms of its record on human rights, and local groups with foreign connections are especially suspect. Organizations that are substantially concerned with human rights are among those least favored. Amnesty International, for example, has not been allowed to establish an official presence in the country.[47] The government is implacably hostile to the Bar Council, and has never forgiven it for its condemnation of the government's destruction of judicial independence. Mahathir told Parliament that it behaved like an opposition party.[48] A National Human Rights Society (HAKAM) exists, but its application to be registered was not accepted for about two years. It seems that this was not occasioned mainly by bureaucratic delays, but reflected the opinions of the Mahathir government.[49] HAKAM publicly criticizes the government from time to time, as do other NGOs, but, unlike the Indonesian Commission mentioned in the next paragraph, it does not investigate individual complaints. It organizes forums and seminars, which are given some notice in the press.[50]

It is surprising that there is no official Malaysian human rights commission. A few years ago, there was some skepticism about establishing such an organization in Indonesia, but, when it was set up, its performance was more impressive than would have been predicted.[51]

Relations between the government and NGOs deteriorated towards the end of 1996. In November, an international conference on East Timor, held in Kuala Lumpur (despite official warnings), was broken up by protesters, including UMNO Youth. Ten foreign human rights activists were arrested and deported. More than a hundred others were arrested, including seven UMNO Youth members.[52] The government reacted strongly against a proposal by nine NGOs to hold a "public tribunal" to discuss allegations of abuses of power by the police. Mahathir claimed that some NGOs were deliberately challenging the government to take action against them and threatened that he would do so, if they had broken the law.[53]

In Mahathir's estimation, NGOs were particularly obnoxious when they threatened to delay large government projects. A prominent example was the hydro-electric Bakun Dam in Sarawak, to be constructed by an international consortium at a cost of $US5.4bn. The agreement was signed in October 1996, and building the dam would take five years. The government made arrangements to resettle 9,400 people as well as animals. Some new techniques were used in this attempt to transmit electricity from Sarawak to Peninsular Malaysia. Not only did accidents and land slips occur, but also the executive chairman of Ekran, one of the participating firms, Tan Sri Ting Pek Khing, suffered a heart attack. There were hostile demonstrations in Kuala Lumpur, as well as protests from some of those due to be resettled, environmentalists, and NGOs. Three Sarawakians succeeded in obtaining an injunction to halt construction, although the Court of Appeal granted Ekran a suspension of the injunction, and, pending a hearing of an appeal by Ekran and other defendants, construction was resumed.[54]

Mahathir correctly complained of the costs of delay: "If we delay any longer, the costs will go up. [It] had been made to look as though I have enriched a friend of mine...Tan Sri Ting Pek Khing." The Prime Minister said it was the NGOs who took the matter to court after taking the cue from their foreign counterparts who were envious of the nation's progress. He added that the majority of the people in the affected area supported the project and would be duly compensated with jobs and land. Their compensation would be more money than they would ever make in their lifetime.[55]

In mid-1997 Bakun's troubles continued. There was a major dispute between Ekran and its contractor, Asea Brown Boveri Holdings. Moreover, it appeared that prospective investors were being deterred by the high risk and the long gestation period. Nevertheless, Mahathir, on his return from a two-month vacation (July 1997), stated that the project had to go on. There was no need to give the impression that it was failing. Then the financial crisis in August 1997 delayed the project (pp. 75–6).

In 1997 the government investigated the ways in which NGOs were being managed. Their use of funds would be scrutinized to find out if they were being diverted from their original purposes for the benefit of individuals.[56] The government's action may have been initiated because of its growing hostility to the organizations, some of which, it believed, were cooperating too closely with foreign governments.

Not only does the government sometimes infringe on human rights, but what is perhaps more distressing to human rights advocates is that it seems to have such low esteem for organizations that strive to protect them.

The environment

The problems of the Penans and of the Bakun Dam might, quite appropriately, have been discussed under the heading of "The Environment." In 1991 the importance of protecting the environment had already been recognized in the *Second Outline Perspective Plan*.[57] Several recent events contributed to an increasing awareness of environmental issues. A haze afflicted parts of Malaysia, Singapore, and Indonesia between August and October in 1994, caused mainly by forest fires in Sumatra and Kalimantan, and threatened to become an annual occurrence. The haze intensified during 1997. About thirty forest fires were listed in north Sumatra in one week, September–October. Malaysian firefighters helped in Sarawak. Schools were temporarily closed in Sarawak, jogging was discouraged in Peninsular Malaysia, and talks were held with Indonesia about how to limit future damage. In Kuala Lumpur the view of the Petronas twin towers was often impaired. Public hospitals in Sarawak dealt with 25,000 cases of respiratory and eye complaints in the first twenty-four days of September. Toward the end of the year conditions had improved because, seasonably, rain and a change in wind direction had helped visibility.[58] The "haze" reappeared in Sarawak in April 1998.

In 1995, several buildings collapsed on Malaysian hillsides. Initial government explanations that these were due to natural causes, or "acts of God," were challenged by allegations that indiscriminate clearing might have been responsible. Top government leaders, including the Prime Minister, made public comments on these disasters, and it was announced that there would be stricter enforcement of building regulations.

Conclusion

The improvement in ethnic relations, made possible by a more accommodating government attitude, has not been matched by a more relaxed government approach towards human rights. To be sure, the number of detentions for political reasons has fallen, but it is not yet apparent that there will be any substantive changes in the ISA, in spite of persistent reports that change is contemplated. There was more openness until 1997, in the press and on television, no doubt related, at least partly, to the increasing influence of communication via satellite. The Prime Minister's toughness on human rights and on human rights organizations is unchanged. Its persistence seems to be related to disagreements over human rights internationally, given some attention in Chapter 6.

6   Foreign policy

Put in the simplest terms, practitioners of foreign policy must operate success-fully in two capacities: they must perform well in the "arena" and they must please the spectators. They are therefore under pressure, both external and internal. These pressures are not steady but shifting, calling for a high degree of anticipation and agility. Apart from these factors, the conduct of foreign policy will be shaped by the idiosyncrasies of its director. In the first section of this chapter the highlights of foreign policy as it evolved, 1957–81, will be followed under Mahathir's three predecessors.

When he became the first Prime Minister in 1957, Tunku Abdul Rahman had little experience of international relations, but had lived and studied for his examinations in law in Britain. He had happy memories of its way of life, which found expression in his liking for Rothman's cigarettes and for kippers. With the exception of his opposition to the Malayan Union proposals, he worked closely with the British, especially during the Emergency and at the time of Indonesian Confrontation. His hatred of communism would have made accommodation with the Soviet Union or China difficult, but he looked ahead in 1959, and foresaw that one day the defense pact with the British would end. He therefore thought it essential that the country should participate with its neighbors in some kind of Southeast Asian friendship and economic treaty.[1] Malaya, along with Thailand and the Philippines, became a member of ASA (the Association of Southeast Asia), which had its first foreign ministers' meeting in 1961.[2] During a lull in Confrontation, the confederal association Maphilindo was founded, which included Malaya, the Philippines, and Indonesia, but it died after the proclama-tion of Malaysia in September 1963 and the subsequent severing of diplomatic links with Indonesia and the Philippines.

By 1966, the Acting Foreign Minister, Tun Ismail, was talking of a possible shift in foreign policy to accord with world trends. In 1968, after he had retired from the cabinet for health reasons, he called for the neutralization of Southeast Asia, guaranteed by the major powers, the signing of non-aggression pacts, and the declaration of a policy of coexistence. The proposals had Razak's support. Tunku was not consulted, but thought that the neutralization idea was worth consideration.[3] In 1968 the British were already planning for total withdrawal from areas east of Suez, to be effected, in stages, by 1970.

From this account it is clear that Razak's spectacular moves in the early 1970s towards neutrality had been considered for a long time. Razak's original proposal took the form that Southeast Asia should be neutralized, partly through guarantees by the great powers, but this did not meet with the approval of Malaysia's regional partners. However, it was replaced by a vaguer (and therefore more acceptable) alternative of a "Zone of Peace, Freedom and Neutrality (ZOPFAN)."[4] The question of neutrality was linked with the need for China to play an appropriate international role. This was accompanied by laying the basis for official relations between Malaysia and China, which was done in 1974.

After Hussein Onn became Prime Minister (1976), two important multilateral agreements were endorsed: the ASEAN Treaty of Amity and Cooperation and the Declaration of ASEAN Concord. Both of these were important, yet they were the product of work in progress in Razak's time and did not reflect new initiatives. Hussein was Prime Minister for only five years, and in poor health for much of the time, so this was essentially a period of consolidation rather than innovation.

Mahathir and foreign policy

All prime ministers, even someone as "iconoclastic"[5] as Mahathir, are bound by constraints on foreign policy, just as they are in other policy areas. Even if their own inclinations do not motivate them to continue with existing policies, they are constrained by commitments, by custom and by bureaucratic inertia. It takes time for the unwieldy ship of state to make a big change of course. This having been said, Mahathir did display activity and did effect changes.

Two possible misunderstandings have to be clarified. An active prime minister with an interest in foreign policy need not be deterred, although he may be dissuaded, by the wishes of his foreign minister. This applied to the relationship between Mahathir and his experienced Foreign Minister, Ghazali Shafie, whose influence was less than it had been under Hussein. It applied even more to Ghazali's successors. Also, the conduct of foreign affairs is not confined to the foreign ministry but is in part in the hands of the ministry of external trade and industry, the ministry of defence, and other ministries.

Mahathir came into office with a favorable disposition towards Japan and a less favorable disposition towards Britain.[6] He is much more pro-Japan than any other Southeast Asian leader. His interest in Japan is shown by his co-authorship, with a Japanese, of a book (see note 70). These inclinations showed themselves in his early policies. He quickly announced a "Look East" policy, which concerned mainly Japan and South Korea (pp. 55–6). He showed skepticism about defense agreements with Britain, and through his low evaluation of the worth of the Commonwealth and its biennial Heads of Government Meeting. He denounced this institution in 1985: "It should admit that it really cannot contribute towards solving the problems faced by its members."[7] He continued by citing apartheid in South Africa, the subjugation of Namibia, and the damage to the economies of poor countries by the policies of rich and powerful countries. Two years later, he announced that Malaysia would host the 1989 CHOGM in Kuala Lumpur. He attributed the change to the persuasion of the Commonwealth secretary-general, Sir Shridah Ramphal.[8] He is also said to have been influenced by the Wisma Putra (Malaysian Foreign Office) and by the advice of the prestigious ISIS (Institute of Strategic and International Studies). Given Mahathir's eagerness to convey his views to "the South", membership of, and speaking in, CHOGM offered great advantages – about three-quarters of its membership of approximately fifty were from developing countries.

Participation in international organizations

As a small country and an emerging "middle power," Malaysia has always favored multilateralism in its foreign policy dealings. This has led to its active participation in numerous international organizations, where it perceives that it gains strength from numbers, and especially in Asian regional organizations, where it commands a forceful voice. Since 1970, Malaysia has endorsed the principle of non-alignment and promoted the neutralization of the region, while at the same time remaining anti-Communist and in fact pro-West. Under Mahathir, Malaysia's preference for non-alignment has become more clear. Malaysia's post-cold war foreign policy goals have assumed the character of championing "the South" in doing battle against the forces of domination emanating from "the North," and challenging the "double standards" of the developed states, particularly the United States, in tolerating the conduct of allies, such as Saudi Arabia, while censuring other states.

The United Nations (UN)

While strongly objecting to the composition of the UN Security Council and the veto power of the permanent members,[9] Malaysia has been very supportive of the UN in general. Mahathir, in his address to the 50th session of the UN General Assembly, concluded that it is still the only truly multinational organization where the "voices of small nations can be heard."[10]

Malaysia was elected to the Security Council as the Asian non-permanent representative in 1988 and had to make some difficult (and domestically unpopular) decisions over supporting the UN mandate for military action leading to the Gulf War. Undaunted by the experience, Malaysia is currently (1998) seeking another Security Council seat for 1999–2000. A Malaysian, Tan Sri Razali Ismail, recently completed his term as president of the UN General Assembly, and Malaysia has participated in the activities of a number of UN agencies, including the Human Rights Commission, and has chaired several high-level committees, for example, on drug trafficking, Indochinese refugees, and the United Nations Educational, Scientific, and Cultural Organization (UNESCO) General Conference. Further, Malaysia has been a generous provider of peacekeeping forces for UN missions (with approximately 2,000 peacekeepers abroad in 1995), so much so that peacekeeping is now, like in Canada, a proud tradition.

Interestingly, since the Gulf War and Malaysia's experience on the Security Council during that period, Mahathir has become more insistent upon reform of the Security Council so that it is not dominated by a few Western powers, particularly the United States, and he has become more vocal as champion of the South.[11] In an address to the General Assembly, he sharply criticized the world body:

> Despite earlier hopes…what we see is still a UN which dances to the gyrating music of the major powers in total disregard for the high principles and objectives pledged at its formation…. The UN presents a shattered image with a threadbare moral authority…. The victors of 1945 have clung tenaciously to the levers of power. They control the high ground, exercising influence and power as nakedly as when they were colonial powers. Only the masks have changed.
>
> …Tell us how have the principles of the Charter on the non-use of force and the illegality of claiming territory acquired by aggression been of help to the Bosnians? What protection or solace has the Genocide Convention been to those slaughtered in Rwanda, Bosnia, Cambodia and Chechnya?…The United Nations Secretariat must take some of the blame for all these brutalities. In Rwanda, it truly shirked its duty while in Bosnia it sent in a protection force which was instructed not to protect the Bosnians…. Of late there has been much talk about reform of the UN…. A more equitable representation on the Security Council is a must. This means that permanent seats should be given to regions…. The veto power should be dropped. Under no circumstances must the Security Council be made an instrument of any one country…. The reform of global institutions must encompass the Bretton Woods organizations…[which] have to cease acting as debt collectors for the mighty and the rich bankers.[12]

Beyond the UN, Malaysia's multilateral foreign policy energies have been directed towards regional security and trade organizations and forums, namely ASEAN, the ASEAN Post-Ministerial Conference (PMC), the ASEAN Regional Forum (ARF), the Asia–Pacific Economic Cooperation (APEC) forum and the East Asia Economic Caucus (EAEC), the Asia–Europe Meeting (ASEM), and also the World Trade Organization (WTO).

ASEAN, the Post-Ministerial Conference and the ASEAN Regional Forum

Malaysia was a founding member of ASEAN in 1967 and has remained strongly committed to the organization since – in fact it is central to Malaysian foreign policy objectives and strategies. The formation of ASEAN formalized the end of Confrontation and signalled a rapprochement, without the involvement of the big powers, among the five, sometimes bickering, neighbors. Although not a formal security arrangement, ASEAN's stated purpose was to promote the peaceful resolution of conflict in the region. Another purpose was to enhance regional trade and economic development.

ASEAN's most important contribution has been in promoting a method of operation and code of behavior, through consultation and consensus, for the non-violent management of intra-regional disputes among the members. Indonesia, by virtue of its size and importance, has become the pivotal actor in ASEAN,[13] with Malaysia emerging as a strong and insistent voice, especially under the determined direction of Mahathir. When Suharto and Mahathir pursued the same objective in ASEAN, they were a formidable, almost irresistible, force within the organization.

ASEAN has been slow in reaching trade and tariff agreements – the first step towards an ASEAN Free Trade Area (AFTA) was taken only in 1992 (with the completion of targets now set for 2003).[14] However, on the political side, ASEAN sprang into action to resist Vietnamese expansionism in Cambodia from 1978, and Thailand, as the front-line state, became a much more involved and stronger force inside ASEAN as a result (as did Singapore through its UN representatives, who became ASEAN's most effective voice in the UN).

The first ASEAN summit was held in Bali in 1976, out of which came a demonstration of resolve in the wake of Communist revolutionary success in Indochina. The summit produced a Declaration of ASEAN Concord (DAC) and a Treaty of Amity and Cooperation (TAC). Both documents spelled out the principles of the non-use of force and the peaceful settlement of disputes, and the TAC was open for accession by the other Southeast Asian states. Johan Saravanamuttu calls the treaty a mini-version of Malaysia's neutralization scheme ZOPFAN, and writes, perhaps with some exaggeration, that these accords "represent the most significant regional multilateral accords to have emerged out of Southeast Asia in recent history."[15]

Since the early 1990s, ASEAN has been very active, setting up the ARF, which with the PMC directly follows on the annual ASEAN Ministerial Meeting (AMM). The PMC allows for multilateral dialogue on regional non-security issues between ASEAN and some of the major powers which ASEAN members have chosen as "dialogue partners." In 1993, concern over US strategic decline and an assertive China led ASEAN to initiate the ARF as a venue for discussions of regional security and defense issues. ASEAN is the organizer and sets the agenda, in consultation with other participants. The idea of the ARF is to discuss security and defense matters jointly with potential adversaries rather than generating insecurity by forming coalitions against them. According to Michael Leifer, one of the main functions has been "to draw China into a constraining multilateral security dialogue."[16] The ARF focuses on confidence-building measures, from coordination of international sea rescues to agreement on advance notice of military exercises so as to reduce suspicion and misunderstandings. The ARF is also viewed by some as a multilateral substitute (as well as a complement) for the old regional system of having a series of bilateral ties with the United States.[17] Interestingly, the ARF has functioned as a facilitator of US–China dialogue. Discussion at the 21-member ARF in 1997 centered on concerns about stability in Cambodia, and criticism by the non-Asian members of ongoing political repression in Myanmar (Burma).[18]

ASEAN was conceived from the beginning to include all ten states in the region eventually, and to avoid the permanent division of Southeast Asia into two ideological blocs. As early as 1975, with the end of the Vietnam War, Razak stated that, when he looked at the map of the world, he saw Southeast Asia as a cohesive and coherent unit. He proclaimed: "Surely the moment has come for that community of Southeast Asia, which has been our dream, to be realized."[19] However, expansion was initially slow and cautious. Brunei was not admitted into ASEAN until 1984, and it was not until 1995 that Vietnam was admitted. Brunei adjusted easily to the familiar consultation and consensus decision-making formula of ASEAN. Vietnam, however, is unused to give and take, concessions, and consensus.[20] It has needed to be socialized into ASEAN's mode of behavior.[21]

Since 1992, Indonesia has pushed for an ASEAN-10 to fulfill the vision of "one Southeast Asia" and also to give substance to the ASEAN policy of "constructive engagement" with Myanmar.[22] However, Malaysia strongly opposed giving Myanmar observer status in 1992 because of its mistreatment of the Rohingya Muslims, and so Myanmar was not invited.[23] Soon after, Malaysia reversed its position and became a strong supporter of Myanmar's admission. In 1994 Malaysia and Indonesia supported Thailand's initiative of inviting Myanmar as an observer to the Bangkok AMM. At that meeting, ASEAN reaffirmed its commitment to expand. In the next few years, Malaysia and Indonesia together powerfully pushed ASEAN into a difficult-to-achieve consensus to admit Myanmar, Cambodia, and Laos in 1997 in Kuala Lumpur on the 30th anniversary of ASEAN. In the face of Western criticism about admitting Myanmar, Mahathir said, "I don't like people telling me who I should have as a friend and who should be my enemy."[24]

It is ironic that the dream of "one Southeast Asia" in ASEAN was upset at the last moment, not by internal discord or by actions in Myanmar, but by violence in Cambodia as a result of a coup by Second Prime Minister Hun Sen, who removed his coalition partner, First Prime Minister Prince Norodom Ranariddh. Malaysia had been the most staunch supporter of realizing ASEAN-10 at the Kuala Lumpur meeting. Obviously disappointed, Malaysia's Foreign Minister Abdullah Badawi announced ASEAN's decision on July 10, 1997, just two weeks before Cambodia was scheduled to be admitted, that its admission was to be deferred indefinitely. Reportedly, Malaysia and Vietnam favored admitting Cambodia on time despite the coup, and Badawi stated publicly that the decision could be quickly reversed.[25] However, that was ruled out when Hun Sen in turn flatly rejected ASEAN mediation, and threatened to withdraw his membership application, saying that Cambodia might not join for many years.[26]

Although ASEAN set some conditions for admission that appear to require a return to the *status quo-ante*, the lure of completing the dream of ASEAN-10 is powerful. From the time of the coup it seemed likely that Hun Sen's rule would be accepted as a *fait accompli* once reasonable stability was restored and so long as

Hun Sen allowed the previously scheduled 1998 election to be held, and conducted with a modicum of international acceptance. ASEAN did not insist upon the reinstatement of Prince Ranariddh as co-Prime Minister since it increasingly viewed him as ineffectual and the power-sharing situation as untenable.[27] The election was held in July 1998 under the supervision of a 500-member Joint International Observer Group. Hun Sen's party emerged with a slim majority, but under Cambodia's complex rules it needs to put together a coalition in order to form a government. Despite widespread allegations of political violence and intimidation, including reportedly the murders of some 100 opposition members, the international observers declared the election "free and fair".[28] This provides Hun Sen with the veneer of international legitimacy insisted upon by ASEAN. It is expected that soon after the new government is installed in the autumn of 1998, Cambodia will be admitted into ASEAN.

One of the questions that arises from the ASEAN-10 configuration is whether the power to persuade will shift from Indonesia–Malaysia to a new mainland bloc led by Thailand, as James Clad believes,[29] or perhaps to a solid four-country "newcomers bloc" behind Vietnam – one "with more muscle than ASEAN ever intended".[30] Although Malaysia has considerable influence, and Mahathir sometimes gets what he wants (or most of what he wants) in ASEAN by sheer single-minded persistence (which, likewise, is not always appreciated by the others), it is unlikely he could ever dominate the organization or hold ASEAN together if consensus failed.

APEC versus the EAEC

APEC is a consultative, non-negotiating economic body of twenty-one (1998) Pacific Rim countries/regions (from East and Southeast Asia, Australia, New Zealand and Papua New Guinea, North and South America), grouped for the purpose of enhancing trade liberalization and diversification. APEC is based on the concept of "open regionalism," meaning that any trade liberalization measure is automatically granted to all other trading partners.[31] When APEC was first proposed by the Australians in 1989, ASEAN initially rejected the idea, believing that it was intended as a regional trading bloc that might diminish ASEAN and the AFTA.[32] However, ASEAN quickly changed its mind in view of the potentially protectionist trade groupings emerging in North America and Europe. At a meeting in Seoul in 1991, relatively easy membership criteria were established, a position that Malaysia supports since it wants greater numbers to counter the influence of the United States.[33] In 1992, Australia proposed an APEC summit to counter the G-7, and the first summit took place in Seattle the next year at President Clinton's initiative. Dr. Mahathir boycotted the occasion because of the lack of prior consultation. Probably the most important breakthrough inside APEC came at the 1994 summit when Suharto secured a free trade agreement (the Bogor Declaration). Mahathir, who attended, went along with this decision, but emphasized the voluntary nature of the agreement.[34]

At the Seattle summit in 1993 the ASEAN decision-making model of "consensus minus x" was adopted, and APEC has become slowly "ASEANized" since then. For example, beyond the consensus decision-making style and voluntary compliance, it was also decided at Osaka in 1995 that there should be a "third pillar" of APEC promoting economic and technical cooperation between the developed and developing members. Further, it is now the accepted practice that the APEC summit meet in an ASEAN state every other year: Seattle, Bogor, Osaka, Manila, Vancouver, and Kuala Lumpur in 1998. This is important because the host has responsibility for setting the agenda. Still, the ASEAN members attend APEC as individual members, and they have been surprisingly reluctant to try to synthesize their views, despite an ASEAN agreement to act as an East Asian-wide caucus inside APEC.

APEC has set some achievable targets, with voluntary compliance, and has reached some agreements (e.g., on technology in 1996), and it has spurred ASEAN to shorten its AFTA timetable for tariff reductions.

In 1993, an "Eminent Persons Group Report," which supported the US position, called for more formal rules, concrete objectives, and enforceable deadlines, but the report was rejected. However, there is still pressure to institutionalize the forum. The former executive director of APEC, William Bodde, noted that there were three contending groups in APEC on the issue: those favoring institutionalization, which includes the non-Asian states and Singapore; a middle group, ranging from moderately reluctant to moderately favorable, but open-minded states, which includes most of the Asian states; and one state adamantly against any institutionalization – Malaysia.[35]

Mahathir remains lukewarm at best about APEC, still preferring his EAEC idea as an alternative. He views the APEC forum as a grouping that will likely come under the dominance of the United States, become institutionalized, and lead to Western economic control in Asia, creating a situation wherein Asian members would become minor players with virtually no voice in the economic affairs of their own region.[36] Hence his act of boycott in 1993. It has been suggested that Malaysia as host in November 1998 may try to divert the emphasis away from trade and investment liberalization and towards so-called "third pillar" goals, emphasizing economic and technical cooperation.[37]

Mahathir proposed his alternative to APEC in December 1990 – an East Asia Economic Group (EAEG) as a counter to the New Zealand and Australia Free Trade Agreement (NAFTA) and the European Union (EU). It was also an expression of Mahathir's desire to forge closer links with Northeast Asia. Mahathir wanted an all-Asian group of countries which had "something in common" as regards culture and attitudes and approaches towards economic development to counter the West and provide Asia with a strong, united voice in international trade negotiations:[38] Japan would take the lead. Apparently, he expected to play a key role in the EAEG.[39] Although the Malaysian media have played up the concept relentlessly, it is not very well understood internationally and "not well conceived" or articulated.[40]

Indonesia and some of the other ASEAN states were not receptive to the EAEG idea (especially since they were not consulted about it beforehand), since they believed that they would be cutting themselves off from important regions and trade partners.[41] The United States was hostile, and apparently urged Japan, which was not very favorable anyway, and South Korea to reject the proposal. Later, Mahathir chided Japan to return to its Asian roots, and said Japan "owed it" to Asia to join the EAEC.[42]

In late 1991, Indonesia suggested at an ASEAN Economic Ministers Meeting that the idea be converted into a consultative caucus known as the EAEC rather than seeming to constitute a trade bloc proposal. This was accepted by Malaysia, and these are the initials currently used (hence the jibe of critics that it stands for "East Asia Excluding Caucasians"). But exactly what form it would take was left unspecified. In 1993, again as a result of strong Malaysian pressure, ASEAN accepted the EAEC as an informal caucus inside APEC. However, by 1997 it had only met once as a caucus, ineffectively, and increasingly Malaysian officials have come to view the move as a way of burying the EAEC, rather than giving it life.[43]

It has been suggested that the EAEC idea was prompted by ASEAN's slow pace on economic matters.[44] However, the concept suggested a potentially anti-Western coalition,[45] and Higgott and Stubbs believe the EAEC was aimed primarily at "combatting the political power of the US and Europe."[46] Unlike APEC, it was not geared to promoting economic liberalization and free trade, something to which Malaysia is less favorable than most of the rest of the original ASEAN states.[47]

In November 1993, Mahathir showed his ire by refusing to attend the APEC summit in Seattle, saying that "perhaps you have to thumb your nose at people before they notice you."[48] However, the next APEC was set for Bogor, and Suharto quietly let it be known that, in the spirit of cooperation among ASEAN members, he "expected" Mahathir to attend.[49] Mahathir duly attended and he has participated in APEC summits since then.

Nonetheless, he has not given up. He has persisted with his campaign for the EAEC and has lamented ASEAN's lack of resolve in getting the EAEC launched.[50] Interestingly, the EAEC has found life at the ASEM, so it is clearly too soon to dismiss it.[51]

Asia–Europe Meeting

Europe greeted the creation of APEC (whose members account for one-half of all world trade and two-thirds of the global GDP) with shock and alarm. Despite the fact that APEC was merely a consultative forum and not a trade bloc, the Europeans viewed it as a "war machine" intended to exclude Europe from the rapidly growing markets of Asia.[52]

The Europeans, therefore, became determined to bury the colonial past and "return to Asia." The mechanism that emerged was proposed by France and Singapore in 1994 for a summit meeting biennially between the Asian states and the European Union. ASEM-1 was held in Bangkok in 1996 and ASEM-2 convened in London in 1998.

Despite the EU's strong desire for an enhanced trade relationship with Asia, progress in ASEM has been slowed by the incursion of social and human rights issues into the discussions. The EU's complex decision-making process has allowed any member with any grievance towards any Asian state to stop ASEM initiatives. As a result, progress on a ministerial declaration and an action plan have been stymied.[53] Initially the EU had more at stake in ASEM than Asia but the balance of interests have altered with the reversal of economic fortunes from mid-1997. However, the forum serves to give Asia more clout in APEC to withstand pressures generated by and in the interest of the United States.[54]

An interesting feature of ASEM is that it has given some substance to the EAEC concept, since the Asian membership includes ASEAN and China, Japan, and South Korea – precisely Mahathir's EAEC composition. Malaysia's main impact on ASEM has been to block Australia's bid to participate in both Asia–European summits, despite the strong support of some Asian states (the Philippines, Singapore, and Japan) and the absence of opposition among most of the other Asian states.[55] This veto is consistent with Mahathir's view that Australia has little in common with Asia other than being geographically close. Although any kind of "payback" has been denied by Malaysia, this was also possibly retribution for Australia's strong promotion of APEC and opposition to the EAEC.

The World Trade Organization

As the successor to the General Agreement on Tariffs and Trade (GATT), following the Final Act of the Uruguay Round concluded in Morocco, the WTO was created in 1995 as a rules-based, vote-taking organization to regulate international trade. With 128 members and another 28 aspiring to membership (as of December 1996), the WTO is now the principal international body concerned with solving trade issues between states and providing a forum for multilateral trade negotiations.[56] Although Malaysia is an advocate of large multilateral settings to dilute the dominance of the major powers, Mahathir remains skeptical about the organization, saying that it "will become answerable only to the world's wealthiest economic powers."[57]

The WTO held its first trade ministerial meeting in Singapore in December 1996. Interestingly, Malaysia and Malaysian External Trade Minister Rafidah played a significant role at the WTO in leading the fight against the most acrimonious issue of the meeting – the US and EU demand, as anticipated, to link social clauses and labor standards to trade agreements.[58] The contest created a genuine multilateral Asian consensus, led by the Group of Fifteen (G-15) developing states (p. 134), and it revived the old North–South split (with Australia and New Zealand backing the South).[59]

In Asia's view, linking labor standards and social clauses to trade was a self-serving form of protectionism being pushed by US and European trade unions.[60] Asia's position was that non-trade issues did not belong in the WTO.

The final Declaration's wording implicitly recognizes the commitment of WTO countries to "core" labor standards.[61] Thus, the United States and the

European Union, and international labor unions, believe that they managed to get the issue of linkages on the table and that this will keep it alive. However, to others, the Declaration seems "unequivocal and clear" that the International Labour Organization (ILO) is the competent authority to deal with labor issues.[62] Rafidah proclaimed that the issue has been "put to rest" once and for all.[63]

Overall, Malaysia's active participation in a number of international organizations has been consistent with its preference for multilateralism. It has also enhanced the country's reputation as a strong and insistent voice for the interests of Asia and the South, and as a sharp critic of Western dominance.

Malaysia's policy toward the major powers

To supplement the account given of Malaysia's interaction with institutions, it may be useful to outline its relations with the major powers, China, Japan, and the United States.

Mahathir believes that China will strive to preserve its present political system in order to maintain its national unity. Moreover, it will avoid democratization, particularly because its adoption in the Soviet Union preceded fragmentation and collapse. If it organizes its human potential properly, and enacts laws to facilitate trade and growth, it will become an economic giant with considerable influence over Asia, including Japan. It will almost certainly increase its arms budget, fueling fears of its military ambitions. In his speeches, Mahathir has been optimistic on this topic. Southeast Asia would welcome a wealthy China because it could share in the wealth produced; fear of China's territorial expansion was largely the West projecting its own greed and hegemonic tendencies onto China.[64] He compared China's military expenditure with the larger expenditures of the United States and Japan,[65] and remarked that Malaysia would rely on China's stance (apparently referring to the Spratly Islands (p. 132)) that it would not resort to aggression regarding territorial disputes in the region.[66]

An external commentator might see the situation differently, observing that an Asian view would certainly be wary of the Chinese but would also be hopeful that its economic interests would cause it to be a responsible member of the Pacific Asia community. The question is whether or not China can be socialized into the regional community. As far as ASEAN is concerned, its international principles are codified in the TAC. Yet unlike, say, Vietnam, it is not clear that China will allow other, similar, states to set the terms for its behavior.[67]

Much depends on the time period under consideration. Belief that China's intentions were probably not aggressive applied to the short and medium term. The effect of China's assurances was shaken by China's occupation of Mischief Reef, in the Spratlys, in 1995. The "long term" seemed not to be so far away. One opinion is that, given the prospects of Chinese assertiveness, no lasting balance of power be achieved without a considerably strengthened Japan, and a commitment to offset China's military growth.[68] So far, however, the ASEAN states, including Malaysia, have not thought it advisable to raise these possibilities in public.

Malaysia's relations with the United States have been clouded by the verbal battles between the two countries in which it fought against US attempts to impose rights and values on Asia and the Third World in general, against their will (pp. 136–9). The deep feelings aroused in this exchange must have affected Malaysia's view of the US security role. Mahathir questioned the conventional wisdom that the US presence in Southeast Asia was necessary for regional security in the post-cold war world.[69] In 1996 there was a policy shift. There was an increase in the number of US warships visiting Malaysian ports, culminating in the first ever visit by a US aircraft carrier. This was expected to be followed by the opening of facilities for US forces as well as by joint exercises. Analysts said that these arrangements might be connected with increasing interest by American firms in the MSC (p. 78).

Mahathir is also optimistic about Japan. In 1988 he remarked that Japan was becoming more and more visible over the horizon and its influence over the world seems bound to increase. Since Malaysia is in the region where Japan is, it is going to feel the impact of that influence. His guess was that Japan would become one of the great powers, but hopefully an economic power and not a military power, or, alternatively, it would become even more dependent on its alliance with the United States. However, he foresaw the danger that Japan might react by becoming more of a military power. As far as security is concerned, Malaysia, like the rest of Southeast Asia, is less worried about the revival of Japanese militarism than formerly.[70] Economically, ASEAN wishes Japan to open up its economy, but also fears that they may be increasingly subject to decisions made in Tokyo without having an input of their own.[71] Even Malaysia, the originator of the "Look East" policy, has suffered some disillusion (p. 56).

Mahathir as champion of "the South"

It is clear why Mahathir took an interest in ASEAN and in other organizations in the region. It is not so easy to see why he took up the cause of "the South." Perhaps he simply wanted to exercise his political talents in a wider field.

It is possible that an early experience of Mahathir's may have strengthened his interest in the Third World, and helped to predispose him to take up the cause of "the South." In 1965, when Malaysia was trying to get all the support it could in the Third World in order to counter Indonesia's efforts to win friends for its campaign of Confrontation, it sent an unofficial delegation to the Afro-Asian People's Solidarity Conference, held in Winneba, Ghana. It attended the meeting, but failed to gain membership for itself. The composition of the Malaysian delegation was unusual; it included people who were not typical government supporters, as well as two supporters who were later detained, Abdullah Ahmad and Samad Ismail (p. 107). The leader of the delegation was Mahathir.[72] Khoo Boo Teik has another, plausible, suggestion.[73] He asks who, in Mahathir's formative years, was "the enemy"? The answer from the Malays' point of view was the Chinese. This was not to underrate the admirable qualities of the Chinese, which were freely acknowledged in *The Malay Dilemma*. Yet these qualities made it harder for the Malays to oppose them successfully. Khoo sees both continuity and change in the development of Mahathir's nationalism. The change took the shape of shifting the target of his Malay nationalism from "the Chinese" to "the West." After Mahathir became Prime Minister, he was distracted by the struggles described in Chapter 2 and the need to control the Islamic resurgence (Chapter 4). He was able, in the 1990s, to use his position as Prime Minister to complete and spell out the consequences of the shift.

Some important aspects of Khoo's aperçu remain to be explored. First, it is significant that Mahathir's shift is described in terms of a change of *target*. With Mahathir, who was driven by a hatred of what he perceived as unjust, what counted was not what he was *for* but what he was *against*. Second, a corollary of the shift was brilliantly, although gradually, actualized by Mahathir. If the Chinese were no longer to be the "enemy," clearly it was best to have them as enthusiastic collaborators. They had to become "one of us." For this to occur, he had to act – as recommended by the MCA (perhaps without much hope) when he was named Hussein's successor – as leader of the nation and not just of the Malays (p. 28). This took gradual shape, first by watering down the pro-Malay emphasis of the NEP through replacing it by the NDP, and by the prospect, later, of eliminating it through *Vision 2020*. Third, the Chinese in *The Malay Dilemma* consisted of a rather limited group of Chinese traders and petty shopkeepers. The corresponding group now contains all kinds of people who are on Mahathir's "hate lists," including practitioners of colonialism, members of the G-7, human rights advocates, the press, Zionists,[74] and, latterly, foreign currency speculators. The larger the range of choice in the target group, the easier it was to find some appropriate target(s) for a given "conspiracy."

In considering the institutions through which Mahathir sought to promote the interests of "the South," it may be convenient to consider first non-explicitly Islamic ones, and, second, those associated with Islam. Mahathir worked through some existing bodies, such as the Non-Aligned Movement (NAM),[75] where he was able to stress issues that were of particular interest to him, such as the Bosnian question. Still, in his opening speech at the NAM 1995 summit, he listed three priority items of wide general interest: outlawing nuclear weapons, enhancing economic performance, and restructuring the UN to make it more democratic. However, he failed to get NAM to act effectively to upset the 1959 Treaty of Antarctica, by which the area was potentially earmarked for control by a small group of countries.

Mahathir was also instrumental in creating some new "South" organizations, including the G-15, a group of developing countries, which was set up in 1989, to extend South–South cooperation, and had its first meeting in Kuala Lumpur shortly afterwards. Its first secretary-general was a Malaysian. Among the Malaysia-initiated projects was a South Investment Trade and Technology Data Exchange Centre and a Bilateral Payments Arrangement (designed to guarantee export payments), located in Kuala Lumpur.[76]

Mahathir was also active, on behalf of the South, at meetings concerned with the environment, including the influential environmental summit of 1992 in Rio de Janeiro, where Mahathir attempted to turn the tables by pointing out that "the North" was really responsible for violations that it had pilloried the South for committing. On damage to the environment, he claimed that the North wanted to have a direct say in the management of forests in the poor South at no cost to itself. Mahathir also stated that, while blaming damage to the environment on the South,[77] the North was at the same time hindering the South's ability to protect the environment by failing to foster a sustainable environment.

He visited a number of developing countries, which he thought could benefit from Malaysia's example, and to which he delivered the "southern" message. Some were relatively close to Malaysia, such as Fiji (he offered assistance to it after sanctions had been imposed on it following a coup by the indigenous army against an Indian-led government), Western Samoa, and Tonga. During visits, he exhorted African countries,[78] to show solidarity with the South and stick together to resist the challenge of globalism. He warned against the stranglehold of the World Bank and the International Monetary Fund (IMF), and against restrictions on child labor which would impede international trade. The former colonizers, he pointed out, were still in control and imposing the use of a playing field that was not level. He cited Malaysian experience as a guide to economic development and an example of good ethnic relations. Malaysia also launched the equivalent of a peace corps in 1997, which would travel to Laos, Cambodia, and some African countries, among other places.[79]

Foreign policy and Islam: Bosnia

In foreign policy, as in other spheres, Islam assumed growing prominence under Mahathir. This was both the consequence of the Islamic resurgence and of the reactions that it aroused in Mahathir. Islam had figured in the foreign policy of his predecessors, but it was pursued with more fervor under his direction. A major forum was the Organization of Islamic Conference,[80] established in 1971, which had approximately fifty members. Mahathir regularly attended its summit meetings. At a 1992 meeting in Kuala Lumpur, speaking as "Asia's representative," he sent a message little different from those intended for internal consumption. He mentioned the need to respond to the challenges of the twenty-first century, and urged that practices that were neither truly Islamic nor relevant should be discarded. He also supported the OIC's associated organizations, such as the Islamic Solidarity Fund, the Islamic Development Bank, and others. He attended meetings of other Islamic groups, such as the Regional Islamic Dakwah Council of Southeast Asia and the Pacific, where he defended Islam against biased critics.[81] In general, he sprang to the defense of Islam when it was criticized, but in the Gulf War, although he had some sympathy for the US intervention, he was subject to cross-pressures. He was steadfastly pro-Palestine and anti-Zionist.[82] In particular, he deplored the Israeli occupation of Arab territories, and was vociferous on the issue of Zionist influence in the international press and opposed the visit of the Israeli President to Singapore in 1986.

However, since the dissolution of Yugoslavia, Mahathir has been preoccupied with the plight of Bosnia Herzegovina. His deep interest is shown by the fact that, in 1995, 1,500 of Malaysia's 2,500 personnel engaged in peacekeeping were stationed in Bosnia-Herzegovina. He was so committed on the Bosnia issue that he defied the West to impose sanctions on Malaysia for selling arms to the Bosnia Muslim forces.[83] Exhibiting his well-known insistence on the West's habit of practising double standards, Mahathir believed that in Bosnia-Herzegovina the righteousness sometimes displayed over minor infringements of human rights was remarkably absent. He did not think that the Western countries had implemented their policy in Bosnia by providing adequate support for the relatively weak government of Bosnia-Herzegovina. An address of his in 1994 brings out clearly his objections to the policies of the United States and the European powers after the UN had accepted Bosnia as a member-state. He blamed the UN for having laid an embargo on the contestants, because this helped to weaken the Bosnian government (p. 125). He denied that the conflict was a civil war between the Muslims and the rest. Both the defenders of Sarajevo and the government included Serbs and Croats. He said:

> The Bosnian government desperately appealed for help from the vaunted defenders of the human rights of the world, but neither the European Union nor the United Nations Security Council took decisive action. Humanitarian aid was offered subject to permission being granted by the Serbian aggressors. And, as can be expected, the Serbs were not quite cooperative…Bosnia-Herzegovina is the victim of designs of certain people and powers who are quite happy to see the emergence of Slovenia and Croatia, but will do nothing for Bosnia, although Bosnia-Herzegovina has as much right as the other two to nationhood.[84]

Mahathir concluded that neither the Americans nor the Europeans cared enough to act. The speech does not specify who "certain people and powers" are, nor does it identify the actual supporters of the Serbs, notably the Russians. But it clearly points to the lack of will shown by some powers, and adds that Malaysia has also felt strongly about the injustices and oppression that have recurred in non-Muslim countries, such as South Africa and Cambodia. This indictment is a good example of Mahathir's polemical skills, and, with the touch of the virtuoso, plays upon a favorite theme – conspiracies. It also alludes to human rights – not a favorite term of Mahathir's in other contexts, suggesting that their violation in Bosnia can be a justifiable reason for protest.

Rights and values – East and West

The dispute that came to a head in the early 1990s over rights and values may be regarded as a reaction to Western pressures by the ASEAN countries, China, and others. The reaction was not only defensive, but also took the form of a counter-attack. Symbolically at least, the peak event was the Vienna Conference on Human Rights in 1993.[85] Before this "climax," two preparatory conferences were held in Bangkok, one at which governments took part, while, at the other, NGOs were represented. The Southeast Asian governments that had most to say about human rights were Indonesia, Malaysia, and Singapore. However, Indonesia was somewhat inhibited by the adverse publicity that had followed the shootings of civilians in Dili, East Timor, in November 1991, so the other two were more outspoken.

The ASEAN states, along with other countries, formed a loose, common front on rights issues, in response to the aggressive tactics of the West, particularly Washington. Values were brought into the debate, and the Asians provided arguments to show that their values were in some respects different from the West's, and had many features in common with each other.[86]

The "Asian" position rested on two premises. Rights must reflect values and, broadly, Asian values differed from Western ones in two main ways. First, they laid greater stress on economic and social rights and emphasized civil and political rights less, compared with the West. Second, they took less account of individuals, and gave more regard to the interests of the community. They thought, unlike the West, that there should be a balance between rights and duties (or obligations). They believed that there should be defined limits to the freedom of the press, e.g., on ethnic and security topics. They were cautious about extending the range of rights to cover too many "grievances," some of which they considered to be relatively trivial. They agreed that the emphasis should be on "basic" rights, such as that no one should be put to death "illegally," or should be tortured.

Democracy is often mentioned in the West almost in the same breath as human rights. In fact, the two concepts are quite different. One has to do with the protection of the individual against the state, while the other determines the extent to which the individual can choose and control the rulers.

The United States attributes its victory in the cold war to the practice of democracy and to its opponent's lack of it; it also considers its own *form* of democracy to be superior. As Mahathir aptly inquired: is there only one form of democracy, or only one high priest to interpret it?[87] Moreover, the United States believes that democracy should be spread to other countries, no matter what the circumstances are. Sometimes it even asserts that there is only one real version of democracy, its own. Whereas the United States sees democracy as an end in itself, some Asian leaders believe, in a utilitarian way, that good governance is more conducive to human happiness.[88]

The ASEAN states and some other Asian countries reacted unfavorably, not just because they objected to the message. They were even more resistant to the unsavory *method* of delivery, which they perceived as indicative of the continuation of colonialism by other means. They resented the one-way method of communication as implying superior status; they were tired of being dictated to through Western agencies such as the press, NGOs, and trade unions. They believed that when the West failed to reach them by one route, it would try another. One method that US governments have tried to use, with the support of the labor unions, is to increase the price of labor in Asian countries. In 1994, Mahathir described the West's switch of tactics in order to impair East Asian economies' ability to compete:

> They would like the East Asian democracies to be weak and unstable like theirs, or worse. Maybe there is no great conspiracy by the West to undermine all the East Asian economies. But conspiracy is not necessary. It is sufficient for everyone to see the danger threatening them for them to act in concert. The early attempts to disguise their intention by talking about democracy, human rights, etc. have now been largely jettisoned. Now they are openly proposing to eliminate the competitiveness of the East Asian economies in order to prevent them from successfully competing with the West. The proposal for a world-wide minimum wage is one blatant example. They know very well that this is the sole comparative advantage of the developing countries.[89]

It seemed to Mahathir that the West was determined to dominate even if it entailed "changing the rules."

He alleged that some Western powers even went as far as supporting opposition parties so that the government would change at every election (thus meeting a so-called criterion for democracy):

> When the government keeps changing, there will be no stability, which will result in investors staying away from the country.... My belief is that the Western powers do not want developing nations like us to outdo them in terms of progress.[90]

In his battle with the West, Mahathir found support from an unexpected quarter. Dr. Chandra Muzaffar, the founder of Aliran, an uncompromising defender of human rights and later the founder and director of JUST (Just World Trust), took a stance on the North–South issue very close to Mahathir's. Mahathir accepted an invitation to deliver the keynote address at a JUST conference in December 1994.[91]

The West, in launching its campaign to further its concept of rights, had expected little opposition. To its surprise, it found that the ASEAN states, not all of which were yet economic tigers, nevertheless fought fiercely in defense of their values. They were buoyed by their economic successes, and in their counter-attack did not refrain from drawing attention to the West's weaknesses: its high rates of violence, crime, and drug trafficking.[92]

Malaysia was particularly outraged by the West's efforts to link human rights with aid or trade. "The term being used is 'conditionality.' In simple words it means the donor countries are saying: You behave in exactly the way we want you to, or we will not help you eradicate poverty."[93] Eventually, these counter-attacks against the West were successful. For example, at the first Asia–Europe Meeting (ASEM-1) in Bangkok, March 1996, the European Commissioner for Asian Relations noted that the EU had moved from confrontation to a normal dialogue on these (human rights) questions.

The debate on human rights showed Mahathir's gift of invective at its best and his exposure of some Western illogicalities was devastating. He was correct in thinking that, while ASEAN (including Malaysia) might accept the rulings of some international body on its human rights practices, it was too much for the West/North to make assessments that would be accorded the same credence. If he were sometimes wide of the mark, it was principally because he sometimes seemed eager to credit the North with a ruthless cleverness which it did not possess.

Mahathir's handling of international disputes

Mahathir's handling of disputes throws some light on how he conducts foreign affairs generally. Three examples have been chosen of recent disputes between Malaysia and Britain, Australia, and Singapore, respectively. In each, no single issue was at stake. Rather, what may have appeared to be a single issue was actually connected with a perception of previous recriminations.

Malaysia and Britain

As has been indicated, Mahathir was not very well disposed toward Britain. He had no fond memories of having studied there, and he was opposed to it as a colonial power. This provided the ammunition for anti-British actions if it were triggered. Just after he became Prime Minister in 1981, British plantations were being bought in order to fulfill a target of the NEP – to provide Bumiputera with a stock of capital.[94] Consequently, Guthries, a prominent plantation holding, was acquired by the appropriate government agency, Permodalan Nasional Berhad (National Equity Corporation). The takeover on the London Stock Exchange was legal, but Guthries and the British government claimed that the customary notice had not been given and the London Stock Exchange rules were changed. The takeover also occurred soon after Britain had raised the fees for overseas students attending tertiary institutions, affecting about 13,000 Malaysian students. Predictably, Mahathir reacted. Among other things, he had to make it plain that he was in control. In future, trade and commercial transactions would have to be referred to the Prime Minister's Office, which would follow the precept "buy British last." The ban was rescinded in April 1983, partly as a result of the efforts of Mrs. Thatcher, the British Prime Minister, who got on well with Mahathir.

However, tension was renewed in 1994.[95] A British loan to help construct a power station in Pergau, Kelantan, came under scrutiny when it was linked, by the press, to a large sale of heavy weapons and aid for construction projects by Britain. A British newspaper alleged that a British construction company had offered a bribe to Mahathir in order to secure a contract for an aluminum smelter. Mahathir resented the allegations of the press and the failure of Prime Minister John Major to defend him publicly. It was soon decided that Malaysia would not award any new contracts to British firms, and a sharp exchange of words followed between Mahathir and the British press. The dispute ended after seven months, more quickly than the previous one. Significantly, the exact timing for the lifting of the ban was decided by Mahathir. It helped that the press was relatively quiescent. Curiously, British exports to Malaysia rose substantially during the ban; the Malaysian use of what were, in effect, sanctions was largely ineffective because they applied only to *government* contracts. On both occasions, the use of sanctions by the South against the North was no more successful than some sanctions that were applied the other way round. By 1997, relations were good, and Mahathir complimented Britain, saying that it was Malaysia's "most comfortable friend," proposing that the two countries should be partners in promoting "high tech" in Third World countries.[96]

However, British press comments – on the ill treatment of refugees and immigrants to Malaysia – once more incurred government censure in April 1998.

Malaysia and Australia

The disputes between Malaysia and Australia, to be discussed here, had shallower roots than their Malaysia–British counterpart. Australia was not the previous colonial power, although its relationship with Malaysia could be described as "quasi-colonial" or "paternal."[97] The leaders of each country aspired to the uncertain status of a "middle power." Cultural issues, rather than economic or political issues, seemed to evoke the strongest expressions of ire from the Malaysian side. Malaysians found Australian views of their country, particularly those expressed on film or television, flawed and offensive. Examples were the film *Turtle Beach*, which showed massacres of Vietnamese refugees by Malay villagers (which had not occurred), and a television series, *Embassy*, which depicted, unflatteringly, a state which was imaginary but, from its location, could have been construed as having been Malaysia. In response, Malaysia's TV3 showed a television series, *The Ugly Face of Australia*, about the treatment of Australian aboriginals and Asian immigrants. Malaysia also resented Australian objections to the death penalty applying to drug-trafficking offences, and to logging in Sarawak which was not friendly to the environment.

At government level, there were two occasions on which normal relations between the two countries were threatened. The first occurred in 1991, when, after the *Embassy* series, the Malaysian government cancelled a number of official Australian visits to Malaysia and suspended all non-essential Australian projects in Malaysia. Also, Malaysia contemplated a "buy Australian last" policy. Australia behaved coolly and correctly, and offered an acceptable apology. The two governments signed an agreement to dissociate themselves from news reports about each other's affairs, and the episode was officially declared to be over.

At first, relations were good between Mahathir and the new Prime Minister, Paul Keating. However, when Keating succeeded in arranging for APEC to hold biennial summits, and rejected Mahathir's idea for an EAEC as an alternative to APEC (pp. 128–30), Mahathir was not happy with Keating's efforts. In November 1993 after Mahathir had announced that he would not attend the APEC meeting in Seattle, Keating responded by saying that APEC was bigger than Australia, the United States, Malaysia, Dr. Mahathir, and any other "recalcitrants."[98] This was regarded as a blunder by most Australian politicians. Mahathir did not take any action immediately but, ominously, said he would seriously consider any call from UMNO for taking action against Australia. The call was duly forthcoming, and measures were adopted, including banning Australian-made television shows and commercials for Malaysian showing. It was also announced that a group of scholarship students would not, as planned, go to Australia. Keating, despite several attempts, did not manage to produce the right kind of apologetic wording to satisfy Mahathir.[99] When Australia seemed likely to take counter-measures, the Malaysian cabinet called off the dispute, leaving Malaysia the clear winner in the battle of words.

A.B. Shamsul thinks that Australian–Malaysian relations will remain in a state of "stable tension" – trouble could flare up at any time.[100] This would almost certainly apply if at least one of the prime ministers concerned had a temperament similar to Mahathir's or Keating's.

Malaysia and Singapore

Malaysia–Singapore relations resembled Malaysian–British relations, because in each, it was impossible to ignore memories of the past; the two countries had been linked under British rule, and had formed parts of a single state, 1963–5. They were forced to cooperate, for the benefit of each, for economic and defense reasons, either bilaterally or through ASEAN. There were numerous disputes between them – on the ownership of an island, about territorial incursions during maneuvers, and so on – but they were resolved peacefully and without too much acrimony. In some respects, however, they were competitive. On several particular issues, although not on a comprehensive view, their relations were zero-sum. This was evident in Malaysia's development of ports, for instance Kelang and Kuantan, which were competitors of Singapore, and in the promotion of the MSC (pp. 76–9). Above all, Malaysia's efforts to improve the condition of the Bumiputera through the NEP resulted in its inability to rival Singapore's proud claim to be a "meritocracy," at least until "Vision 2020" was realized.

In Singapore, Lee Kuan Yew had raised the matter of its "re-merger" with Malaysia in reply to questions after a dinner with the local and foreign press. He said that it would be difficult to achieve for a very long time, but added that he hoped that it would happen. A condition for re-merger would be that meritocracy must prevail; no race could have a privileged position.[101] He may have been engaging in speculation, or the difficulties he foresaw may have been underlined, in an election year, to reassure Singaporeans about the advantages of their existing arrangements.

The matter of re-merger then became a widely debated topic in Singapore, with Malaysia at times being disparaged. Before long, Malaysian officials became annoyed at being portrayed – for Singapore election purposes – as the "bogeyman." An angry Mahathir complained, and some Malaysians called for retaliatory action. However, in the absence of serious provocation, tempers cooled. Singapore reassured Malaysia that it had not intended to show Malaysia in a negative light, the matter was dropped, and good relations were restored.

The second incident, which took place only a few months later, originated from Lee Kuan Yew's dislike of Tang Liang Hong, a defeated opposition candidate in the 1997 elections whom the PAP labelled a "Chinese chauvinist" during the campaign. Tang had taken refuge for a while in Johor Baru during a defamation suit against him, and Lee, believing his remarks were confidential, referred to Johor Baru as notorious for "shootings, muggings, and car-jackings." Lee apologized twice, and applied successfully to have the statement in question removed from the record.[102] Mahathir expressed his displeasure and remained calm. He admired many of Lee's traits, and exercised restraint when dealing with a fellow member of ASEAN. However, several Malay politicians wished to intensify the pressure; branch elections for UMNO were starting, and it was thought that political capital could be gained. Some members of the cabinet wished to freeze bilateral ties or "cool off" relations for a time. A media war broke out, and Lee was called names. Side issues were pursued, such as the respective crime rates in Johor Baru compared with Singapore, and whether the UMNO Youth leader Datuk Ahmad Zahid Hamidi should have apologized for certain crude statements or not. By about mid-1998, relations had improved somewhat, but differences soon arose, or were revived. Prominent among them were disputes about competition between Singapore and Malaysian ports, and about immigration and customs procedures for the Malaysia–Singapore rail link. It seemed that verbal attacks were becoming addictive, and that relations had reached their lowest point for some time.

These disputes had one reassuring feature in common. They were not pushed to extremes – maybe because some of them, on the long view, were not far removed from triviality. It was in the interests of both parties that they should not continue. In all the incidents, the press and UMNO Youth, or its equivalents, fanned the flames. Yet "face" was often an issue. The Malaysian government disliked its internal processes being discussed in a foreign press. Keating made an insulting comment about a fellow prime minister. Lee Kuan Yew asked a possibly speculative question, which was taken up as perhaps a proposal for action. In the second incident he maligned Johor Baru, as he thought, off the record, and his apology did not put an end to recriminations.

In all the incidents, initially Mahathir restrained himself but did not silence the voices that were raised, sometimes stridently, in his support. One has the impression that they were called off only at what he judged was the optimum moment.

Foreign policy: conclusion

Mahathir is capable of exhibiting pragmatism, for instance, in supporting UN Resolution No. 678, sanctioning the invasion of Iraq, in spite of the opposition of younger members of UMNO,[103] and of accepting institutions such as the Five-Power Defence Arrangements (including Malaysia, Australia, Britain, New Zealand, and Singapore), a modified "colonial" pact, originally set up to protect Malaysia and Singapore from Communist attack.[104]

How does a politician so innovative, eccentric, and iconoclastic preserve a degree of continuity and predictability in his foreign policies? He is equipped with "brakes" by the personnel of the Wisma Putra (foreign office), which help to safeguard good relations with Malaysia's major partners in security and trade issues, and yet, on a less worldly plane, allows Mahathir to champion Third World causes. Beyond this, he sometimes takes advice, such as that from the ISIS which helped to convince him that it was advantageous for Malaysia to remain in the Commonwealth and attend its Heads of Government Meetings.

His major innovation was to supplement iconoclasm with "icon-erecting," above all by promoting the cause of the South. There was in fact a "two-track" policy. For example, in 1995, a huge rally was held at which Mahathir and representatives from all twenty-five political parties denounced France's nuclear testing in the South Pacific. A few months earlier, Mahathir had visited France to pursue continuing and successful negotiations to obtain French help for Malaysia's third "national" car.[105] Likewise, Mahathir regularly criticizes the United States, yet it remains one of Malaysia's largest and most important trading partners.

It would seem obvious that foreign policy should help to provide benefits for the people of a country. What other need could it serve without being irrelevant or subversive? In some cases it must serve these needs by conforming to external changes, or by resisting them. An example might be recognition of China in the mid-1970s, consequent upon the withdrawal of British forces from the area. A "political" way of putting it would be to say that foreign policy must be shaped in order to maintain the government comfortably in power. In Malaysia this tactic is apparent in strengthening links with Muslim countries and letting electors know that government policies are approved of by Muslims outside the country. Additionally, good relations with China are appreciated by most Chinese electors, particularly in facilitating visits to relatives in China. On more complex issues, such as the role of the EAEC/EAEG, few electors are qualified to judge. The "spectators" applaud because they have been convinced that they ought to, not because they appreciate the finer points of the performance.

7   The succession to Mahathir

Anwar Ibrahim

In October 1971 Mahathir reflected on one aspect of Tunku's "feudalism." According to Mahathir, he chose to play the feudal ruler and named Razak as his heir apparent. The party was not to be allowed to choose its next leader. The Tunku kept Razak waiting, while he hinted, repeatedly, that he was not going to step down after all. At one stage, Mahathir wrote, Razak despaired of ever becoming Prime Minister and mentioned to several people that he might take a post abroad.[1]

In the late 1990s, the theme has been repeated under Mahathir but with variations. Mahathir did not hint that he would not step down. He asserted that Anwar would succeed him, but declined to say when. In the mid-1990s, conflict was postponed, but by 1998 tension was mounting, uncomfortably. It was much more a subject of speculation than the Tunku–Razak transfer of power was in the mid-1960s.

The rise of Anwar

The rise of Anwar,[2] in UMNO and the government after he became active in national politics from 1981, was not only rapid, but assumed an air of inevitability. In the party, he became successively president of UMNO Youth, party vice-president, and then deputy president (1993). In the government, after a few years in minor posts, he quickly became Minister of Education, then Minister of Finance (1991). The only near-check he sustained in general elections or party elections occurred in 1982, when he won the UMNO Youth presidency by a margin of only ten votes.

He owed his entry into UMNO, and his subsequent progress, largely to Mahathir. He received additional help from UMNO members who, like himself, were previously in ABIM. Although his supporters formed a wide support base, the nucleus had been composed of ABIM members.

On the debit side, such a promising recruit to UMNO, sponsored by its president, sent an immediate danger signal to aspirants for the succession. They all started counting relative ages, likely promotions, and possible allies, in order to deal with the new element introduced. If Mahathir remained in control of UMNO for another decade or so, Anwar could expect to be among the frontrunners for the succession not long after that time. Daim, Musa, Razaleigh, and others had reason to fear the new competitor. Anwar's prospects of advancement became even better when Razaleigh and Musa removed themselves from the list of competitors – Razaleigh by leaving UMNO and Musa by leaving competitive politics. On the other hand, their actions improved, to a limited degree, the chances of Ghafar Baba, the former Chief Minister of Malacca.

Anwar could not have run ABIM as successfully as he did, without a talent for organizing and mobilizing people. But, in spite of this, and the experience gained in negotiating with government over the amendments to the Societies Act, some aspects of UMNO politics seem to have been new to him. "The first time at a political meeting the non-partisan Anwar was surprised at the amount of politicking, winks one government source. We will have to bring him gradually into the political arena."[3]

Anwar had changed in ways other than by acquiring a political sense during the previous fifteen years. By the time he wrote *The Asian Renaissance*,[4] he had greatly expanded the range of his interests.

The Asian renaissance

Anwar has always been an idealist, although he seems to have been an organized, and organizing, idealist – a rarity. Now he has extended his interests to include not only Islam, but also Confucianism, Hinduism, and other Asian religions, civilizations, or systems of belief. He has surveyed Western cultures, and made comparisons with their Asian counterparts. He has pushed his range beyond history and the social sciences to contemplate art, literature, and aesthetics. His reading is reflected in the large number of speeches he has made in the 1990s, some of which were reproduced in *The Asian Renaissance*.

The book has two main themes. The first is the reflowering of Asian culture in the last century or so. He wished to introduce people who evaluated Asia's recent accomplishments only in terms of its economic successes, to wider horizons. On the airplane to China in 1994, he insisted that *Farewell to my Concubine* [sic] should be shown to the accompanying top Malaysian industrialists to make them aware that China was more than "just one huge consumer market."[5]

The second theme is an approach to a "common vision, shared by East and West." This may be secured by shedding prejudices, including those based on Western arrogance.

If a dialogue does take place, and is successful in going beyond economic questions, Asia would emerge as a major contributor to globalization:

> The idea of what constitutes Asia is elusive to some, because of the diverse nature of Asian culture. Yet it is this very diversity that is decisively needed in a world where cultural boundaries are in fact disappearing. I am convinced that the reflowering of Asian culture will be a powerful counter movement to the tendency towards homogenization, the kind of cultural reductionism that goes along with globalization. There is no point in being

hysterical against cable networks or by the threat of cultural domination via the web of the new electronic superhighways. The threat is real enough, but censorship and closing the sky is not the answer in this late twentieth century. Only creativity and imagination will provide the Asian societies with cultural empowerment, not only to withstand the new and more subtle and pernicious forms of cultural imports but to acquire the capacity to offer the world our own cultural output.[6]

Two topics discussed by Anwar are important for understanding government in Malaysia: democracy, and liberty in conjunction with human rights. "Democracy," increasingly conjoined with the notion of a civil society, is strongly appealing to the United States. Anwar sees this as linked to the high degree of religious, cultural, and ethnic diversity in that country. However, he remarks that in Asia there must be a foundation for democracy which consists of a strong economy, based on a stable social and political order. If these conditions are absent, there will tend to be chaos, and unbridled individualism will paralyze attempts at nation-building through consensus.[7]

Anwar also perceives that democracy should not be regarded as an end in itself, but merely as a means for ensuring humane governance. (It might be added that it may not be the only, or the best, way of securing this.) In 1994, he cited, as an example of the need to curtail democracy, the government's crack-down on the religious sect, Darul Arqam (pp. 87–8). "We give as much freedom as possible to religious groups to carry on their dakwah activities, but, once they deviate, we have to stop them."[8] He esteems civil society, constitutional principles, and the needs of the poor and the oppressed, as deserving a higher priority than democracy:

> The hallmark of leadership…is to act on conviction based on principles rather than pander to the whims and fancies of the mob, as measured by public opinion polls. Much too often these days the *leitmotif* of leadership is to do what is politically expedient rather than what is morally right…the case can easily be made for lending a receptive ear to the voices of the politically oppressed, the socially marginalized and the economically disadvantaged. For, ultimately the legitimacy of a leadership rests as much on moral uprightness as it does on popular support.[9]

The Asian Renaissance is skeptical about advocating liberty without qualification. Not only must rights be accompanied by duties, but additionally liberty should not be allowed to degenerate into immorality and permissiveness.[10]

In his discussion of rights, Anwar plays down the importance of their origins. Many Asians, he believes, reject the idea of human rights because they regard it as Western, and hence alien to their cultures.[11] The central issue is not origins but the balance of civil and political rights, on the one hand, and economic, societal, and cultural rights, on the other. Anwar, like the Malaysian government and many other Asians, condemns the West for having "lectured and hectored"

Asians,[12] for linking human rights with the application of sanctions, and for using allegations of human rights infractions in order to protect the West's commercial interests. Anwar is one of the most outspoken Asian leaders on the subject of human rights. It is shameful, he thinks, to hold up Asian values as an excuse for autocratic practices and the denial of basic rights and civil liberties. Asians place great emphasis on social stability, but the individual should not constantly be sacrificed on the altar of society.[13]

Regarding freedom of the press, Anwar thinks that there are many conflicting considerations. A free society must be vigilant about those who seek to perpetuate their dominance by keeping a stranglehold on the press.[14] He envisages the model of a free press as being one committed to societal ideals and traditional values, and not, as in much of the Western press, thriving on sensationalism and mud-slinging. On the other hand, the media must play their part in checking possible excesses by leaders, and a line has to be drawn where racial hatred and religious animosity are concerned.

Relations between Anwar and Mahathir

The links between Anwar and Mahathir were both constitutional and personal. They were both members of the government, and this tie was reinforced by their membership of UMNO. That, however, was not enough. It had not made for an easy relationship between Musa and Mahathir, nor had it linked Mahathir so tightly to Ghafar that he was determined to defend him as deputy at all costs. An additional Anwar–Mahathir factor was that Anwar was Mahathir's choice, although he was not pinpointed as an immediate successor to Mahathir. Nevertheless his relationship with Mahathir seems to have been not exactly close, but, rather, candid. By 1984, Anwar believed that the relationship was firmly grounded. Mahathir, he said, was very honest and gave straight answers, which he saw as among the main qualities of a leader. One might disagree with him very strongly, but one knew that he could be trusted.[15] Later, Mahathir perceived the relationship in similar terms. In 1996, he said that negative reports about Anwar sometimes troubled him. He wondered if they were true, and at times carried a "slight doubt" about it overnight. His style was that if he heard something, he went directly to him and asked if it were true. If he said that it was not true, that would be the end of it.[16]

Anwar–Mahathir policy similarities and differences

Accompanying basic agreement between the two, there were greater or lesser degrees of enthusiasm expressed by Anwar over specific policies. Government policies on corruption may be used as an illustration. UMNO and the government had long expressed concern about corruption, especially about the prevalence of "money politics" in UMNO. More thought, and some action, had resulted after Mahathir's startling denunciation of it at the 1996 General Assembly. Anwar stated his opposition to the practice in 1997: "The Prime

Minister, before going on leave, sent a message to me that there should be no compromise in the firm measures to wipe out corruption," he said, adding that Mahathir had said that it was immaterial whether the wrongdoing involved the leaders in UMNO, other Barisan parties, or in higher government offices.[17]

One speculation was that Anwar had been very outspoken on the topic, and that Mahathir's absence would present an opportune time for him to tell Anwar to take action on it for a while. The anti-corruption drive continued, although few charges were laid (1998). No "big fish" were involved.

Anwar is one of the few leaders to draw attention to the fact that the incidence of corruption rose in step with the euphoria stimulated by the country's rapid economic growth.[18]

Anwar has also stood out by his vigorous denunciation of immorality. UMNO Youth leader Rahim Tamby Chik was at first backed politically by Anwar, and he was part of his "Vision Team" in 1994, but after charges had been brought against him for having had sex with an under-age girl, Anwar and his followers successfully pressed for his resignation, even though he still had Mahathir's backing.[19]

There was close agreement between Mahathir and Anwar on government policy toward Islam. Like Mahathir, Anwar in his statements was careful to say that the sentiments and sensitivities of non-Muslims must be taken into account. He was also critical, as Mahathir was, of the "traditional" Islamic educational system. He believes that "Islamic slogans, exhortations and rituals, the obsession with superficialities and the whipping up of religious sanctions cannot cover up our psychological and educational weakness."[20] Comments like these might well have been made by Mahathir himself (p. 84). Possibly, if Mahathir had been in Malaysia in June–July 1997, he might have been more outspoken than Anwar in condemning the clumsy way in which Islamic laws were invoked, concerning beauty contests (p. 88).[21]

Like his predecessor, Musa, Anwar was skeptical about some of Mahathir's expensive heavy industry projects. He did not, during Mahathir's absence abroad, attempt to conceal the difficulties encountered by the contractors of the Bakun Dam,[22] nor encourage going ahead with it at a time when funding it was difficult. Also, while attending the annual meeting of the World Bank and the IMF in Hong Kong in September 1997, Anwar had to reassure investors emphatically that Malaysia would not impose restrictions on currency trading, despite Mahathir's threat made during his address to the annual meeting to do so. When Anwar was asked whether he or Mahathir should be believed, he replied that it was a tricky question, but essentially he defended Mahathir's denunciation of foreign currency speculators and said, therefore, that both of them should be believed.[23]

On democracy, liberty, and the press, Anwar's opinions, outlined earlier, are close to Mahathir's; however, they are less aggressive. In foreign policy, too, Anwar's tone is more measured. He is not so anti-West; anti-colonialism affected him less than it influenced Mahathir. He supports Malaysia's role in ASEAN. He has said little about APEC, but was reported to have been unhappy about Mahathir's decision not to attend the APEC summit in Seattle (1993).[24] He has waxed less rhetorical than Mahathir in questioning the need for the US naval presence in the region.

On defending the right to disapprove of arbitrary measures against the person, he is much more forthright than Mahathir: "I do not think that we should deny the right of Asians or Americans to question arbitrary arrest or torture. I see no reason why I am expected to condone or defend."[25]

If Anwar had become Prime Minister would his policies have been very different from Mahathir's?

One difficulty that affects a prediction is that Anwar is said to have a reputation for sometimes telling people what he thinks they want to hear. Of course, this may be an indication of his politeness, or use of the "Malay way." An alternative phrasing might be that he talks about what he thinks the listener is interested in, or is able to relate to. (By contrast, Mahathir is apt, on occasion, not to talk about what the listener is interested in, but on what he himself feels like complaining about.) Two academics and one of Anwar's closest political confidants have been cited concerning Anwar's possible policy changes. Dr. Chandra Muzaffar believes that, as Prime Minister, Anwar would be more ready to accept differences of opinion in society and the need for consultation. Another academic said that, although Anwar believes that some of the main provisions of the Internal Security Act would have to go, that he still favors preventive detention, and would not be more liberal. Kamaruddin Jaafar, head of Anwar's Institute of Policy Development, thinks that there would be a push for programs that were humanitarian and were not in contradiction to Islam.[26] It was quite widely felt that, if Prime Minister, he would move toward "Islamization" (not always clearly defined), but some close to him are convinced that there was no hidden Islamic agenda. At the OIC he placed less emphasis on questions of doctrine and more on humanitarian issues, such as lessening the gender gap and the inequalities between rich and poor.[27]

A trap to avoid is to take at face value statements that, on his accession, there would be a change in style rather than in substance. Mahathir used these words after his succession as Prime Minister, but, considering his innovative, even iconoclastic, bent, his remark was an imperfect guide to his performance. After all, the style is the man.

Rifts in Anwar's relations with Mahathir

Stories of rifts or imagined rifts between Anwar and Mahathir became common toward the end of the 1990s. They peaked at various times, for instance before the UMNO General Assembly of 1995, and during Mahathir's absence from Malaysia in July–August 1997. Tension and rumors are inherent in a situation where a leader has been long in power, and where the likely successor has been identified, but the timing of succession has not been specified because of the prime minister's fear of being regarded as a "lame duck." Rumors were played up by Anwar's supporters, putting pressure on him to speed up the succession, which would advance their own political careers. They were also, perhaps unwittingly, suggested by Mahathir when he helped to publicize a rumor in 1997 that Anwar had resigned, by denying it publicly. Rumors might also be spread by trouble-makers, who, for example, might wish to influence the stock market. Some rumors, current in 1994, were denied by both politicians. One of them was that Anwar was unhappy about the way that Mahathir had handled the suppression of the Darul Arqam movement (pp. 87–8). (In fact, Anwar had backed him publicly on this.) Another was that they had disagreed on whether a particular Chief Minister should resign or not. (They agreed that he should be removed.)[28]

Another rift obtained publicity: that between Anwar and his predecessor as Finance Minister, Daim. The latter was no longer a minister seeking to win a seat in Parliament. But he exercised power by being close to Mahathir, being his financial adviser, and as the UMNO treasurer. He had numerous business connections,[29] some of which cooperated with Anwar's corporate links. At other times, a competitive relationship existed. Clashes were reported concerning the Bakun Dam project, where Daim's associates were included, while Anwar's were not,[30] and there was competition over some privatization projects. By extension, the Anwar–Daim rift could be construed as part of the Anwar–Mahathir rift.

Daim retained his economic power, and, through Mahathir, much of his political clout. The issue of *Asiaweek* that ranked Mahathir as number two, with reference to power in Asia, ranked Anwar as thirty-fourth, but Daim as thirty-second.[31]

Tensions were somewhat defused by Mahathir and Anwar making it a point in public to affirm confidence in each other. Mahathir said that he had good relations with his deputy, and met him almost every morning: "He tells me what he is doing, and asks me for my advice, and I sometimes ask him for his advice. We get on very well together."[32] Outsiders were not aware of this relationship, he said. He was reciprocating Anwar's assurances that he consistently supported Mahathir's policies. Anwar had to refer all his decisions to him. Anwar had always regarded Mahathir as his leader and "father," because he came from a younger generation.

At the UMNO General Assembly of 1995, when the prospects of competition for office in the near future had somewhat receded, gracious compliments were paid. When Anwar's winding-up speech was accompanied by ringing applause, Anwar said that he was touched by Mahathir's confidence in him: "If I am asked to go back to university, I am not sure there is a university which can provide training as good as you have given me."[33] He then recited a *pantun* (a Malay poem).

Mahathir was inclined to make jokes about Anwar – good-humored, but sometimes with a bite – just as Tunku used to do with Razak. When asked in an interview if he had come to terms with Anwar, he said that he had had to "Apparently he has the support. I can't be changing deputies all the time. If you change deputies too many times, it must be because you are wrong and not them."[34]

He also compared his reading habits with Anwar's. On one occasion, Mahathir said that he had not read Machiavelli or Clausewitz. There was no need to read them in order to be a successful politician.[35]

Mahathir said he was a low-brow reader, preferring authors such as Sidney Sheldon and Tom Clancy. Anwar's tastes were more literary:

> He reads more: I think more…. Anwar says things in a different way, perhaps because the words he uses are more conciliatory, but his views are exactly the same as mine. He is very academic. He likes to quote but he says the same thing. I just give my opinion. I don't read very much.[36]

The 1997 UMNO General Assembly ended with some light-hearted badinage. Mahathir gave assurances that Anwar would succeed him but explained that his deputy sometimes got "panicky" about the timing. They also exchanged remarks about Anwar's goatee beard and Mahathir's forehead, nose, and sideburns.[37]

Anwar acts for Mahathir, but Mahathir maintains contact

In July–August 1997, Mahathir went overseas. It was partly a vacation, but he also engaged in government business, for instance by promoting foreign investment, particularly in the Multimedia Super Corridor. Anwar was made Acting Prime Minister, and also acting president of UMNO.

Had Mahathir simply given power to the obvious person to take over, while keeping in constant touch with and directing him through a tele-conferencing apparatus installed in Anwar's office? Or was Mahathir setting Anwar a test to see if he was worthy of taking charge when the time came? He had to walk a tightrope between being assiduous in supporting Mahathir, or challenging him. To cite a particular issue, when Mahathir instructed Anwar to mount an anti-corruption campaign during his absence, should he have gone the extra mile in pursuing a cause that was known to be very close to his heart? Or was the "test" intended to find out whether he might be over-zealous and provoke criticism? The verdict on Anwar's performance generally was that he behaved well. He did not act as decisively, on such issues as dealing with religious authorities' banning of beauty contests, as Mahathir might have done (p. 88). But he covered himself by taking the approach that he was in constant touch with Mahathir, and followed his instructions as carefully as he could.

The Australian journalist Greg Sheridan has likened Mahathir to "the Malay Magician" and Anwar to "the Sorcerer's Apprentice."[38] The comparison is striking, but valid only up to a point. In the original tale, it was almost disastrous for the sorcerer to absent himself and leave the feckless apprentice in charge. However, Mahathir's temporary absence enabled Anwar to provide a happier ending at that time. He seemingly proved himself capable of being more than just an "acting magician."

Anwar stakes his claims to be Prime Minister

Anwar's successful bid to be deputy president, 1993

At this point, it may be useful to show how the attitudes and ambitions of Mahathir and Anwar were revealed from 1993 onwards, when the two leaders assumed a competitive, as well as a cooperative, relationship, revealed, notably, at UMNO General Assemblies.

When Musa resigned as Deputy Prime Minister in 1986, the number of eligible choices for Mahathir in selecting a replacement was small. Anwar was too young and only recently active in the party. To nominate Razaleigh would be to choose a possible challenger and rival, who actually announced his opposition in the following year. Ghafar seemed a safe choice. To be sure, he was on Hussein's "short list" of three possible successors in 1981, but his high rank in UMNO – vice-president – was not matched by his international experience or his appeal to the younger generation. He was unlikely to challenge Mahathir. He could become deputy president/Deputy Prime Minister only with Mahathir's approval.

Anwar's strategy, after Ghafar's appointment, was not too difficult to predict: in order to take the first step to becoming Deputy Prime Minister, he had to dislodge Ghafar without appearing to press so hard that Mahathir would be forced to act quickly against him. To achieve surprise, Anwar had to conceal that he was challenging Ghafar for as long as possible. He claimed that he had not intended to challenge him, but that he had been compelled to do so by the enthusiasm of his followers. Mahathir's strategy was defense in depth. Ghafar had to be fought for, but in the end he was expendable. Anwar had been very effective in mobilizing support, as the published results of the UMNO deputy-presidential nominations showed. Originally, Mahathir had said that he did not want the post to be contested (in 1989 he had assured Ghafar that he would be his successor),[39] but as Anwar's strength became evident, he declared that he was neutral. It was too late to stem the tide. Mahathir stated later that he would have been happy to have had Ghafar continue as deputy, but that some in the party wanted change, so he felt he could not be disloyal to so many party members.[40] Ghafar at first tried to continue the contest, but before the actual election took place, he resigned his party and government posts.

The 1993 General Assembly

The 1993 UMNO General Assembly met with the deputy-presidential election already decided. However, other elections, especially those for the vice-presidents, could help to determine the top leadership of the party in the future. Anwar coopted the word "vision" from "Vision 2020" and named his team for the vice-presidential election, "the Vision Team."[41] It consisted of Najib, Muhyiddin, the Menteri Besar of Johor, and Tan Sri Mohammad Taib, Menteri Besar of Selangor. They benefited not only from the "vision" theme, but also from invoking Mahathir's concept of the "new Malay," the "Melayu Baru."[42] Anwar and his supporters claimed that the team should be elected because it would contribute to Mahathir's goals, as expressed in "Vision 2020" and else-where. Anwar's tactics of aligning his own goals with Mahathir's appealed to many in UMNO who wished to support both. They did not realize what was evident to those near the top of UMNO, who saw that, in one sense, the two were now rivals. With Ghafar's exit, alignments were changing.

All three members of the team were elected, Muhyiddin obtaining the highest vote. Two incumbent vice-presidents were defeated, Badawi and Sanusi. The team also won the presidency of UMNO Youth (won by Rahim Tamby Chik) and a majority of the supreme council seats.

Mahathir makes appointments and changes the rules

After the general election of 1995, Mahathir provided additional evidence of the power of a Prime Minister to modify the choices of the General Assembly through his ability to determine appointments. Muhyiddin, in spite of his winning vote, was "banished" to the low-profile Ministry of Culture, Youth, and Sports. Najib, however, was not penalized, but was rewarded with the prestigious Ministry of Education. (He was probably the most powerful check remaining against Anwar.) Rahim Tamby Chik, also a member of the "Vision Team," retained his post of Chief Minister of Malacca, but after a sex scandal was forced to resign it (p. 148). Anwar (because of his alleged conduct) was unwilling, and Mahathir seemingly unable, to save him. Mahathir used another tactic to put Anwar supporters on a tight leash; some were made deputy ministers in the Prime Minister's Department, where he could keep his eye on them.[43]

Mahathir was less able to exert his power effectively at the divisional elections for UMNO held late in 1995. Two of the most disturbing setbacks occurred in Kedah, his own state. Daim was opposed for election as divisional chairman, and declined to contest. Sanusi, switching from the federal to the state level, had the backing of Mahathir and was intended to become the Kedah Menteri Besar. However, he was narrowly defeated in the divisional elections, and it took over a year of pressure and maneuvering by Mahathir for him to reach that destination.[44]

With the next UMNO elections in view (to be held at the 1996 General Assembly), Mahathir also decided that changes in the rules were needed to protect his own position. His powers in the UMNO Baru had been enlarged soon after the reconstituted party began to function (p. 29). The system of "bonus votes," that is, votes for contestants for the top offices acquired just for having been nominated, had been instituted (p. 45).[45] However, this was not enough. Anwar, after his impressive performance against Ghafar, could hope to do almost as well against Mahathir. Procedures for the election had to be centralized and tightened. For the 1996 UMNO elections, divisions would no longer have the power to make nominations; candidates would have to register directly with UMNO headquarters. A time limit was also set. Prospective candidates had to announce their candidacies by May 7.[46] Unregistered candidates would be ineligible for election, even if they were nominated by UMNO divisions. Moreover, the campaigning period would be reduced. Mahathir announced that it should not begin until July. Campaigning was actually banned by the supreme council in July.

These measures embodied the experience that Mahathir had gained from Anwar's defeat of Ghafar. His successful tactics were not going to be allowed to work a second time. There would not be any surprise announcement, at short notice, that Anwar had decided to contest because of the overwhelming pressure from his supporters. The conduct of the campaign would be more transparent – to the eyes of UMNO headquarters. The restrictions on campaigning were represented as being necessary to reduce the often denounced evil of money politics. The circle of the argument was complete. Campaigning had been infected by money politics, so, in order to protect democracy, it would have to be curtailed.

The UMNO General Assembly, 1995

In September, two months before the Assembly, Mahathir said that the party tradition, by which the deputy president takes over when the time comes, would continue. It was not true that the deputy would challenge him next year. He told reporters that Anwar would confirm this. He did so, and said that his support should not be questioned.[47] Asked whether there would be no contest for both the top two posts, Mahathir agreed, but said that the vice-presidential posts would be contested.

At the General Assembly, Mahathir put these decisions in context, saying that he did not want UMNO to be split. He also said:

> Two things could happen if there is a contest. First, I may win, at least from my point of view. It's okay, too, if I lose. After all, I've led the party for fourteen years, been a Prime Minister that long. But imagine if Anwar loses, that's the end of his career.

Anwar interjected by saying, "I've made the right decision, so the matter is closed," to the laughter of all present.[48]

Comments on the proceedings agreed that, technically (subject to accepting the revised rules), there was nothing to stop Anwar from doing, essentially, the same thing that he did against Ghafar in 1993. But by this time the no-contest agreement was morally binding. It had been affirmed several times, for example, at the Youth and Wanita assembly meetings, and it had been stated, without dissent, that anyone who nominated another candidate would be seen as a traitor to the Malay cause.[49]

The 1996 General Assembly

At the 1996 Assembly, since the deputy's post was not contested, the relative degrees of support for Mahathir and Anwar, respectively, had to be assessed from the performances of their supporters. There was a marked contrast between inferences to be drawn from the results of the Wanita and Youth wings, on the one hand, and those for the vice-presidential posts and for the supreme council, on the other. The former contests, on the whole, favored Anwar, while the latter were, in general, pro-Mahathir. Anwar's supporters were the winners in both the Wanita and Youth elections. Rafidah was displaced from the women's presidency by Dr. Siti Zahara Suleiman. Rafidah was close to Mahathir and well respected internationally for her management of the Ministry of International Trade and Industry. However, the requirements of her job made grass-roots activities difficult for her. Moreover, she was both bright and tough, and her exhortations to women to be equally tough and self-sufficient were not attractive to some women accustomed to more conventional roles. The Youth president, Rahim Tamby Chik (p. 153), was defeated by Datuk Ahmad Zahid Hamidi, an outspoken businessman, who was close to Anwar.[50]

There were seven vice-presidential candidates for three positions. Two incumbents were victorious, Najib and Muhammad Taib. These two were no longer thought to be necessarily pro-Anwar, but rather "free agents." Muhyiddin came only sixth out of seven, compared with first, three years before. He was replaced by Badawi, who was now, once more, a vice-president. Consequently the advantage, which had at first been Anwar's, had been overcome a day later. Much of the reversal may be attributable to the intervening speech by Mahathir, in which he wept, assailed money politics, and was warmly applauded.

If Anwar's initial success had been sustained, he might have been encouraged to press for a rapid succession. As it was, the leadership issue had "become a little more murky than it was."[51]

The 1997 General Assembly

The 1997 Assembly produced little that was new. This was symbolized by pleasantries between Mahathir and Anwar, although they were accompanied by one innuendo when Mahathir repeated that Anwar was his successor, and said that talk that his deputy was quitting should stop,[52] thus giving it more publicity. He said, "he is still my deputy and he is my potential successor." After loud applause, he continued: "I hope that the applause is an endorsement of what I have just said."[53]

Some delegates thought that in 1999, when elections would normally be held, the two top posts should once again be uncontested, but no resolution was introduced to give effect to this suggestion. Mahathir tried to influence UMNO's

1998 divisional elections (which will affect who will be entitled to vote at its 1999 General Assembly elections for its top office-holders) by limiting challenges to incumbents. However, the strategy may not be wholly effective. Another issue, which has been mooted for some time, to strengthen stability by having elections held less frequently than every three years (perhaps every four or even five years),[54] is still unresolved.

Until 1998, it seemed that the Mahathir-Anwar rivalry over the succession might continue on a predictable path. By ensuring, year by year, that the top post should not be contested, Mahathir, by the judicious use of rewards and deprivations, and by adjusting the rules of UMNO elections, could hope to block Anwar's bid until the new century had arrived and his own projects were substantially completed. A number of events, however, induced him to employ a bolder tactic – a preemptive strike. On 2 September 1998 he dismissed Anwar as Deputy Prime Minister and as Finance Minister, and he was quickly expelled from UMNO by the supreme council. Mahathir took over the Finance Ministry, and the Deputy Prime Minister's post was left vacant.

There were three main reasons for Mahathir's change in strategy: economic policy differences with Anwar; signs of militancy among Anwar's lieutenants; and the perception that Anwar had been weakened because of character attacks on him. Anwar's economic policies were too conservative for Mahathir, whose urge to attempt simple – some thought simplistic – solutions had reasserted itself. He decided to achieve monetary stability by fixing the value of the ringgit (pp. 177–8). The aggressive mood of Anwar's followers was expressed by the UMNO Youth leader at the 1998 General Assembly. Datuk Zahid fiercely denounced the government's favoritism and nepotism in the allocation of contracts. Mahathir, obviously forewarned of the attack, blunted it by publishing a list of names which showed that Anwar's relatives and followers had also benefited substantially from privatization contracts. Anwar himself, although he knew what Zahid was going to say, did not voice any direct criticisms of government policies at the Assembly, and made an affirmation of allegiance to Mahathir after the Assembly was over.

Additionally, Anwar had recently become vulnerable because of allegations about his personal behavior, including philandering and homosexuality. These reports had been spread by poison-pen letters, but during the General Assembly they were supplemented by a book claiming that such behavior should preclude him from becoming Prime Minister. Mahathir said that he had heard such allegations nearly a year previously, but had dismissed the stories until they came to him from so many sources that he thought that they ought to be investigated, which he did, by speaking to seven witnesses.[55] Anwar, on the other hand, did not take any official action until the book attacking him was published, because the poison-pen letters, by their nature, did not identify an author or publisher.[56]

When Mahathir did decide to act, as was his custom he carefully prepared the ground first. He took a number of steps designed to weaken Anwar. In June 1998 Daim was appointed to the post of Minister for Special Functions. The functions were mainly economic, and therefore infringed on Anwar's sphere of influence (as well as making the central bank – with which he specially concerned himself – less autonomous). In July two pro-Anwar editors resigned.[57] Mahathir also traveled selectively to solidify the loyalty of key UMNO figures. These preparations also included Mahathir's plans to stabilize the ringgit (pp. 177–8), so that Anwar's dismissal would not trigger a steep fall in the currency or in the stock market.

Charges were prepared against Anwar, and his residence was surrounded by police. However, he was permitted to carry out a nation-wide speaking tour in mid-September. Action against Anwar was apparently not planned until after the end of the Commonwealth Games. However, after discovering the extent of the support for Anwar, Mahathir had him arrested, under the ISA, at his residence on 20 September, shortly after he had addressed a crowd of about 50,000 in Kuala Lumpur. Four top office-holders in ABIM and others, including Zahid, the UMNO Youth president, were also arrested under the ISA.

Alternatives to Anwar

There are few politicians of the necessary caliber to replace Anwar. There was an infusion of young blood into UMNO after Mahathir became Prime Minister in 1981, but casualties have been heavy, partly because of the elimination of some "Team B" contenders. Mahathir, in September 1998, said he would prefer not to appoint a Deputy Prime Minister before the UMNO General Assembly elections in 1999. The most likely choice remaining is probably Najib. He entered Parliament in 1976, and in 1983 he became Menteri Besar of Pahang, where the ruler needed careful handling. Not yet 30, he was then the youngest Menteri Besar. He bore a well-known name, was elected deputy president of UMNO Youth in 1986 and president in 1988, and was appointed Minister of Education in 1995. He became an UMNO vice-president in 1993 as a member of Anwar's "Vision Team".

During the UMNO split, he was the most prominent member of "Team B" to switch to "Team A" (p. 43). He was also active in the ethnic conflict of 1987, when, as acting-president of UMNO Youth, he was militant in affirming Malay claims (pp. 108–9).

Abdullah Badawi was a member of "Team B", but has proved his durability by surviving a defeat while vice-president by winning the party post back three years later in the next election. Against him is the fact that his government ministry, Foreign Affairs, offers minimal opportunities for influencing the grassroots or patronage. For him is that his state is Penang, so that, in a general election he might draw support away from Anwar. An unlikely, but ironic situation might be reached if Najib were preferred, and, after he became Prime Minister, Badawi were to be made his deputy. The irony would consist in the two top posts being occupied by former members of "Team B", constituting a victory of a kind for it beyond the grave.

The Anwar dismissal, occurring at the highest level of government, raises two issues which transcend parties and personalities. One concerns civil liberties. Will any charges made against Anwar take place in open court or be discussed openly by an independent Royal Commission of Inquiry of Parliament, or UMNO? Or will openness be precluded by the use of a State of Emergency, the Internal Security Act, or the Official Secrets Act? In any case, the power of the media will certainly be employed against him, including the suppression of opposing views, and those seen supporting Anwar could face retribution.

The other issue concerns the procedures for choosing leaders in Malaysia. How can one explain a system in which (with rare insight) a "rebel" is recruited into the political establishment, performs ably in rising through the system, with an untarnished moral reputation, yet is brusquely rejected before reaching the highest level? What aspects of such a system could lead to so bizarre an outcome?

8 Mahathir as Prime Minister

Mahathir's personal characteristics

Mahathir is a believer in strong government, especially if exercised by himself. He enjoys power, and he fights to win. One judgment on him was: "In the Mahathir lexicon of politics, power has to be absolute, and if one takes that seriously, there could be very dangerous tendencies."[1]

Control and determination

In an interview he said that he did not care whether people would remember him or not after he was dead. He added (what perhaps seemed to worry him more) that, even when still alive, he found that people were passing all kinds of judgments over which he had no control.[2] He is tenacious, and is prepared to exert seemingly boundless energy in pursuit of his goals. Anxious to have the prestigious Formula One motor-racing championship held in Kuala Lumpur by 1999, he flew to London to lobby the organizers. One of the executives said that his enthusiasm "more than convinced" the organizers. Even on this apparently non-political issue, there was, seemingly, a degree of overkill. Mahathir's determination to exercise power is fortified by his belief that he has never been wrong.[3]

Checks and balances within the executive

Mahathir uses "checks and balances" to make sure that holders of government posts are kept aware of the presence of a potential rival for the Prime Minister's favor. A classic example occurred when Musa was elected UMNO deputy president over Razaleigh (p. 40). Mahathir, although he favored Musa, refused his request that Razaleigh should be dropped from the cabinet. Apart from his value as a minister, Razaleigh was also useful to retain as a check in case Musa became too independent-minded. Later, when Anwar became increasingly likely to succeed Mahathir as Prime Minister some time in the future, Mahathir made sure that this would not occur inconveniently soon by appointing Ghafar as his deputy. Even in 1996, Razaleigh briefly resumed the role, not exactly of a threat, but rather of a shadow threat, after he disbanded his party, and, with the majority of his followers, rejoined UMNO.

More generally, Mahathir adopted a technique that had also been used by his predecessors, except, possibly, Hussein. In the more important states, an UMNO Menteri Besar was usually checked by another prominent UMNO politician from that state. This might be the head of the UMNO state liaison committee (if, atypically, the Menteri did not hold that position) or a cabinet minister. Confusingly, "checks and balances" in Malaysia has a totally different meaning than it has in the United States. There, the term indicates the separation of powers between the executive, the legislature, and the judiciary. In Malaysia, on the other hand, it is a weapon to ensure the supremacy of the dominant power, the executive.

Dislike of competition

Although once in a contest, he is set on winning, he prefers that no contest should occur. His dislike of competitive games was apparently evident as a schoolboy when he preferred reading, which resulted in his good scholastic performance. Later on, his main hobbies included wood-carving and boat-building, although he also engaged in horseback-riding with the Sultan of Johor. His dislike of competition was illustrated by his policies in government, as well as in his choice of personal pursuits. Although in a broad sense he favors "capitalist" systems, within this description various sectors of Malaysia's economy operate with varying degrees of competition.[4] One of his main economic policies was privatization, but many of the privatized activities are no more competitive than they had been when they were in the public sector. Nor, in privatizing them, were the people chosen to operate them selected on objective, competitive criteria or for their suitability (p. 59).

In the operation of government, he has not been deterred by any regard for checks on the executive power. According to Chandra Muzaffar, "Mahathir doesn't seem to appreciate the importance of autonomous ideas or institutions. His style isn't conducive to the growth of a culture that values popular participation, debate or dissent."[5]

Politically, the best recent example of Mahathir's successful avoidance of competition occurred at the 1995 UMNO General Assembly, when he asserted, without any signs of dissent, that he would not be challenged for the top UMNO post until 1999 (p. 154).

Mahathir's vision – far and near

According to a biography of Mahathir,[6] Anwar thought that Mahathir would be remembered mainly for his vision and courage. The word "vision" will always be associated with him, because of his blueprint for the attainment of developed-country status by 2020, and the replacement of ethnicity by a truly national feeling.

Remarkably, Mahathir's capacity to envisage the broad outlines of the future is accompanied by his scrutiny of small details in the present. He keeps note-books handy,[7] and, if some incident or fact attracts his attention, he jots it down, whether it is a blocked drain, a pile of litter, or instances of red tape which impede smooth administration. He is interested in the condition of public toilets, especially at airports. He has actually invented an Islamic toilet,[8] no doubt because it combined the challenge of observing Islamic precepts with his interest in things mechanical.

Confrontational aspects

On occasion, Mahathir's mode of speech is confrontational: "I'm not a very nice personality. I like to speak my mind, and I may offend people in the process."[9] "He...thrives on crisis and confrontation," stated Razaleigh.[10] There are elements of the street-fighter in him, as is shown in his battles against the rulers, and in opposing Team B of UMNO in 1987 and, subsequently, the judiciary. It was understandable that, when in power, he would be able to relax more than when he was the writer of the denunciatory letter of 1969: "We're the same people, only a little older. The only thing is that, when you're outside, there is a need to shout in order to be heard and this gives the impression of anger."[11] He probably was more self-effacing when taking the oath of office as Education Minister in 1976 when he was no longer "out" but not yet completely "in." His style was "quiet and unassuming."[12]

The examples just quoted are of Mahathir to Malaysians on internal topics. His gift of invective is most evident when he is speaking about foreign affairs, and has available customary targets, such as "colonialism," "the West," or the Security Council of the UN. He has been so outspoken about the UN that some of his drafts have had to be toned down, according to a high-ranking official who specializes in writing many of his key speeches.[13]

Some qualifications are necessary. Mahathir's remarks are sometimes abrasive or mordant, but he rarely loses his temper. When he does, it may be for strategic reasons.[14] He is said to "let himself go" when the issue does not really matter very much, for instance in a trade dispute, if the sum concerned is small. On one notable occasion, the UMNO General Assembly of 1995, tears were used rather than denunciation to indicate that he spoke more in sorrow than in anger (p. 150). In informal conversation he can be sympathetic toward a distraught politi-cian, such as Australia's former Prime Minister, Bob Hawke,[15] or puzzled researchers, such as the authors of this book. Anwar gives a fair summary, although it should be remembered that when he was speaking he was Mahathir's deputy:

> He learns a lot, he reasons a lot. He even changes his position. I don't see how much more democratic one can be. But he has to be firm. He is tough, I agree, but we require firm and tough leaders.[16]

Mahathir has a trait that surely limits his effectiveness. In an interview, he did not seem to see that previous disasters merited study in order to avoid similar errors in the future. He shrugged off mention of the tin fiasco (p. 70), and said that no one talked about it now. Bumiputra Malaysia Finance had been a problem (pp. 68–70), but they resolved it and Bank Bumiputra was doing very well. "We can overcome these so-called disasters…. We mismanaged but recovered."[17] It is quite in keeping with Mahathir's character that on special occasions, or for charities, he can be persuaded to sing his favorite song, "I Did It My Way."[18] In view of his defensiveness about some miscalculations, he should follow it with an encore, a song immortalized by Edith Piaf, "Je ne regrette rien."

Mahathir's temperament is not fitted to the requirements of avoiding crises. One opinion is that the "rulers' crisis" would have been managed more amicably if Tunku or Razak had been Prime Minister.[19]

Mahathir gives the impression that he is not much interested in the political process. He does not follow the example of other Malay politicians who relive each moment when retelling a political anecdote in which they were involved, a joy to researchers. He is not fascinated by the "game" of politics. To him, politics is an intrusion into his aims of smooth governance and development. He sees himself as a builder, a developer, a promoter of Malay achievements, an interpreter of Islam, and a promoter of ethnic harmony. Politics are an unwelcome distraction from such aims, as are sections of the press, pressures from the West, and the clamor from human rights bodies.

Mahathir's broadening horizons

Mahathir, conscious of his abilities, was not long engaged in politics before he was attracted to playing a more important role in Malaysia – subsequently even beyond its horizons (pp. 133–6). His ambitions to operate in a wider sphere were expressed partly in a denial, when in a 1973 interview he agreed that he did not want to be Menteri Besar of Kedah:

> That I do not want to be Menteri Besar of Kedah does not mean that I want to be Prime Minister – or something like that…I am interested in so many things, I have so many ideas which I would like to put to people, and if I am asked to confine myself to Kedah, it will cramp me up. My main job is to think and to find out, to bring up new ideas…. I feel I should be contributing to every sector.[20]

The Malay Dilemma; *the importance of time; polemics*

The Malay Dilemma not only was intended to portray some Malay traits that Mahathir deplored and wanted to change. It also provided the key to some of his own behavior. He was guided to behave in a way consonant with preferable patterns of Malay conduct. For example, in the book he contrasted the Malays' high valuation of life, but their failure to know what to do with it, that is, their failure to realize the value of time.[21] This derived partly, maybe, from the inclusion of the hereafter in calculations; it is possible to see this life as only a preparation for it. On the other hand, if this life is considered to be also important, it is necessary to plan ahead and not to do so would be a serious handicap in competing economically with societies that are time-conscious.

There are implications here that are congruent with other ideas of Mahathir also contained in his books. One is his condemnation of "polemics." His conception of polemics goes beyond the usual dictionary definition: the art or practice of disputation or controversy, of which Mahathir himself is a master. When he applied it to Malay behavior in *The Challenge*, he saw it as a lengthy debate on proposals for action, which, because they were so lengthy, effectively prevented any action from being taken.[22]

Mahathir has complained that he has not got the time to do all that he wants to do. He took over the premiership when he was fifty-six, with the NEP due to end in nine years. He thought that if you wanted everyone to agree before you started something, you would not get anything done. That was not what leadership was about.[23]

He restated the point later, somewhat differently: when you wanted to do something, you found that a number of people thought they knew all about the subject and gave reasons that they thought you were wrong.[24] He insisted, however, that such criticism would not deter him. He would try to overcome it. If he could achieve a fraction of what he set out to do, it would be satisfying.[25]

Mahathir has had no patience with lengthy preparatory discussions. The important thing is not to consider ideas in order to find shortcomings. For improvement, what is needed is not to exhibit polemical skills, but to accept what is practicable and put it into practice.[26]

One might even speculate that this criticism could be associated with criticisms that he did not proceed through seeking to achieve consensus: "The doctor is one cause of the illness he is now trying to treat. In his six years as Prime Minister he has favored the politics of confrontation in a culture that believes in consensus."[27]

The idea of the "new Malay" was born from the desire to eradicate some undesirable traits of the "old Malay." Quite early in his prime ministership, it was perceived that the Bumiputera would be disappointed because he would not pamper them.[28] When his apparent non-observance of the "Malay way" was referred to in an interview with a Malay politician, the reply was brief: Mahathir is not a Malay.[29]

A possible speculation is that Mahathir's preference for confrontation over consensus may be that ample consultation (pp. 168–70), and even planning, in some projects, resembles polemics too much for it to form part of his style.

The mellowing of Mahathir?

It might be expected that, with age, Mahathir would show signs of mellowing. This should not be confused with incapacity, as shown by the examples of the last years in office of Woodrow Wilson and Winston Churchill. Rather, in Mahathir's case, mellowing might show itself in some softening of his abrasiveness and some checking of immediate instinctive reactions when problems presented themselves.

So far (1998) there seems to have been little mellowing. Since 1987, which may be considered the climax of his authoritarian behavior, there has been no descent into liberalism or any perceptible failing of the will. There are three arguments to support this point of view: he remains deeply devoted to his favorite projects, particularly the Multimedia Super Corridor, although other projects were hurt by the economic crisis that began in mid-1997; his determination to vanquish his opponents whether electorally, by application of the law, or by other means, has not wavered; and his will to remain in office seems as strong as ever.

There are two important exceptions to these hypotheses, yet, in both, it appears that changes in policy, while slowing down the pursuit of some objectives, represent more urgent movement toward other objectives. The first of these is increased tolerance and support of Chinese and other non-Malays, as shown in "Vision 2020" (pp. 165–8). The second is a greater concern for the environment (p. 135). In both these cases, the change will aid Mahathir's policy of supporting the South, as opposed to the industrialized countries. The first point is developed later in this chapter. The second policy change can be briefly summarized here. Mahathir believes that the industrialized countries' abuse of the environment is greater than the South's and he has supplemented defense with attack on this issue.

Following his quadruple bypass operation in 1989, he seemed more patient. However, some of the change may have been occasioned, not by the operation itself, but by some of the public relations measures intended to "humanize" him afterwards, such as his attendance at a football game.[30]

Mahathir's devotion to his projects has been tested by the economic crisis of 1997. His most dear project, the MSC, has survived, but others, including the Bakun Dam, have been postponed; the economic crisis, added to its accumulation of misfortunes, was too damaging to make it immune. Other, long-term plans, for example "Vision 2020", are unlikely to be realized. His most esteemed policies, especially international policies, as opposed to projects, do not appear to have suffered. He is still supportive of the South, especially Bosnia, which is economically part of the South and religiously partly Muslim. Also, although it has not achieved the institutional form he desired, he is still campaigning for his version of the EAEC (pp. 129–30).

Nor, when sufficiently aroused, does Mahathir relax pressure on those he regards as threats or nuisances. This was true of his determination to crush Joseph Pairin, politically, after 1994 (p. 101) and to have Lim Guan Eng brought to trial, convicted and his appeal refused because of his comments on Rahim Tamby Chik, a favorite of Mahathir (p. 114). This was eminently true of his dismissal of Anwar.

The third sign of Mahathir's undimmed resoluteness is provided by his determination to remain in office. This was once more demonstrated, if a demonstration were needed, by his campaign against Anwar in 1998 (see pp. 165–7). His aim, on which the 1997 economic crisis inflicted severe damage, is to last long enough to make the success of his projects secure.

Maybe Mahathir has not mellowed. Maybe it is simply that those who have observed him for a long time have become used to him. It may be their judgments of him that have mellowed.

"Vision 2020": developed-country status and the end of ethnicity?

"Vision 2020" is an attractive title, presenting appealing concepts. It was so attractive, according to Mahathir, that it caught on in all kinds of contexts which had not been thought of when it was conceived. Mahathir suggested that perhaps there was *too* great an interest shown, although, of course, nothing could have been achieved if it had been ignored. Some people talked of a 2020 Walkathon, whatever that might mean, he said. Maybe, he mused, somebody would produce a 2020 toothpaste, but we should not be unduly bothered about that.[31] The date in the title refers to the year when it is planned that Malaysia will become a fully developed country. Speaking about it in 1993, Mahathir reminded his listeners that the hall in which he was addressing them had been designed, planned, and built in two and a half months and this augured well for the completion date of the Vision being achieved.

The Vision is quite different from the regular five-year plans. It is not detailed, with statistical tables and appendices. It is intended to seize the imagination and to inspire. Mahathir launched the idea in a publication in 1991,[32] and restated it later, particularly in a similarly titled keynote address in April 1997.[33] The main themes remained throughout. There were two main sections, one economic and one social, as well as a list of related "challenges," which Malaysia had to surmount. All was written so that it could be understood by a wide range of people. Targets were numerical for the economic section. They were realistic at the time, not long before the economic/financial crisis that began in August 1997. The Gross Domestic Product was to double every ten years between 1990 and 2020. It would be eight times larger at the end of the period than at the beginning, rising from 115bn. ringgit to 920bn. ringgit, in real terms. This would require a growth rate of about 7 percent in real terms over the period. Ingeniously, for demonstration purposes, Mahathir made the growth targets somewhat hard to reach, but said that a little extra effort would make it attainable and not beyond the capacity of Malaysians. In 1998, these targets seem optimistic. The rate had been achieved in Malaysia over the last decade or so, but this period had not included a recession. The 1997 crisis makes it unlikely that such a growth rate can be reached, at least in the early years.

He also elaborated the "challenges", which included: establishing a united Malaysian nation with a sense of common and shared destiny; fostering and developing a mature democratic society; creating a fully moral and ethical society; encouraging a scientific and progressive society; and creating an economically just society.

The first "challenge" is by far the most formidable, and stands out from the surrounding material. In effect, it constitutes the second main section. It means that the ethnic principles underlying Malaysian society are to be transformed. The system of ethnic relations, competitive sometimes to the verge of violence and occasionally beyond, is to end. It is the government's objective to establish a united Malaysian nation, with a sense of common and shared destiny. It must be at peace with itself, and territorially and ethnically integrated, living in harmony and in full and free partnership, made up of one "Bangsa Malaysia" (Malaysian race) with political loyalty and dedication to the nation.[34]

In spite of the violence in 1969, with time, government accommodation toward non-Malays has become more pronounced. In 1981 Mahathir gave a personal view. "I never was against the Chinese and other non-Malays. I just wanted to correct the imbalance."[35] Soon afterward, he identified a trend: he thought that the concept of racial politics would diminish to a certain extent. He added that he did not know how long it would take; a lot would depend on the NEP. Such sentiments were increasingly expressed by UMNO members, particularly toward and during the 1995 election. At the 1995 general election Anwar reiterated the message of "Vision 2020" (pp. 125–8) on the theme of ethnicity. Speaking to a mainly Chinese crowd in Sabah for an hour (in English, Malay, and Mandarin), he said he meant it when he referred to Malaysia as one big family, and appealed to them to make it work.[36] Since then, there have been further examples of greater ethnic liberality under the NDP, as opposed to its predecessor, the NEP. One recent example is that the Amanah Saham national savings scheme, previously restricted to Bumiputera, was opened to non-Malays as well.

Reactions to "Vision 2020" in July 1997 covered a wide spectrum. Several "opinion leaders" commented quite spontaneously, not in answer to questions. A non-Malay politician said that it kept people looking toward the future, not brooding on the past; a Malay politician took an instrumental approach – anything that he wanted to get approved, he linked closely to attaining the goals of "Vision 2020." A Malay academic asked that Dr. Mahathir himself should explain what it was really all about; a non-Malay politician remarked that they should have to see if race could be "pushed aside."[37] Not yet fully clear is the relation of "Vision 2020" to another concept of Mahathir's, the idea of a "New Malay" (Melayu Baru), mentioned in his speech to the UMNO General Assembly in 1991. The "New Malay" would have to meet exacting criteria: he or she had to be capable of meeting all challenges, had to be able to compete without assistance, must be knowledgeable, sophisticated, honest, disciplined, trustworthy, and competent.[38] This idea makes the effects of "Vision 2020" hard to predict. On one interpretation, the non-Malays by the year 2020 could also be described as "New Malays." Would they now resemble Malays as they had been, or some "New Malays," who would conform to higher standards of ability and behavior?

Some other questions remain concerning "Vision 2020." The NEP could have been implemented more slowly so that the process of transferring wealth and other benefits, such as employment, would have been gradual. As things happened, some non-Malays underwent dislocations in their lives (and some Malays had their expectations aroused, more than would have happened under a less drastic scheme than the NEP). If a slower course has been followed, perhaps the social/ethnic provisions of "Vision 2020" would not have seemed so startling. On the other hand, given the state of mind of some influential Malays in 1969, including Harun and Mahathir, something like the NEP was probably needed to defuse Malay feelings and contain possible further violence. As it is, the transition from the present ethnic arrangements, in which some residue of the NEP persists, to a future based on "Vision 2020" may be difficult.

A sensitive issue may be: can there be only one race, if there is more than one religion? Some Malays may believe that one race entails one religion.[39] The basic problem may be expressed in more general terms: after 2020 will life in Malaysia be lived in an integrated system or an assimilated one?[40]

Yet another important question is: should all existing examples of ethnic divisions in institutions be abolished? Should the Barisan, for example, be abolished because it is an "overarching party," with separate ethnic sections? Should other parties have to be multi-ethnic? If existing practices were changed, there might be great dissatisfaction on the part of some existing officeholders.[41]

In general, most objections to "Vision 2020" are likely to come from Malays. The leader of UMNO Youth accepts some features of "Vision 2020," but not all. He has argued that the ethnic quota system should be abolished so as to give all Malaysians equal opportunities by 2020. He claims that the country did practise meritocracy already, but that it should be expanded so that they will not be accused of favoring one ethnic group. He added that healthy competition internally would help Malaysia to maintain its competitive edge internationally. However, in his opinion, there should be no drastic measures, such as removing Malay privileges that are in the federal Constitution. He said that they want them to be retained, as the foundation of the Constitution.[42]

A question that goes to the roots of Malaysian political behavior is the effect that dismantling ethnic barriers will have on the class system and on voting behavior. It is often said that class as a basis for political affiliation is shut out, or attenuated, by ethnicity.[43] If ethnic divisions are weakened, or nullified, just how will the effects be manifested?

The easing of ethnic restrictions, envisaged by "Vision 2020," may be viewed from different aspects. It is clearly an attempt to strengthen national unity so that greater cooperation will improve Malaysia's economic capabilities and competitiveness. Also (pp. 133–4), it seems that, since the Malays' former "enemy" (the non-Malays, especially the Chinese) have been replaced, so to speak, by the West, the non-Malays should be coopted in a national struggle to promote economic prosperity and Asian values, and the Chinese are willing to cooperate.[44] The cooperation of the Chinese is even more vital than it was, because of their contacts with China, whose world status is on the rise. The coopted Chinese are now part of the solution to a "Malay dilemma" of today.

Mahathir; ideology; sources of advice on policy

Khoo advances the ingenious idea that there is a relatively coherent political ideology, "Mahathirism," although he immediately qualifies this by saying that it contains tensions, contradictions, and paradoxes.[45] The point is ably argued, and appropriate components are suggested: nationalism; capitalism; Islam; populism; and authoritarianism. (Liberalism is not included.) The links among the components are difficult to work out without seeing their place in Mahathir's own ordering of things. In other words, "Mahathirism" is not a guide to Mahathir's thoughts or actions. Rather, Mahathir's thoughts and actions are a guide to constructing "Mahathirism." Mahathirism is an exercise in allocating his thoughts into logical categories with the aim of achieving intellectual satisfaction and understanding.

The cabinet

Prime Ministers do not, and cannot, rule alone. There is cabinet collective responsibility for government policy. Moreover, it is physically impossible for the Prime Minister to examine, and act on, the whole range of policy decisions. There must be delegation via a "chain of command." Without scrutinizing the details of the machinery of government, some key institutions and persons are worth mentioning to indicate other main sources of advice on which Mahathir has relied.

The cabinet is the obvious place to start. Accounts of how it operates under Mahathir vary considerably. Sometimes one almost wonders if the ministers and ex-ministers are speaking about the same institution. Those who have had substantial differences with Mahathir give the impression that there is not much consultation, while those who get along with him better, tell a different story. Nevertheless these different versions of events are not irreconcilable. There seems to be broad agreement on a number of points. Apart from cabinet meetings, a relatively small number of ministers seem to have been consulted by Mahathir regularly. At cabinet meetings, not many ministers have displayed close knowledge about the agenda. One conscientious, and able, minister used to spend several hours familiarizing himself with it the night before, but this was exceptional.[46]

When in the cabinet, both Razaleigh and Musa had spoken knowledgeably and often. Other frequent participants included Daim, Anwar, Rafidah, and, on occasion, Samy Vellu. Before he ceased to be Deputy Prime Minister, Ghafar denied that Mahathir had practised "dictatorial" leadership in cabinet or elsewhere.

Daim, because of his experience and his closeness to Mahathir, was important because he could act as a brake on some of Mahathir's more impulsive actions. This was especially so in the early stages of the 1997 crisis when Daim performed this function temporarily, in conjunction with Anwar. (When Mahathir was criticized for lack of consultation on some issues, he retorted that Tunku had sometimes not consulted either, for instance on the important question of Singapore's separation from Malaysia.)

Several critics of Mahathir's handling of cabinet meetings have complained that the decisions reached were stated in general terms only. One cabinet member claimed that nothing beyond broad outlines was agreed on at that stage; the details came afterwards. Sometimes when a government policy was announced, he failed to recognize it as having been agreed to by cabinet.[47]

At party level, meetings of UMNO's supreme council are even less "consultative." Its membership overlaps with the cabinet's but some members are not in close touch with the direction that government policy is taking. supreme council meetings have been summed up as "government by fait acccompli."[48]

In both cabinet and the supreme council, the subject matter concerned tends to be more complex or technical than in previous administrations. Almost every member has ideas on what farmers are most unhappy about, but few are cognizant of developments in heavy industries, or have ideas about how to interest more foreign firms in the advantages offered by the MSC. Those who venture constructive views on such subjects are likely to be versed in economics, either by training or by experience.

Mahathir has other advisers, including the Japanese economist Kenichi Ohmae, who has given talks to the cabinet and senior civil servants. Mahathir has also made use of think-tanks, notably the Kuala Lumpur-based ISIS, particularly on foreign affairs.

The centralization of power which has occurred under Mahathir reflects not only tendencies that often become evident in organizations as they grow older, but also Mahathir's growing self-confidence, and perhaps also an increasing disinclination to suffer fools gladly.

The civil service

Because some of the members of the higher civil service have duties consisting of the administration and supervision of policy, it might be assumed that it plays no part in the formulation of policy. However, this would be incorrect. Those in the higher echelons of the service have been traditionally expected to advise ministers, including the Prime Minister, on policy.

What is different under Mahathir may be summarized in two statements. First, additional sources now play a greater part in supplying policy advice. Second, although some highly placed civil servants still advise ministers, the minister–civil servant relationship has changed.

The Malayan Civil Service (now the Malaysian Administrative and Diplomatic Service) was modeled on the British pattern. From that source, it inherited traditions of impartiality, high standards of honesty, and conscientiousness. It also had a (sometimes excessive) reliance on tradition and precedent.

Additionally, by 1957 (the date of independence), it was hierarchy conscious, and even before 1957, was obliged, by law, to give Malays (later, Bumiputera) preference in hiring.[49]

The civil service, particularly the Malaysian Administrative and Diplomatic Service, is expected to be politically neutral and to follow the orders of the government in power.[50] Real problems would arise, as they have done in some countries, if there were a change in the party in power; however, this has not yet happened at federal level in Malaysia. Originally the social classes from which the top Malay civil servants were appointed coincided quite closely with those from which the leading Malay politicians were drawn. Common social origins contributed to harmonious collaboration. Recruitment and promotion nowadays are more dependent on merit. Yet, because of UMNO's persistence as the dominant partner in government, it is hard for civil servants to conceive that any other party would be in power, federally, in the near future.

There do not seem to be any differences in principle between Mahathir's view of how the civil service should operate and those of his predecessors. But it appears to be affected by his general program for "modernization." On taking office, he was committed to a program of making it more efficient (p. 29). He seemed to be determined to eradicate complacency. By 1994, he had raised the standards required, and believed that he had convinced the civil service of the need for excellence.[51] In 1997, Anwar, in his capacity as Acting Prime Minister while Mahathir was abroad, initiated surprise visits to check on whether operations were proceeding in accordance with plans.[52]

The ideal relationship between the Prime Minister (and other ministers) and the civil service is hard to delineate. Basically, civil servants must give their unbiased advice to a minister, bearing in mind what the government policy is. Yet the final decision must be the minister's/Prime Minister's. Before Mahathir took over as Prime Minister, possibly the minister–civil servant relationship was too close, and the bureaucracy was perhaps aggrieved that the new government wanted the type of relationship to change. Later it was reported that changes were occurring; politicians were now making decisions that, previously, had been taken by civil servants, and there was now a tendency to make some civil service appointments on the basis of political and personal loyalties rather than on professional merit.[53]

Partly because of the rise of competing sources of advice, and Mahathir's tendency to consolidate power in his own hands, the influence of the civil service has been reduced since 1981.

Mahathir's non-achievements in policy

In two important areas, Mahathir's policies have been non-existent or non-successful. In one of these, supporting and encouraging respect for the judiciary and the rule of law, he has done nothing to indicate that his views on the subject have substantially changed since 1987 (pp. 46–9). In the second area, corruption, a campaign against it was launched in 1997, but so far (1998) with few apparent results.

The judiciary and the rule of law

Reports that Mahathir was anti-British and may have come to underestimate the study of law because he was rejected for a scholarship in Britain, do not seem to be easily verifiable.[54] Soon after he became Prime Minister, a biographer revealed him as something less than a staunch supporter of law. A chapter in this biography, entitled "The Rule of Law is Sacred," contains no quotes by Mahathir, although Musa and others are cited.[55] Two of his subsequent remarks after 1987 may be quoted, although the first is qualified and the second is cryptic. In 1994 he stated that members of the judiciary must be free to discharge their responsibilities, but added that there could not be 100 percent freedom in doing this.[56] In 1997 he said that he wanted people to accede to the rule of law, and linked discipline to observance of the rule of law. The government had to ensure orderliness. "We do not wish for a government so powerful that it could arrest people it did not like."[57]

Not only does Mahathir seem to have limited regard for the judiciary, he also thinks that medicine as a profession provides better training for politics than does practising law.[58] While accepting the cogency of some of his arguments, two comments may be relevant. A doctor can have a more immediate power of life or death over a patient than a lawyer usually has for a client. This is not to suggest, of course, that doctors abuse this power, but only that they might carry the consciousness of it into other spheres of activity such as politics. Also, he is "unaccustomed to having his patients dispute his diagnosis."[59]

Corruption

Perhaps Mahathir's greatest weakness in policy has been that he has failed to stem the growth of corruption, especially in the form of "money politics" in UMNO. This is not a new phenomenon (p. 26), but it has never been as widespread as in the late 1990s. Mahathir denounced it at both the 1994 and 1995 UMNO General Assemblies, and at the latter meeting his speech culminated in tears. The magnitude of the problem has been acknowledged. Yet the disciplinary action taken against UMNO transgressors has been limited. The practice continued at the 1996 UMNO General Assembly elections, although there were modifications in the methods used.[60]

Although money politics has probably been the most publicized form of corruption practised in Malaysia, it is not the only one. Yet, perhaps to avoid discouraging foreign investment, the Prime Minister and the government tend to play down other examples of corruption. Mahathir denied that corruption was rampant in Malaysia, although his rhetorical question, "How can we achieve an 8.5 percent growth rate over the last seven years, if we are as corrupt as is made out by the Western newspapers?"[61] fails to meet the point. Allegations of corruption are directed not toward the issue of growth but are attacks on illegal practices and on a distorted pattern of the ownership of wealth. Critics who allege corruption blame, possibly cynically, the example of the ruling group at any particular time.[62] By 1997, the question of corruption was too obvious for the government to ignore.

The problem came to a head – though not the solution – during Mahathir's absence from Malaysia in 1997, when he directed Anwar, who was Acting Prime Minister, to launch an attack on corruption. He did so, and in addition to intensifying investigations of corruption (though not apparently of the "big fish"), forums were held on the causes of corruption, attended by members of government, opposition parties, and research institutions and other groups.[63]

There were no quick or spectacular results from the new campaign against corruption. Some limited evidence of long-term improvement in government activity against corruption was found in statistics provided by Anti-Corruption Agency (ACA), although it was stated that most cases probably remained undetected. While over two thousand people were arrested, 1977–86, nearly three thousand were arrested in the ten years after that, and the number of prosecutions also rose.[64] This suggests greater vigilance on the part of the ACA, and also more government interest in combatting corruption.

In 1997, Chandra Muzaffar highlighted once more the crucial role of elites. There was, he claimed, often an unwillingness on the part of ruling elites to move deliberately against corruption, particularly where their own interests were concerned.[65]

Mahathir himself had written on the evils of corruption in the mid-1970s. He defined corruption as a practice that enabled someone in office to obtain remuneration through illegitimate means.[66] His analysis of its causes, the forms that it assumed, and the difficulties of dislodging it once established, was well grounded. He dramatically envisioned the frightening possible consequences for a country's government: it could lead to its downfall and a state of chaos; eventually corruption might become a way of life.[67]

Unfortunately, he did not advance any suggestions on how the problem should be tackled. The determining factor in fighting it was not the method or machinery used against it, but the system of values of the society. A relevant consideration, he stated, was to prevent elections from encouraging competition for benefits which led to corruption. The conclusion must surely be that the book is of little help as a guide to how to suppress corruption. In retrospect, the NEP may be judged as having been *too* successful insofar as it implanted the desire to make money, without also inculcating the balancing virtues of honesty and social responsibility (p. 71).

Mahathir's achievements and limitations: innovation versus rationality?

Mahathir believes, correctly, that innovation is one of the outstanding characteristics of leadership: "for me, at least, it is the ability to provide guidance. And your guidance should be something superior to what your people can do by themselves. You must have initiatives and ideas that are not common."[68]

Some of Mahathir's ideas that were acclaimed as innovative, were not really so. "Look East" was an assortment of ideas, loosely held together by the choice of a catchy title. Privatization consisted of the adoption of ideas already put into practice elsewhere. What was really novel was its controversial close association with UMNO's corporate activities. Technically, for the most part, privatization was well planned and implemented, the Economic Planning Unit being largely responsible. The heavy industry policy, as exemplified by the Proton Saga and other vehicles, was innovative in Malaysia, and justifiable, provided that the need for subsidies was accepted. Other examples fall into various categories. Perwaja steel was proceeded with on the basis of untested assumptions, and, saddled with the added burden of "mismanagement," was continued with only because of dedication to "sunk costs," and it has constituted a continuing drain on Malaysia's resources. The Bakun Dam had more than its share of bad luck, but also was managed by firms, some of which lacked appropriate experience, and which did not work well together. When scrutinized according to more market-oriented criteria after the 1997 crisis, its financial weaknesses were revealed, as well as the heavy cost to the taxpayers. Another example, his penchant for grandiose buildings, is reminiscent of the disposition of former President Sukarno.

Policies that were not concerned directly with physical construction warrant a more favorable appraisal. Among these were Mahathir's consistent encouragement of foreign investment. Also, although Mahathir disliked competition in several domestic sectors (p. 160), his expressed view was that free trade was of benefit and protectionism was an evil,[69] which, however, seemed at variance with his policies toward Malaysia's car industry. He encouraged foreign investment by liberalizing NEP restrictions on investment, particularly in 1986.[70]

On ethnic relations inside Malaysia, the climax, for this century, was his statement and restatement of "Vision 2020," yet, even before that, there had been a relaxation of practices that were distasteful to the non-Malays, and the replacement of the NEP by the less discriminatory NDP (pp. 72–3). If the direction of policy changes followed during the 1990s can be continued, it will indeed augur well for the implementation of "Vision 2020;" however, there are signs that there may not be wholehearted endorsement of the new, more tolerant, ethnic policies by Malays (p. 167).

Mahathir's policy on Islam followed the trends established by the governments that preceded his (p. 85), yet his determined bid to take over control of how Islam should be interpreted and implemented in Malaysia illustrated very well how political will could have truly innovative effects on policy.

Mahathir's capacity for innovation has been also apparent in his foreign policy. His championing of his own vision in the form of the EAEC was not entirely successful (pp. 128–30). However, he established the reputation of being one of the most steadfast promoters of Asian values in the debates with the West concerning human rights and democracy. He also enlisted, and often led, the

"South," and was recognized as a leading exponent of its point of view. He invoked the support of the South to help the East reach a balance with the West. This acknowledgement of leadership was a remarkable feat, given the size of Malaysia's population and resources, and even led to it being ranked by some as a "middle power."[71]

Innovationary measures in Malaysia's tertiary education have met with less international publicity than they deserve, but they merit attention because they attempt to lay out a comprehensive policy in an area where there are quite deep-seated conflicts. The present policy, put together by Najib, the Education Minister, tries to reverse previous policies which have threatened to marginalize English, a key element in Malaysia's economic future. In doing this, it also hopes to pacify the powerful Malay-language lobby, which is sustained by the mystique enjoyed by *Bahasa Malaysia*. The aim is to reconcile these objectives with the aspirations of non-Malays by making Chinese (and Tamil) more accessible in primary schools, even for Malays. This is in accord with the objectives conveyed in "Vision 2020," and also takes account of China's growing economic ascendancy and its growing importance for Malaysia. Additionally, at the tertiary education level, there will be more emphasis on science and technology, compared with arts.[72] There is to be a technical university, and foreign universities are now opening branch campuses in Malaysia. All these measures should contribute to keeping Malaysia educationally equipped to derive the optimum rewards from growing economic opportunities.[73]

Decision-making: rationality

It may be useful to look at Mahathir's methods of decision-making and the varying degrees of difficulty that problems presented for him. Sometimes it has been easy for him to rectify an omission, simply by fiat:

> I saw Kuala Lumpur when I first came here, and thought it was a very bleak town. I said, "why don't you plant trees?" I kept on saying this but it never happened…until you have the authority to say, "Plant!"[74]

Once Mahathir was Prime Minister, problems of this sort presented fewer difficulties. However, it is easier to see whether a tree is present or not, than to assess the cleanliness of a toilet without close personal inspection. Mahathir fought a continuing battle on this topic, especially on airport toilets. As a doctor, he had a special interest in this. Yet even a problem of this kind can be kept under control, if persistence is sustained. The intractable cases concern mainly forces outside of Malaysia, and therefore beyond Mahathir's jurisdiction. An obvious example of the former was encountered when his concept of the EAEC met with opposition (pp. 128–30). The barriers to the exercise of political will are much stronger externally than internally. That is what sovereignty is all about.

Unfortunately, when Mahathir has set his heart on a project, such as the MSC, or the Bakun Dam, he has acted as if cost–benefit considerations did not apply. He has certainly implied as much by identifying some projects as "national" projects, and indicating that they could not be allowed to fail. Such language is not compatible with that of an economist, who thinks in terms of cost–benefit, "sacrificed alternatives," and so on. No amount of political will can compensate for an approach that is not rational. Political will is a necessary, but not a sufficient, condition for success.

The uncertainties surrounding both costs and benefits concerning the MSC are so great that it seems almost impossible to quantify them. In mid-1997, Mahathir's track record could have been taken into account as a plus factor in estimating the chances of the MSC's success. Now (1998) this seems to be not such a safe assumption as it was previously.

In 1986 the Malaysian writer Rehman Rashid identified the non-quantitative element in Mahathir's policy-making, but thought that experience might have curbed it:

After five years as Prime Minister...confidence has been distinctly tempered with realism. Dr. Mahathir has not let go of his vision of what Malaysia could and should be in the future, but the vicissitudes of the past couple of years seem to have given him a new and possibly valuable pragmatism regarding Malaysia as it is now. The dreamer has come down to earth.[75]

This conclusion may have been premature, as the events of 1997 suggest.

Mahathir's handling of the 1997 economic crisis; 1998, stablilizing the ringgit

Mahathir's decision-making style during a period of crisis is best illustrated by his actions during the economic crisis, which started in August 1997 and has still to run its course (pp. 175–8). This section seeks to pose three questions. First, what were the main reasons for the crisis? Second, what did the Malaysian government do in order to deal with it? Third, what did Mahathir's responses reveal about his approaches and adaptability in reacting to such situations?

First, the following features are identifiable as having contributed to Malaysia's problems: (1) the current account deficit was high; (2) the banks were under-regulated; (3) the government was too much inclined to bail out firms that were in trouble, e.g., United Engineers Malaysia (pp. 59–62) and Ekran, a key player in the consortium that was building the Bakun Dam; (4) too many big structural projects were being attempted at one time. To a large extent, the crisis occurred in the private sector, but many of the firms involved were closely linked with the government, and even more closely linked when the public sector bailed them out, that is, took over some of their debts. Bailouts took the form of transferring liability to solvent governmental agencies, such as Petronas. Allegedly, such "rescues" often favored government leaders, or their relatives, or firms with de facto links to UMNO. Sometimes organizations which were non-Bumiputera-owned assumed liability by relaxing existing rules, thus benefiting the economy.

In spite of these weaknesses, the Asian economies concerned, including Malaysia, had strengths which were obscured by the waves of panic that swept from country to country. Among them were: high savings, budget surpluses, flexible labor markets, and low taxation.[76]

Second, for Malaysia to join the "orthodox" stream of international economic thinking, Mahathir had to soft-pedal his original public complaint that the crisis was caused mainly by the activities of "rogue speculators" rather than market forces that had their origins in weaknesses of certain Asian economies. He had to agree to adopt retrenchment measures in some existing projects. This was done, and was seemingly based on cost–benefit principles. Expenditure was halted, or postponed, on Bakun, and on some not really essential road, port, and airport schemes, although later this seemed uncertain. The MSC emerged substantially unscathed, although some ancillary projects were affected. Mahathir's enthusiasms were checked, although it might be argued that there was a trade-off, Mahathir's *quid pro quo* being the continuation of the MSC. Mahathir had to change his entire frame of reference. He had looked at things from a construction-engineering perspective. There was a "real world" of bridges, ports, airports, highways, dams, and corridors.[77] How could this be made to vanish into thin air merely by the manipulation of money? How could finance possess a life of its own? This belief was in contrast to the pragmatism that he often practised.

Malaysia's responses did not encourage confidence, because initially they were not coordinated. They were, rather, a "resultant" of pulls in one direction by Mahathir and of pulls in another direction by Daim and Anwar. This was evident in budgetary policy. While Mahathir was still repeating his conspiracy theories and trying to save his pet projects from cuts, Anwar and Daim were quietly taking action along "orthodox" economic lines. Anwar's first "extra" budget (October 17, 1997) did not cut expenditure deeply enough, as shown by the reactions of the stock market and the exchange rate. Its successor (November 5, 1997) received approval because it checked the fall in share prices and in the value of the ringgit.

In spite of these measures, there was no immediate improvement in the economy. On the contrary, the IMF estimate of the 1998 real GDP growth per head (8 percent in 1997) was revised to 2.5 percent at the end of December 1997, and in January 1998 the ringgit to US dollar rate reached the level of nearly 5 to 1, before falling back down to only just over 4 to 1. As mid-1998 approached, it seemed that growth for the current year would be negative, and would perhaps reach minus 5 percent.

In May 1998, Mahathir said that he was unsure that Malaysia could achieve its goal of becoming a developed nation by 2020. However, Malaysia, unlike South Korea, Indonesia, and Thailand, has not sought direct help from the IMF. In March 1998, the IMF signified its approval, in general terms, of Malaysian economic policies, according to the Malaysian press. Yet, in May, it commented that rapid growth in money supply should be tightened and that there should be greater fiscal transparency.

In November 1997, it was announced that a National Economic Action Council (NEAC) would be set up. The executive secretary would be Daim, and Mahathir and Anwar would be the chairman and deputy chairman, respectively. The NEAC's exact role was not specified. It drew up plans, and may have been intended primarily to concentrate economic power in Daim's hands. Reporting on the crisis has been limited by the government; indeed newspaper editors have been told not to use the term. In January 1998, Datuk Nasri Abdullah, editor of *Berita Harian*, considered an Anwar supporter, was compelled to resign.[78] He was reinstated, but in July was forced to resign again. Among other things, newspapers in his group had referred to conflicting statements by government leaders.

It is not clear how much Mahathir has learned from the crisis. He continued to voice his early complaints of dangers from international speculators at the G-15 developing countries summit, held in Kuala Lumpur in late November 1997. In his opening speech, Mahathir attacked currency speculators who represented a "new imperialism," worse than the old.[79] He was supported by President Suharto. However, it seemed that his early "denial" of the problem was being replaced by circumspection. At the Commonwealth Heads of Government Meeting in Edinburgh in November 1997, replying to a question about speculation and the ringgit, he observed: "I have been told not to shoot my mouth too much, because, any time I do, the ringgit falls down."[80] By December 1997, he sounded uncharacteristically plaintive, telling reporters after the ASEAN informal summit that Southeast Asia had to accept that there was no equality in the world, and that "might" was still "right."[81] He might, at last, have come down to earth. His failure to do so earlier could have been a fatal flaw. The gloomier economic statistics, accompanied by the difficulties experienced by business, sometimes resulting in bankruptcies, led to dissension in the leadership over how to deal with what was now recognized as a major recession. While the immediate Malaysian response to the crisis in 1997 was to cause Anwar and Daim to work together temporarily to check some of Mahathir's less conventional economic ideas, by the middle of 1998 Daim supported Mahathir's expansionist policies as opposed to Anwar's emphasis on restraint, illustrated, for example, by their contrasting views on interest rates.

The division of opinion was exacerbated by disagreement about the time when Mahathir should hand over power to Anwar, while Suharto's recent forced resignation from the Indonesian presidency must have induced concern in Mahathir to avoid a similar fate. He decided that Malaysia's partial adoption of IMF-type policies was apparently not succeeding; they were causing widespread distress, which might alienate electoral support. He revived his 1997 theme; the ringgit had to be protected from speculators. Now he believed that the best way to achieve this was to prevent fluctuations in the exchange rate, which he fixed, for the time being, at 3.80 ringgit to the US$. Ringgit outside the country would become worthless after September 30, 1998, and foreign portfolio investments would earn no return unless they remained in the country for at least a year. Appropriate exceptions were made, for instance, to pay for student tuition abroad and for foreign travel. The controls would operate for an indefinite period. [82]

As might have been expected, "orthodox" economists (including the governor and deputy governor of the Bank Negara, the national bank – who resigned – and, reputedly, Anwar) did not agree with the new policy. The arguments used against the controls were predictable. Foreign investments, heavily relied upon by Malaysia, would be reduced; if too rapid economic expansion were attempted, the sustainability of the new rate would be called in question; experience had shown that such controls were conducive to the creation of black markets and to evasion through corruption.

Paul Krugman, an "unorthodox" economist, whose views partly coincided with Mahathir's, warned that such policies could succeed only under certain conditions. The controls should only be temporary, for several reasons. The longer they lasted, the more the economy would be "distorted" away from market forces; if used to defend an over-valued currency, they could lead to a permanent system of trade protection; they should not be regarded as a substitute for necessary institutional reform, for instance in the restructuring and recapitalization of banks. [83] Whole-hearted approval for Mahathir's measures was accorded, perhaps, only by "ordinary people", who were suffering from the existing market-driven policies. [84]

By definition, changes in the (now fixed) exchange rate could not be used to measure the effects of the policies. Changes in stock market prices were not explainable without knowing the background. In early September 1998, these prices shot up. Some dealers, however, attributed the rise, not to public support but to "orchestrated" government intervention. [85] The government was also responsible for the rise in another way. It was expected that companies with strong government connections would benefit from bailouts or the awarding of official contracts, so the expectation was that their value would appreciate; they would be a "good buy".

In the long run, the success or otherwise of Mahathir's changes in economic policies will tend to be reflected in growing or diminishing electoral support. However, if economic woes can be convincingly attributed to external influences, the effects on government popularity may be moderated. Also, increasingly authoritarian rule, suppression of dissent, and more pressures on the judiciary, may make elections less important.

Democracy and authoritarianism in Malaysia

Scholars are driven by a perpetual urge to classify their material, and political scientists are no exception. One of their longest (as old as Aristotle) and perhaps most frustrating quests is to compare various types of rule. How many people rule a country? Is the result beneficial or otherwise? The quest is frustrating because definitions have become more and more detailed in order to capture the nuances of various systems of government,[86] and because the evaluation of benefits and disadvantages depends a good deal on individual interpretation.

Discussion of types of rule may necessitate new terminology or imagining two "poles" and a spectrum which stretches between them.[87] At one end lies the "democratic" pole, and at the other is the authoritarian. At the former, a high proportion of government decisions reflect high participation, or input, from a substantial proportion of the citizens. At the latter, fewer citizens make, or influence, a smaller number of decisions. Third World countries, like Malaysia, are in some respects, or at some periods, more democratic, or less so, than at other times, but the estimation of the type of rule fluctuates. A related meaning is to speak in terms of government responsiveness to groups' demands: from the point of view of non-Malays, the government would be behaving more democratically if it became more responsive to their demands. In Malaysia, the situation is complicated by ethnicity, which, in spite of "Vision 2020," cannot at present be left out of consideration.

There is one other element to take into account. It is useful to talk about "authoritarian" rule as a contrast to "democratic" rule. However, there are other meanings of "authoritarian," for example, to describe behavior that is linked to the use just mentioned, but in a different context. One is related to the characteristics and behavior of a *person*. The term could be applied to certain aspects of Mahathir's behavior as described at the start of this chapter, or later in the section on "Consultation" (pp. 168–70). There is yet another possibility: "authoritarianism" is sometimes intended to describe a government that acts so as to restrict freedom, or rights. "Authoritarianism," in one context, is contrasted with democracy; in another it is contrasted with approval of, or the promotion of, rights or freedoms. The distracting fact is that a government action could be authoritarian in both senses.[88] An example would be the arrest of Malaysian opposition leaders in 1987. This, of course, would inhibit the freedom, or rights, of the persons concerned. But, also, because their actions helped to preserve democracy by providing competition at elections, their arrests were harmful to the democratic process. Here we shall be using "authoritarian"/"authoritarianism" mostly as constituting a contrast to democracy.

If the government uses its powers of detention sparingly, it is quite possible that it has curtailed human rights and freedoms, without having been deliberately anti-democratic. But if there are large-scale detentions, as in 1987 in Malaysia, it is very likely that a main motive has been to limit the competition of opposition parties, which strikes at the heart of democracy.

A government may combine repression with responsiveness. Crouch cites the example of government reactions to protests over toll increases for the North–South Highway in 1990.[89] Five DAP supporters, headed by its candidate for a forthcoming election, were detained for using violence. However, shortly afterwards the toll was suspended and later the amount was halved. The messages seem to have been: we agree that you have a grievance, but we do not want to seem to be taking action just because of your protests.

Major steps towards, or away from, authoritarianism are usually well marked. The former could be detected in the government's actions after May 13, 1969, which clearly curtailed human rights. In striking contrast was the trend in governmental policies in the early 1990s, which became increasingly responsive to some non-Malay grievances (p. 96). If "Vision 2020" is implemented as planned, this would be a convincing demonstration of receptiveness to some deep-seated non-Malay sources of discontent, although, unfortunately, it would not be responsive to the wishes of some Malays (p. 167).

If the role of ethnicity is indeed diminished, a consequence may be that class differences, at present, as it were, preempted by ethnic factors,[90] might assume greater importance in determining political behavior.

Unfortunately, the existence of governmental repressive instruments, and those who wield them, adopted mainly to meet the Communist threat some fifty years ago, affords a constant temptation to governments to use them against its opponents. Yielding to this opportunity provides an authoritarian bias to the system. Many of the detentions in 1987 were examples of this abuse.

Until the economic crisis of 1997, it seemed that there were two tendencies that might help to make Malaysia more democratic. One, the growth of a middle class, or classes, is perhaps too optimistic (pp. 62–4). However, the other is that, if "Vision 2020" proceeds as planned, the influence of ethnicity in politics may be diluted, and a more fluid party system may develop. Coalitions might be formed that are more viable than the "shotgun" versions attempted for the 1990 and 1995 elections (p. 46). However, with the crisis, if there is inequality in the distress suffered by different ethnic groups, ethnic tensions could increase. The Malaysian economy will probably suffer a recession in 1998. If, as in the mid-1980s, the government then loses so much support that its tenure of office is imperilled, even remotely, it may adopt more authoritarian measures.

Mahathir's use of such measures is compatible with his skeptical views on democracy. These were discussed earlier, when they were contrasted with Western views, which he felt were being aggressively thrust upon Malaysia and some other Asian states. His reactions are consonant with some of his personal authoritarian traits (pp. 180–4). More explicitly, he has stated his unflattering opinions on democracy in the Malaysian context. His ideas in August 1969 were forthright: "we must accept that there is not going to be democracy in Malaysia, there never was and there never will be."[91] After May 13, he expressed a congruent belief: authoritarian rule can at least produce a stable and strong government.[92]

He was also skeptical about a variation, "limited democracy," which he claimed was introduced in Malaysia in 1971, when constitutional restrictions were introduced, aimed at minimizing inter-ethnic violence.[93]

Mahathir believes that democracy is only a means to an end, which is stability and freedom from fear:

> If democracy in its liberal form can deliver that, well and good. But if liberal democracy only results in insecurity, fear and poverty, then democracy must be tempered with responsibility so that it delivers what it is supposed to deliver.[94]

When dealing with the relationship between democracy and authoritarianism, Mahathir makes some statements particularly relevant to Malaysia. In his classic address at Trinity College, Oxford, in 1985 (a model for speech-writers), he stated: "In fact many authoritarian regimes have been the expression of the electorate's will freely exercised. Many authoritarian governments have been elected by the will of the people who want strong no-nonsense administration."[95] There are difficulties with this statement. What "the people" want may be difficult to ascertain precisely, but did they really want the government to override the opinions of the judiciary? In other words, does the fact of having been elected entitle a government to do whatever it likes? Mahathir certainly has behaved as if being elected conferred absolute power.

Under the first four prime ministers, authoritarian measures were in fact used against political opponents. Also, perhaps most obviously in 1987, they were used, principally but not exclusively, to contain ethnic violence. Mahathir, for this purpose, avoided the harder alternative of restraining his own top followers, mainly Najib, and preferred to detain smaller fry on the government side, as well as opposition supporters and non-political figures. Even when only *threatened*, detention was a powerful weapon, not only against persons, but against human rights and democracy.

In Malaysia, then, the degree of democracy varies over time. Yet the regime is not unstable. It may relax its control somewhat, but it has the means, and under Mahathir the will, to make "corrections," so that the degree of control that it desires is established.[96]

Democracy inside UMNO

It is interesting to speculate on the democracy/authoritarianism relation, not only in Malaysia, but also in UMNO, its dominant political party.[97] It has become a cliché to say that the "real" elections in Malaysia are the UMNO elections. Actually there are two possible meanings of the statement. The first is that in general elections, under present circumstances, the Barisan is bound to win; what is at issue is only the *extent* of the win and the shifts in power within its component parties which are assessable from variations from area to area. The second is that there is more "democracy" in UMNO elections than in general elections. However, it can be contended that, over time, not only has there been a decline in democracy in Malaysia, there has also been a decrease in democracy inside UMNO.[98] It would appear that these two trends are not related in any simple way.[99] Each appears to result from the "iron law of oligarchy."[100] As organizations grow older, power tends to become more and more concentrated. In both country and party there has been a tendency to make changes for expeditiousness and convenience, even if they have restricted discussion and consultation. The point is that it has been mainly the same person – the president of UMNO who is also Prime Minister – who has benefited from (and also often promoted) the concentration of power at the top of government and party. He has had the advantage of being able to influence voting for the top posts in

UMNO. He has also been able to accelerate or decelerate the rise of aspiring UMNO leaders through allocating the important or dead-end jobs in government. His actions in one of these areas may be undertaken in order to influence events in the other.

It is true that, even after the Communist threat receded, Tunku, Razak, and Hussein successively constrained the activities of opposition parties, as well as the freedom of particular political opponents. Mahathir's authoritarianism, which perhaps reached its apex in 1987, was therefore not without precedents. Nevertheless, it was distinctive in two ways. By 1987, the menace of Communism was negligible, and the need for repression less justified than previously. Also, the scale of the 1987 detentions was so great, and the activities of some detainees were so remote from direct political significance, that the arrests amounted to a giant leap toward the authoritarian pole of the spectrum.

Democracy is not an ideal form of government. Mahathir is well aware of its imperfections and he has not invested it with any mystique, unlike the leaders of the United States. It seems that he was not sufficiently attached to it to deter him from behaving in an authoritarian manner. The Prime Minister/UMNO president has to assess where the threats to his power are coming from. If they come from opposition parties, an appropriate response has been to become more authoritarian in the exercise of governmental powers. If they have been for power inside UMNO, then he has had to make his rule in UMNO more authoritarian, that is, increase the power of the incumbents. This was Mahathir's strategy when UMNO Baru was registered, and "bonus votes" were invented.[101] When this seemed not to benefit Mahathir in fighting off the challenge of his deputy, Anwar, the two, at Mahathir's insistence, agreed to "freeze" their respective positions by having no contests for the top positions before 1999. To avoid a clash between these two strong personalities, democracy was put on hold at UMNO's highest levels. It was openly said that unity in UMNO was more important than democracy: "Democracy without a strong party is meaningless," according to Mahathir.[102]

Populism

"Populism" is not a term that springs to mind in describing Mahathir's style of government. It would suggest that he values the beliefs and opinions of the people, which is not otherwise evident. It is true that he has enjoyed visiting rural areas, in order to keep in touch with rural people's feelings and grievances. But he has not needed to obtain the support of the people directly, except on special occasions. The government apparatus and UMNO are both efficient organizations, which are regularly working to ensure his popularity and sustain his power.

However, during Mahathir's struggles in the 1980s, first against the rulers, and then with the Team B faction of UMNO, headed by Razaleigh, Mahathir became quite deeply involved. These were not the equivalent of the recurring general elections, they were essential to protect UMNO against the "feudalism" of the monarchy, and then against its being taken away from his control. They

were contests that were vital for his retention of power. Mahathir, who is generally shy, and who distrusts crowds, found that he likes addressing people who
come to welcome and hear him.

He enjoyed similar experiences from participating in the SEMARAK (loyalty
with the people) movement,[103] which was launched in 1988 ostensibly to
strengthen the rapport between the federal and state governments, and bring
leaders at all levels closer to the people. It may be seen as an effort to consolidate
the victory of UMNO Baru, and establish its legitimacy for the next (1990)
general elections. Mahathir and other leaders took part in a variety of well-
publicized rural activities, such as threshing and driving tractors. In fact, the
SEMARAK campaign was more than just this. Individuals and organized
groups were mobilized to express undivided loyalty to Malaysia through
Mahathir, and to extol his virtues at feet-stomping, raised-arm salute, pledge-
taking ceremonies across the country. The Information Minister announced that
the private sector and individuals contributed about one-fifth of the costs.
Mahathir's speeches to audiences in "the South" might also be classified as
populist.

Of course, there is no discrepancy between being a populist and also being
authoritarian. Populism is acting so as to secure the support of the masses.
Authoritarianism is one of the styles of rule used in order to govern. Marshal
Sarit, one of Thailand's most effective authoritarian leaders of the 1950s, was
also a master of populist techniques.[104]

The methods used in November 1997 to rally support for Mahathir during
the financial/currency crisis in Malaysia were reminiscent of the SEMARAK
campaign. However, most of the demonstrations that occurred relied more on
the support of existing organizations than SEMARAK had done.

Conclusion

Malaysian academic Johan Saravanamuttu, when listing factors that enter into
Malaysia's formulation of foreign policy, uses "idiosyncratic" to refer to the influence of individual actors.[105] Dictionary definitions agree that the word refers to
a characteristic, habit, or mannerism that is particular to an individual. It would
seem that Mahathir could be described as an idiosyncratic person within an
idiosyncratic category. His beliefs and actions are unusual, constituting a pattern
that has been fascinating to previous, as well as the present, writers. He has a
sharp mind rather than an intellectual or academic mind. He is happiest when
dealing with the world of objects, construction, and gadgets. He is captivated by
the way things work. His interest is greater if they are huge or fast, or both. He is
less at home in the world of economics, although he performed well as Minister
of Trade and Industry before becoming Prime Minister. Many of his *aperçus* and
evaluations have been built on the basis of analogies, such as the likening of the
Malays in the 1960s to the inhabitants of the "South" in the 1990s.

By the time he became Prime Minister, he had accumulated an assortment of
idées fixes, or stereotypes, mostly unfavorable, concerning such groups as

members of the British Commonwealth, journalists, Jews, human rights activists, and, latterly, speculators in foreign exchange. Occasionally, he has uttered intemperate statements. After seeing the "North" breaking down national barriers through globalization, he thought that the "South" should retaliate: "We should migrate North in the millions, legally or illegally.... Masses of Asians and Africans should inundate Europe and America." He hoped, however, that the "South" should not have to resort to this action.[106]

To many foreign observers, Mahathir's extreme statements detracted from his attainment of *gravitas*, a favorite term of Lee Kuan Yew's when assessing politicians in Singapore, indicating that the person's opinions carry weight and should be listened to.

Sometimes, however, statements by Mahathir are intended to shock; the aim is to get attention. A 1979 example was Mahathir ordering Malaysians to shoot on sight the boat people who had escaped from Vietnam who entered Malaysian waters and then tried to land. Mahathir wished to alert the United States to the size of the problem. Other Mahathir outbursts have not been too productive. His verbal attacks on speculators in 1997, combined with his inappropriate initial response of trying to prohibit the export of capital, contributed to the weakening, instead of the strengthening, of the ringgit.

Mahathir combines the conviction that he is always right, with a firm determination to stay in power. (After all, the latter follows from the former.) For his sustenance, power is as necessary as food. He is a workaholic, and during his "Look East" campaign, and afterwards, he urged Malays to work hard as well, although many may have derived less enjoyment from their work than he has from his.

Mahathir has looked back, as well as forward, when he has considered his own possession of power. To UMNO politicians who were eager for advancement, he has urged patience and has told them that he himself had been in UMNO for twenty-eight years before he became a minister.[107]

Even before Mahathir became Prime Minister (1981) he repeatedly told UMNO members that, if they felt that a leader was no longer suitable, they could always get rid of him.[108] This might have been applicable to some leaders. Others, Mahathir himself included, would have been quite resistant to being dislodged.

In Indonesia, a reason often given to explain Suharto's unwillingness to resign was that his children's extensive business holdings would become vulnerable after his departure from office.[109] However, in Malaysia, although Mahathir's sons own large assets[110], these are not so widely known about, and the owners not so likely to become a target of popular feeling after Mahathir's retirement.

In 1995 Mahathir was asked what he thought was his greatest achievement and what he considered his greatest disappointment.[111] His answer to the first question was that he had brought the races together. The reply was quite well founded. To be sure, "Vision 2020," though announced, had not yet started to be implemented. Yet the Barisan's success in attracting a greater share of the Chinese vote at the 1995 general election (maybe 10 percent more compared with 1990) justified his point. Mahathir's answer to the second question was that he was disappointed because the Bumiputera had not benefited sufficiently so far. This also was an apposite judgment; the targets of the (now superseded) NEP had lagged behind schedule. However, if one might rephrase the question so that it would relate to *several* items that ranked as achievements and several others that might evoke disappointment, some additions might be suggested. Other achievements include the government's handling of Islamic issues and some of its construction projects (not the Bakun Dam). Another is his successful "wooing" of the "South."

Of the additional disappointments, the most obvious is growing corruption. It almost seems as if either the government is unable to contain it, or that its political will, however strong on most issues, in this instance is not very strong. In either case, this reflects adversely on the government. Another disappointment is the authoritarianism in Mahathir's government, particularly seen in the dismantling of the independence of the judiciary. Also, meritocracy is not pronounced in the government's dealings with business. Yet another disappointment, of course, is that the 1997 economic crisis caught the government by surprise, and the early responses to it were inappropriate. Until then, Malaysia's economic development had constituted an outstanding achievement.[112]

There is also reason for sadness because factions in UMNO became more acrimonious than those under any previous president, so acrimonious that the party split, was declared an illegal organization, and had to be reconstituted. Moreover, there was a swift transition from traditional deference in UMNO to an era of rampant money politics without any perceptible intervening period of democracy in the party in which money played only a limited role. He also disrupted the process of succession to the leadership which, until then, had been widely admired internationally as a model for the smooth transition of power.

Nevertheless, until August 1997, Mahathir's achievements had outweighed his deficiencies. Political experts and Malaysian business people thought that he had scored, numerically, 80 percent "plus," as opposed to 20 percent "minus." Since the 1997 crisis, the figures may be less favorable.[113]

Some last thoughts on Mahathir may be mentioned, along with speculations about "might have beens." Mahathir may not have "mellowed" very much, but there have been recent nuanced changes in his interests and his style. He has become more conscious of his roots in Kedah, and has shown deep interest in the development policies of Sanusi, the Menteri Besar.[114] Projects in the state were encouraged by the federal government, although they were slowed down by the 1997 crisis. Mahathir is coming to resemble Tunku in several respects, although the essence of Tunku is inimitable. The UMNO constitution has been repeatedly amended (as Mahathir formerly attacked Tunku for having done). His contacts with well-off Chinese have increased – Mahathir censured Tunku's close association with them in 1969. As Mahathir has become more esteemed and prosperous, his lifestyle has become more upper class.

It is interesting, but fruitless, to speculate on what Musa or Razaleigh might have done, if either had become Prime Minister. Almost certainly, neither would have been as innovative, and both would have managed things more conservatively. They would have taken fewer risks. Yet the question assumes that either of them could have triumphed over Mahathir. Even if Mahathir had temporarily lost office, his determination would have been so strong that he would not have given up easily.

During his tenure of power he has defeated every threat to his rule in a masterful fashion. However, in so doing he has eliminated from the political scene just about any possible successor approaching the caliber of the best he has eliminated.

Postscript

Little has occurred since Anwar's arrest (September 20, 1998) to point the way to what the outcome of the Mahathir–Anwar struggle may be. Mahathir's determination to wield the unseparated powers of government to the full has been demonstrated yet again. After Anwar was detained under the ISA, before being held for trial under less strict conditions, he was shown to have been physically abused and to have suffered head injuries while in police custody. Rallies after his arrest, some very well-attended, were increasingly marked by violence, sometimes encouraged by provocateurs, and the police became less tolerant. Arrests were made of persons close to Anwar, and his wife, Dr. Wan Azizah, was warned not to make political speeches.

The timing of some important events is not yet known. One exception is that Anwar's trial before a single judge, in accordance with the law, will be a long one, extending into the second half of 1999. Corruption charges will precede sex charges. By the first week of the trial, Anwar had provided, from prison, examples of Mahathir's techniques of dealing with people. Some of the prosecution's early witnesses' evidence lent credibility to Anwar's allegations that there was a conspiracy against him by certain political and business leaders.

Mahathir has been evasive about when he will appoint a deputy; a possible date might be around the 1999 UMNO General Assembly, at which time the party's regular elections will be held. That date is, as yet, also uncertain.

It is likely that the next general election will not be held until late 1999 or 2000. This date is based on the surprisingly high degree of support shown for Anwar now and government hopes that it will fade over the next year or so. Another factor in the calculation is the state of the economy, which may be politically influential, especially as Mahathir's economic policies are so distinctive and unorthodox. The election timing contemplated would allow Mahathir's policies to provide short-term benefits without the long-term costs becoming so pronounced as to weaken his election strength.

Mahathir benefits from official UMNO backing, and support by those among all ethnic groups in politics and government who have been favored by his policies, those who believe that he stands for "stability" and others who do not dare to oppose him. He is supported by the mass media, so uncritically that their credibility has become impaired.

The Anwar debacle has led to the creation of an informal coalition, which constitutes the chief opposition to Mahathir. It is based on PAS; the DAP; the small Malaysian People's Party, led by Husin Ali; and about a dozen NGOs. The group has tried to move away from the single-issue theme of defending Anwar to also espousing "reform," particularly opposition to nepotism, corruption, and "cronyism." It lacks coverage by the mass media, but exercises some influence under various guises through the Internet and by word of mouth. The nature of the opposition, unfortunately, makes it susceptible to efforts to divide its components through appeals to ethnicity.

Mahathir also has a weapon in reserve which he might conceivably use if necessary – declaring a state of emergency.

External support for Anwar has been surprisingly strong. It has been expressed inside ASEAN by President Habibie (Indonesia) and President Estrada (Philippines) and by NGOs and the press in these countries and in Thailand. Western and international officials have also deplored his imprisonment. Mahathir has striven to show that such support really constitutes an attack on Malaysian nationalism.

Given Mahathir's tight grip on Malaysia and his ruthlessness toward opponents, it seems doubtful whether, failing a (another?) major Mahathir miscalculation, Anwar – for all his ability and courage – can wrest control from him. A proper question may be: how can the damage to the economy, the polity and the legitimacy of the government's rule be repaired?

Notes

Introduction: leadership in Malaysia

1 F. Riggs, *Thailand: The Modernization of a Bureaucratic Polity*, Honolulu: East–West Center, 1966.
2 D. Mauzy, "Malaysia: Shared Civilian–Military Interests," in C. Danopoulis (ed.) *Civilian Rule in the Developing World*, Boulder, CO: Westview, 1992, pp. 225–42.
3 W. Case, *Elites and Regimes in Malaysia: Revisiting a Consociational Democracy*, Clayton: Monash Asia Institute, 1996, p. 17.
4 K. von Vorys, *Democracy Without Consensus: Communalism and Political Stability in Malaysia*, Princeton: Princeton University Press, 1975, pp. 342–4.
5 R. Stubbs, "Reluctant Leader, Expectant Followers: Japan and Southeast Asia," *International Journal*, vol. xlvi, Autumn 1991, pp. 649–53.
6 *Asiaweek*, May 9, 1997, p. 39.
7 Mahathir Mohamad, *The Malay Dilemma*, Singapore: Donald Moore for Asia Pacific Press, 1970.
8 D. Mauzy, "Malaysia in 1987: Decline of 'The Malay Way'," *Asian Survey*, vol. xxvii, no. 2, 1988, p. 213.
9 *Straits Times*, March 26, 1987.
10 G. Sheridan, *Tigers: Leaders of the New Asia-Pacific*, St Leonards: Allen and Unwin, 1995, p. 215.
11 Tun Ghafar Baba, who reached the rank of Deputy Prime Minister, also played golf, which, reputedly, he learned as a caddy (interview with a diplomat, July 1986).
12 Interview with Tan Sri Musa Hitam, May 1970.
13 Interview with Tun Abdul Razak, June 1967.
14 *New Straits Times* (hereafter *NST*), 23 October 1976; *Star*, July 22, 1978.
15 G. Means, *Malaysian Politics: The Second Generation*, Singapore: Oxford University Press, 1991, pp. 56–7.
16 R. Milne and D. Mauzy, *Politics and Government in Malaysia*, Singapore and Vancouver: Times Books International and University of British Columbia Press, 1980, p. 364.
17 *NST*, August 15, 1979.
18 L. Pye, *Asian Power and Politics: The Cultural Dimensions of Authority*, Cambridge, MA: Harvard University Press, 1985, p. 225.
19 Interview with Tunku Abdul Rahman, May 1975.
20 Interview with a Menteri Besar, July 1988.

1 Malaysia: how Mahathir came to power

1 R. Stubbs, *Hearts and Minds in Guerrilla Warfare: The Malayan Emergency, 1940–1960*, Singapore: Oxford University Press, 1989.

2 R. Milne, *Politics in Ethnically Biopolar States: Guyana, Malaysia, Fiji*, Vancouver: University of British Columbia Press, 1981, pp. 1–4; D. Horowitz, *Ethnic Groups in Conflict*, Berkeley: University of California Press, 1985, p. 185; J. Kahn, *Class, Ethnicity and Diversity* in J. Kahn and F. Loh (eds) *Fragmented Vision: Culture and Politics in Contemporary Malaysia*, North Sydney: Area Studies Association of Australia, with Allen and Unwin, 1992, p. 162; E. Nordlinger, *Conflict in Plural Societies*, Cambridge, MA: Harvard University Press, 1992, pp. 1–14.

3 J. Nagata, "Introduction," in J. Nagata (ed.) *Pluralism in Malaysia: Myth and Reality*, *Contributions to Asian Studies*, vol. 7, Leiden: E. Brill, 1975, p. 3.

4 Khan, op. cit., p. 171.

5 J. Jesudason, *Ethnicity and the Economy: The State, Chinese Business and Multinationalism in Malaysia*, Singapore: Oxford University Press, 1989, p. 11.

6 H. Crouch, *Government and Society in Malaysia*, Ithaca: Cornell University Press, 1996, pp. 35–6, 41–4.

7 K.S. Jomo, *A Question of Class: Capital, the State and Development in Malaya*, Singapore: Oxford University Press, 1986, pp. 247–9.

8 Khoo Boh Teik, *Paradoxes of Mahathirism: An Intellectual Biography of Mahathir Mohamad*, Kuala Lumpur: Oxford University Press, 1995, p. xvii.

9 B. Walsh, "Attitudes Toward Democracy in Malaysia: Challenges to the Regime," *Asian Survey*, vol. xxxvi, no. 9, 1996, pp. 882–903.

10 R. Milne and D. Mauzy, *Politics and Government in Malaysia*, Singapore and Vancouver: Times Books International and University of British Columbia Press, 1980, p. 25.

11 Heng Pek Khoon, *Chinese Politics in Malaysia: A History of the Malaysian Chinese Association*, Singapore: Oxford University Press, 1988.

12 R. Vasil, *Politics in a Plural Society: A Study of Non-communal Political Parties in West Malaysia*, Kuala Lumpur: Oxford University Press, 1971, pp. 92–221.

13 Milne and Mauzy, op. cit., p. 36.

14 V. Purcell, *Malaya: Communist or Free?*, London: Gollancz, 1954, pp. 192–3.

15 A. Lijphart, *Democracy in Plural Societies: A Comparative Exploration*, New Haven: Yale University Press, 1977, pp. 25–176; Milne, op. cit., pp. 160–9, 176–80; Nordlinger, op. cit., pp. 10–11, 21–36.

16 Lijphart, op. cit., pp. 25–103.

17 I. Lustick, "Stability in Deeply Divided Societies, Consociationalism versus Control," *World Politics*, vol. 31, April 1978, pp. 308–33; D. Mauzy, "Malaysia: Malay Political Hegemony and 'Coercive Consociationalism'," in John McGarry and Brendan O'Leary (eds) *The Politics of Ethnic Conflict Regulation*, London: Routledge, 1993, pp. 106–27.

18 Milne and Mauzy, op. cit., pp. 36–43.

19 M.N. Sopiee, *From Malaysian Union to Singapore Separation: Political Unification in the Malaysia Region, 1945–65*, Penerbit Universiti Malaya, 1974, pp. 126–35.

20 R. Milne and K. Ratnam, *New States in a New Nation: Political Development of Sarawak and Sabah in Malaysia*, London: Frank Cass, 1974, pp. 1–68.

21 R. Milne, "Singapore's Exit from Malaysia: The Consequences of Ambiguity," *Asian Survey*, vol. 6, no. 3, 1966, pp. 175–84.

22 *New Straits Times* (hereafter *NST*), July 4, 1969.

23 K.J. Ratnam and R. Milne, "The 1969 Parliamentary Election in West Malaysia," *Pacific Affairs*, vol. xliii, 1970, pp. 203–36.

24 *The May 13 Tragedy: A Report of the National Operations Council*, Kuala Lumpur, 1969.

25 K. von Vorys, *Democracy Without Consensus: Communalism and Political Stability in Malaysia*, Princeton, NJ: Princeton University Press, 1975, pp. 372–4.

26 *NST*, July 4, 1969.

27 Khoo, op. cit., p. 23.

28 Interview with Datuk Seri Dr. Mahathir Mohamad, May 1970.

29 Mahathir Mohamad, *The Malay Dilemma*, Singapore: Donald Moore for Asia Pacific Press, 1970, pp. 8–15.
30 Khoo, op. cit., pp. 34–6, 81–8.
31 *The Rocket*, vol. 5, no. 1, 1970.
32 D. Mauzy, *Barisan Nasional: Coalition Government in Malaysia*, Kuala Lumpur: Marican, 1983.
33 *NST*, May 23, 1984.
34 W. Case, *Elites and Regimes in Malaysia: Revisiting a Consociational Democracy*, Clayton, Victoria: Monash Asia Institute, 1996, p. 153.
35 *NST*, May 3, 1975.
36 *NST*, May 7, 1984.
37 *NST*, May 26, 1984.
38 J. Funston, *Malay Politics in Malaysia: A Study of UMNO and PAS*, Kuala Lumpur: Heinemann, 1980, pp. 172–6; Mahathir, op. cit., p. 9; Milne and Mauzy, op. cit., p. 174.
39 *NST*, June 21, 1975.
40 *The Guardian* (MCA), vol. 8, no. 2, 1976, p. 2.
41 *NST*, March 7, 1976.
42 *NST*, March 6, 1976.
43 Interview with Tunku Abdul Rahman, July 25, 1986.

2 Mahathir's assertion of executive power

1 D. Mauzy and R. Milne, "The Mahathir Administration: Discipline through Islam," *Pacific Affairs*, vol. 56, no. 4, 1983–4, pp. 617–48.
2 Khoo Boh Teik, *Paradoxes of Mahathirism: An Intellectual Biography of Mahathir Mohamad*, Kuala Lumpur: Oxford University Press, 1995, p. 275.
3 The fall in the numbers in detention between 1981 and early 1983 may have indicated a liberal trend (Mauzy and Milne, op. cit., p. 622). But some of the credit should probably be given to Musa, who was Home Minister at that time.
4 H. Crouch, "Authoritarian Trends, the UMNO Split and the Limits of State Power," in J. Kahn and F. Loh (eds) *Fragmented Vision: Culture and Politics in Contemporary Malaysia*, North Sydney: Asian Studies Association of Australia in association with Allen and Unwin, 1992, pp. 35–9.
5 Liak Teng Kiat, "Malaysia: Mahathir's Last Hurrah?", *Southeast Asian Affairs 1996*, Singapore: Institute of Southeast Asian Studies, 1996, pp. 217–37.
6 The rulers' interference in state political matters has been a recurrent problem. Even the Tunku had troubles with the rulers of Perak, Selangor, Kelantan, Terengganu, and Pahang. The *New Straits Times* (hereafter *NST*), December 12, 1983, noted that the unconstitutional acts of some rulers have led to the federal government agreeing to the resignations of four Menteris Besar, who were sacrificed, while the rulers were permitted to "ride roughshod" over constitutional principles.
7 Interview with a minister in 1984.
8 Interviews with several UMNO ministers, July 1984; David Jenkins, "Proud and Prickly Princes Finally Meet Their Match," *Far Eastern Economic Review* (hereafter *FEER*), February 23, 1984, p. 12.
9 Interview with a Malaysian journalist, June 1984.
10 "The Constitutional Crisis and Democracy," *Aliran Monthly* (hereafter *AM*) (special commentary issue), December 1983; *AM*, July–September 1983. They discuss the pros and cons of the various amendments and the history of changes to Article 150. *AM* on the whole seemed to agree with the need to amend Article 66, but objected to Article 150 as placing too much power in the hands of the Prime Minister (in fact, *AM* disagreed with the 1981 amendment to Article 150).

11 "Going to the People," *Asiaweek*, December 9, 1983, pp. 33–44.

12 Tunku Abdul Rahman, "As I See It," *Star*, October 17, November 7, and December 6, 1983. The Tunku did add that the paradox was that the amendment was brought about by the unconstitutional behavior of the rulers themselves (November 7, 1983). Also see *New Sunday Times*, 23 October 1983, and *NST*, October 29, 1983.

13 Interviews with a Chinese former minister and with a UMNO deputy minister, June and July 1984. See also note 22.

14 *New Sunday Times*, December 4, 1983.

15 *Star*, December 20, 1983.

16 Interviews with UMNO politicians in July 1984.

17 *Star*, July 2–3, 1984.

18 *NST*, May 26, 1984.

19 *Berita Malaysia*, January–February 1985, pp. 1 and 3.

20 Khoo, op. cit., p. 292.

21 *NST*, November 15, 1983.

22 Mahathir Mohamad, *The Malay Dilemma*, Singapore: Donald Moore for Asia Pacific Press, 1970, p. 35.

23 Khoo, op. cit., p. 204.

24 *NST*, January 21, 1993; H. Crouch, *Government and Society in Malaysia*, Ithaca and London: Cornell University Press, 1996, pp. 147–8.

25 G. Means, *Malaysian Politics: The Second Generation*, Singapore: Oxford University Press, 1991, p. 351.

26 *Christian Science Monitor*, December 20, 1976.

27 *NST*, July 3, 1976.

28 Interview with Tan Sri Musa Hitam, May 24, 1988.

29 Khoo, op. cit., p. 229.

30 Interview, August 4, 1986.

31 Interview with Tan Sri Musa Hitam, July 17, 1986.

32 Interview with Tengku Razaleigh Hamzah, July 11, 1988.

33 Interview with Tunku Abdul Rahman, August 1, 1988.

34 Interview with a minister, July 24, 1988.

35 *Straits Times* (hereafter *ST*), April 23, 1987.

36 R. Kershaw, "Within the Family: The Limits of Doctrinal Differentiation in the Malaysian Ruling Party Elections of 1987," *Review of Indonesian and Malaysian Affairs*, vol. 23, 1989, pp. 125–87; D. Mauzy, "Malaysia in 1987: Decline of 'The Malay Way'," *Asian Survey*, vol. xxvii, no. 2, 1988, pp. 213–16.

37 *ST*, April 5, 1987.

38 Crouch, "Authoritarian Trends," p. 30.

39 Khoo Kay Jin, "The Grand Vision: Mahathir and Modernization," in J. Kahn and F. Loh (eds) *Fragmented Vision: Culture and Politics in Contemporary Malaysia*, North Sydney: Asian Studies Association of Australia in association with Allen and Unwin, 1992, pp. 62–3.

40 *FEER*, May 7, 1987, pp. 12–16.

41 *ST*, May 14, 1987.

42 Interview with Tan Sri Sanusi Junid, July 22, 1988.

43 *ST*, April 26, 1987.

44 Crouch, *Government and Society*, pp. 126–7.

45 Means, op. cit., pp. 226–7.

46 *FEER*, April 28, 1988, p. 40.

47 *ST*, March 28, 1988.

48 Crouch, *Government and Society*, pp. 125–8.

49 T. Thomas, "The Role of the Judiciary," in Tan Chee-Beng (ed.) *Reflections on the Malaysian Constitution*, Penang: Aliran Kesedaran Negara, 1987, p. 69.

50 See D. Mauzy, "The Corrosion of Checks on Executive Power: Deinstitutionalization in Malaysia," in B. Matthews (ed.) *The Quality of Life in Southeast Asia: Transforming Social, Political and Natural Environments*, Montreal: CASA/McGill University, 1992, p. 2.

51 *AM*, vol. 9, no. 1, 1989, pp. 36–40.

52 *Asiaweek*, October 9, 1987, p. 18.

53 *Asiaweek*, April 1, 1988, p. 9; *NST*, July 23, 1988.

54 *AM*, vol. 8, no. 1, 1988, p. 10.

55 *FEER*, April 26, 1990, p. 19.

56 See *AM*, vol. 8, no. 4, 1988, pp. 22–4; *ST*, June 8, 1988; *Asian Wall Street Journal*, June 14, 1988. The contents of that letter have not been revealed. However, in his affidavit, Salleh stated that he had noticed that, over time, the attacks against the judiciary by the Prime Minister were becoming more intense and repetitive, and he was concerned that the public should not get the wrong impression about the integrity and impartiality of the judiciary.

57 *AM*, vol. 9, no. 11, 1989, pp. 5–11. Abdul Hamid never gained the respect of the legal community. In 1988, the Malaysian Bar Council passed a resolution of no confidence in him by a vote of 1002 to 0. In 1992, a Bar Council "motion of reconciliation with the Lord President" was defeated, 809 to 52. See *AM*, vol. 12, no.3, 1992, pp. 2–4.

58 *FEER*, April 26, 1990, p. 19.

59 A great deal has been written about the dismissal of the Lord President and the other Supreme Court judges. See Tun Salleh Abas (with K. Das), *May Day for Justice*, Kuala Lumpur: Magnus Books, 1989; *Malaysia: Assault on the Judiciary*, New York: Lawyers Committee for Human Rights, 1990; Raja Aziz Addruse, *Conduct Unbecoming*, Kuala Lumpur: Walrus, 1990; M. Gillen and T. McDorman, "The Removal of Three Judges of the Supreme Court in Malaysia," *UBC Law Review*, vol. 25, no. 1, 1991; G. Robertson, "Malaysia: Justice Hangs in the Balance," *The Independence of Judges and Lawyers Bulletin*, vol. 22, October 1988, pp. 8–12. There is also a book defending the dismissals: P. Williams, *Judicial Misconduct*, Petaling Jaya: Pelanduk, 1990.

60 *Time*, July 25, 1988, p. 22.

61 *AM*, vol. 15, no. 7, 1995, pp. 36–9.

62 *AM*, vol. 17, no. 3, 1997, p. 37.

63 Interview with Tunku Abdul Rahman, July 26, 1986.

64 Interview with a foreign business executive resident in Malaysia, July 1988.

3 The economy and development

1 D. Leipziger and V. Thomas, *The Lessons of East Asia: An Overview of Country Experience*, Washington, DC: The World Bank, 1993, pp. 1–15.

2 *New Straits Times* (hereafter *NST*), November 27, 1993.

3 R. Stubbs, *Hearts and Minds in Guerrilla Warfare: The Malaysian Emergency, 1949–1960*, Singapore: Oxford University Press, 1989, pp. 232–3.

4 R. Stubbs, "Geography and the Political Economy of Southeast Asia," *International Journal*, vol. xliv, 1984, pp. 525–6.

5 *Second Malaysia Plan 1971–1975*, Kuala Lumpur: Government Press, 1971, pp. 4–6.

6 *Straits Times* (hereafter *ST*), January 2, 1965.

7 *Second Malaysia Plan*, op. cit., p. 1.

8 Ibid., pp. 6–7.

9 *Mid-Term Review of the Second Malaysia Plan*, Kuala Lumpur: Government Press, 1973, pp. 81–8.

10 R. Milne and D. Mauzy, *Politics and Government in Malaysia*, Singapore: Times Books International, 1978, pp. 331–7.

11 *Straits Times*, April 5, 1973.
12 *Mid-Term Review*, op. cit., pp. 80–8.
13 Milne and Mauzy, op. cit., pp. 346–7.
14 G. Means, *Malaysian Politics: The Second Generation*, Singapore: Oxford University Press, 1991, pp. 59–60.
15 *Asian Wall Street Journal* (hereafter *AWSJ*), July 13, 1982.
16 Mahathir Mohamad, "New Government Policies," in K.S. Jomo (ed.) *The Sun Also Sets*, Kuala Lumpur: Insan, 1985, p. 305.
17 *NST*, March 31, 1982.
18 Zakaria Ahmad, "Malaysia," *Asian Survey*, vol. xxv, no. 2, 1985, pp. 209–10.
19 J. Saravanamuttu, "Look East Policy: The Real Lessons," in K.S. Jomo (ed.) *Mahathir's Economic Policies*, Kuala Lumpur: Insan, 1987, p. 27.
20 K.S. Jomo, "Overview," in K.S. Jomo (ed.) *Privatizing Malaysia: Rents, Rhetoric, Realities*, Boulder, CO: Westview, 1995, pp. 42–4.
21 Zainuddin Maidin, *The Other Side of Mahathir*, Kuala Lumpur: Utusan Publications, 1994, pp. 6–7.
22 *Seventh Malaysia Plan 1996–2000*, Kuala Lumpur: National Printing Department, 1996, p. 206.
23 Interview with a Malaysian economist, July 1997.
24 *NST*, September 19, 1995.
25 *NST*, March 24, 1997.
26 Jomo, "Overview," p. 54.
27 *NST*, March 31, 1995.
28 *NST*, November 27, 1995.
29 Lim Kit Siang, *The RM 62b North–South Highway Scandal*, Petaling Jaya: DAP, 1981. There was further trouble about tolls in 1997, when the DAP complained that the North–South Highway arrangements placed an unduly heavy burden on users.
30 A former UMNO official said he had not been informed about the details of UMNO's revenues from business (interview, July 1997).
31 E. Gomez, *Politics in Business: UMNO's Corporate Investments*, Kuala Lumpur: Forum, 1990, p. 166. For the MCA's role at the start of the Alliance and MCA and MIC activities in business, see pp. 1–9. On Barisan finance, see also Gomez, *Money Politics in the Barisan Nasional*, Kuala Lumpur: Forum, 1991, pp. 97–104. Gomez, in *Politics in Business*, remarks that Malaysia is one of the few countries in the world where the ruling parties own such a wide range of business interests (p. v). The latest book on the topic is E. Gomez and K.S. Jomo, *Malaysia's Political Economy: Politics, Patronage and Profits*, Cambridge: Cambridge University Press, 1997. Among other things, it discusses the effects of factionalism in UMNO on conflicts in the corporate sector (pp. 183–4).
32 H. Crouch, *Government and Society in Malaysia*, Ithaca and London: Cornell University Press, 1996, pp. 85–7.
33 *Malaysian Business*, August 1–15, 1990, p. 11.
34 *NST*, July 19, 1991.
35 Cheong Mei Sui and Adibah Amin, *Daim: The Man Behind the Enigma*, Petaling Jaya: Pelanduk, 1995, pp. 24–5.
36 *NST*, November 27, 1995.
37 *Straits Times Weekly Edition* (hereafter *STWE*) (Singapore), May 24, 1997.
38 *Aliran Monthly*, vol. 17, no. 11, 1997, pp. 9–14.
39 M. Brennan, "Class Politics and Race in Modern Malaysia," in R. Higgott and R. Robison (eds) *Southeast Asia: Essays in the Political Economy of Social Change*, London: Routledge and Kegan Paul, 1985.
40 J. Jesudason, "The Syncretic State and the Structuring of Opposition Politics in Malaysia," in G. Rodan (ed.) *Political Oppositions in Industrialising Asia*, London and New

York: Routledge, 1996, pp. 129, 146–8. The data are compiled from the *Mid-Term Review of the Sixth Malaysia Plan, 1991–1995*, Kuala Lumpur: Government Printer, 1994, and from the *Third Malaysia Plan, 1976–1980*, Kuala Lumpur: Government Press, 1976. The middle class is defined as persons in professional, technical, administrative, managerial, clerical, and sales sectors. In some countries, but apparently not yet in Malaysia, it has been possible to go beyond such "objective" criteria of class and use data concerning respondents' identification, or non-identification, with particular classes.

41 Crouch, op. cit., p. 181–6. His data come from *The Second Outline Perspective Plan 1991–2000*, Kuala Lumpur: National Printing Department, 1991; *Fourth Malaysia Plan, 1981–1985*, Kuala Lumpur: National Printing Department, 1981; and K.S. Jomo, *Growth and Structural Change in the Malaysian Economy*, Houndsmills: Macmillan, 1990, p. 82. The data in *Seventh Malaysia Plan*, op. cit., do not indicate any change in trends.

42 Jesudason, op. cit., pp. 146–8.

43 *NST*, July 26, 1997.

44 *ST*, April 25, 1997.

45 K. Machado, "Japanese Transnational Corporations in Malaysia's State-Sponsored Heavy Industrialization Drive: The HICOM Automobile and Steel Projects," *Pacific Affairs*, vol. 62, no. 4, 1989, p. 507.

46 Chee Peng Lim, "The Proton Saga – No Reverse Gear! The Economic Burden of the Malaysian Car Project," in K.S. Jomo (ed.) *Mahathir's Economic Policies*, Kuala Lumpur: Insan, 1987, pp. 57–8.

47 *Far Eastern Economic Review* (hereafter *FEER*), December 24, 1982, p. 31.

48 *FEER*, June 16, 1983, p. 101.

49 *AWSJ*, March 1–2, 1990.

50 *NST*, August 2, 1994.

51 *NST*, February 22, 1984.

52 *FEER*, September 1, 1988, p. 56.

53 *FEER*, May 2, 1996, pp. 64–6.

54 Machado, op. cit., p. 511.

55 *FEER*, May 29, 1997, pp. 61–2.

56 *STWE*, October 5, 1996.

57 *ST*, March 23, 1987.

58 *New Sunday Times*, May 6, 1984.

59 P. Bowring and R. Cottrell, *The Carrian File*, Hong Kong: Far Eastern Economic Review, 1984; R. Milne, "Bumiputra Malaysia Finance: Levels of Corruption in Malaysia," *The Asian Journal of Public Administration*, vol. 9, no. 1, 1987, pp. 6–73.

60 Milne "Bumiputra Malaysia Finance", op cit., pp. 62–3.

61 Means, op cit., p. 149, fn. 28.

62 Milne, op cit., p. 64.

63 *STWE*, May 18, 1996.

64 *Berita Malaysia*, November 1984.

65 Milne and Mauzy, op. cit., pp. 205–7.

66 *ST*, April 3, 1987.

67 Means, op. cit., pp. 172–3.

68 *Malaysian Business*, August 1–15, 1990, p. 6.

69 *AWSJ*, April 30, 1986.

70 Means, op. cit., p. 140.

71 Reuters, 24 June 1998, forwarded from the Internet: sangkancil@malaysia.net, subject: "Malaysia's Daim among Wealthiest and most Powerful" 25 June 1998. It states that Daim's estimated wealth is 1–2 billion ringgit (250–500 million $US).

72 *ST*, January 12, 1987.

73 *Aliran Monthly*, vol. 17, no. 5, 1997, pp. 8–9.
74 Interview, July 1997.
75 D. Mauzy, "The Tentative Life and Quiet Death of the NECC in Malaysia," in J. Bernardi, G. Firth, and S. Neissen (eds) *Managing Change in Southeast Asia: Local Initiatives, Global Connections*, Montréal, Université de Montréal, 1995, pp. 77–92.
76 *OPP2*, op. cit., pp. 3–5.
77 Ibid., p. 12.
78 Heng Pek Khoon, "The Chinese Business Elites of Malaysia," in R. McVey (ed.) *Southeast Asian Capitalists*, Ithaca and London: Cornell University Press, 1992, pp. 128–37; Crouch, op. cit., pp. 206–18; W. Case, *Elites and Regimes in Malaysia*, Victoria: Monash Asia Institute, 1996, pp. 177–9; J. Jesudason, *Ethnicity and the Economy: The State, Chinese Business and Multinationals in Malaysia*, Singapore: Oxford University Press, 1989, pp. 128–65.
79 *OPP2*, op. cit., p. 8.
80 Ibid., pp. 8–10; *Seventh Malaysia Plan*, op. cit., p. 98.
81 *ST*, June 18, 1997. The Anti-Corruption Agency investigated the role of a cabinet minister about allocations to ministers' relatives, but found insufficient grounds for taking action.
82 Economic Intelligence Unit, *Country Report. Malaysia, 2nd Quarter 1997*, pp. 23–4; *Seventh Malaysia Plan*, op. cit., pp. 14–17, 37, 127.
83 *STWE*, May 31, 1997; *NST*, June 25, 1997.
84 *FEER*, September 18, 1997, p. 5.
85 *Asiaweek*, June 13, 1997, p. 42.
86 *Star*, March 25, 1997.
87 Mohd. Azman Shariffadeen, "Information Technology Development in Malaysia – Focus on Malaysia's Multimedia Super Corridor", *Malaysia Today*, Petaling Jaya: Asian Strategy and Leadership Institute, 1997.
88 Interview, Datuk Leo Moggie, Minister of Energy, Telecommunications and Posts, July 1997.
89 *Asiaweek*, May 9, 1997, p. 38.
90 *NST*, July 22, 1977.
91 *AWSJ*, June 11, 1997, and October 30, 1997.
92 *NST*, April 10, 1977.
93 Interview, Datuk Leo Moggie, July 1997.
94 Lim Kit Siang, *IT for All*, Petaling Jaya: DAP, 1997, p. 14.
95 Ibid., p. 1; interview with Lim Kit Siang, July 1997.
96 *ST*, June 19, 1997.

4 Containing ethnic dissent

1 G. Means, "The Role of Islam in the Political Development of Malaysia," *Comparative Politics*, vol. I, no. 2, 1969, pp. 264–84.
2 Chandra Muzaffar, *Islamic Resurgence in Malaysia*, Petaling Jaya: Penerbit Fajar Bakti, 1987, pp. 1–42.
3 S. Barraclough, "Managing the Challenges of Islamic Revival in Malaysia," *Asian Survey*, vol. xxiii, no. 8, 1983, p. 961.
4 J. Nagata, *The Reflowering of Malaysian Islam: Modern Religious Radicals and Their Roots*, Vancouver: University of British Columbia Press, 1984, p. 50.
5 Zainah Anwar, *Islamic Revivalism in Malaysia*, Petaling Jaya: Pelanduk, 1987, p. 9.
6 A.B. Shamsul, "Religion and Ethnic Politics in Malaysia," in C. Keyes, L. Kendall and H. Hardcore (eds) *Asian Visions of Authority: Religion and the Modern States of East and Southeast Asia*, Honolulu: University of Hawaii Press, 1994, pp. 99–116.

7 G. Means, *Malaysian Politics: The Second Generation*, Singapore: Oxford University Press, 1991, pp. 61–4.

8 K.S. Jomo and A. Cheek, "Malaysia's Islamic Movements," in J. Khan and F. Loh Kok Wah (eds) *Fragmented Vision: Culture and Politics in Contemporary Malaysia*, North Sydney: Asian Studies Association of Australia in association with Allen and Unwin, 1992, p. 93.

9 Jomo and Cheek, op. cit., pp. 96–7.

10 Shamsul, op. cit., pp. 99–116.

11 Barraclough, op cit., p. 964.

12 *New Straits Times* (hereafter *NST*), July 27, 1984.

13 Khoo Boh Teik, *Paradoxes of Mahathirism: An Intellectual Biography of Mahathir Mohamad*, Kuala Lumpur: Oxford University Press, 1995, p. 165. This point is repeated in his speech at the UMNO General Assembly, 1997 (*NST*, September 6, 1997).

14 Mahathir Mohamad, "Islam Guarantees Justice for all Citizens," in Rose Ismail (ed.) *Hudud in Malaysia: The Issues at Stake*, Kuala Lumpur: Sisters in Islam Forum (Malaysia), 1995, pp. 66–9; J. Nagata, "How to be Islamic without being an Islamic State," in Akbar S. Ahmed and H. Donnan (eds) *Islam, Globalization and Post-Modernity*, London and New York: Routledge, 1994, pp. 71–2.

15 *Straits Times* (Malaysia) (hereafter *ST*), August 20, 1983.

16 *NST*, April 21, 1993 and May 2, 1984.

17 Interview with Dato Dr. Halim Ismail, Managing Director, Bank Islam Malaysia, July 1988.

18 Khoo, op. cit., pp. 175–7.

19 D. Camroux, "State Responses to Islamic Resurgence in Malaysia: Accommodation, Co-option and Confrontation," *Asian Survey*, vol. xxxvi, no. 9, 1996, pp. 861–2.

20 Means, *Malaysian Politics*, pp. 128–9.

21 Interview with Tan Sri Musa Hitam, July 17, 1986.

22 Camroux, op. cit., pp. 864–5.

23 *Aliran Monthly* (hereafter *AM*), vol. 17, no. 1, 1997, p. 38.

24 D. Mauzy and R. Milne, "The Mahathir Administration: Discipline through Islam," *Pacific Affairs*, vol. 56, no. 4, 1983–4, p. 644.

25 *NST*, July 27, 1997; *Far Eastern Economic Review* (hereafter *FEER*), September 11, 1997, p. 20.

26 Khoo, op. cit., pp. 162 and 174–5.

27 Interview with a minister, July 1982.

28 *New Sunday Times*, September 22, 1997.

29 Jomo and Cheek, op. cit., p. 105.

30 Ibid., p. 104.

31 *AM*, vol. 17, no. 6, 1997, pp. 25–7.

32 Means, *Malaysian Politics*, pp. 280–1.

33 *FEER*, September 5, 1973, pp. 23–4.

34 Interview, July 15, 1986.

35 Heng Pek Koon, *Chinese Politics in Malaysia: A History of the Malaysian Chinese Association*, Singapore: Oxford University Press, 1988, pp. 254–8.

36 Interview with Tun Tan Siew Sin, May 1975. He added that when the government was proposing to set the share of corporate wealth, under the NEP, projected for Chinese and other non-Malay ownership at 30 percent, he succeeded in having this altered to 40 percent.

37 *ST*, June 2, 1973.

38 *Asiaweek*, June 1, 1986, p. 47.

39 Interview with Lim Kit Siang, July 1997.

40 *Asiaweek*, February 14, 1987, p. 27.

41 Khoo, op. cit., p. 312, fn. 105.

42 Heng, op. cit., p. 270. The obvious explanation is that Lee was socially close to Tengku Razaleigh, an opponent of Mahathir.

43 W. Case, *Elites and Regimes in Malaysia: A Constitutional Democracy Revisited*, Victoria, Australia: Monash Asia Institute, 1996, p. 140.

44 Means, *Malaysian Politics*, p. 185.

45 *Straits Times Weekly Edition*, March 8, 1997.

46 *The Future of Malaysian Chinese*, Kuala Lumpur: MCA, 1988.

47 *ST*, August 26, 1987.

48 Interview with state MCA officials, May 1964.

49 H. Crouch, *Government and Society in Malaysia*, Ithaca and London: Cornell University Press, 1996, p. 167.

50 *NST*, October 25, 1996.

51 Datuk Seri Dr. Mahathir Mohamad, *Vision 2020: The Way Forward*, Kuala Lumpur: Kongres Kebangsaan Wawasan 2020, April 29–30, 1997. Significantly, the Chinese educational associations, which usually supported the DAP, declared that they were neutral at the 1995 election (Liak Teng Kiat, "Malaysia: Mahathir's Last Hurrah?" *Southeast Asian Affairs, 1996*, Singapore: Institute of Southeast Asian Studies, 1996, p. 222).

52 *FEER*, August 14, 1997, p. 13.

53 Interview with former MIC office-holder, July 1997.

54 *Tamil Malar*, March 4, 1973.

55 Lim Kit Siang, *The Maika Scandal*, Petaling Jaya: DAP, 1992, pp. 91–160.

56 M. Leigh, *The Rising Moon: Political Change in Sarawak*, Sydney: Sydney University Press, 1974: R. Milne and K.J. Ratnam, *Malaysia – New States in a New Nation: Political Development of Sarawak and Sabah in Malaysia*, London: Cass, 1974; M. Roff, *The Politics of Belonging: Political Change in Sabah and Sarawak*, Kuala Lumpur: Oxford University Press, 1974.

57 J.A. Jawan, "The Sarawak State General Election of 1991," *Kajian Malaysia*, vol. XI, no. 1, 1993, pp. 1–23.

58 Means, *Malaysian Politics*, pp. 168–9.

59 *AM*, vol. 16, no. 6, 1996, pp. 5–6.

60 F. Loh Kok Wah, "Modernisation, Cultural Revival and Counter-Hegemony: The Kadazans of Sabah in the 1980s," in Kahn and Loh (eds), *Fragmented Vision: Culture and Politics in Contemporary Malaysia*, North Sydney: Asian Studies Association of Australia in association with Allen and Unwin, 1992, pp. 225–50.

61 *AM*, vol. 12, no. 11, 1992, pp. 2–12.

62 Tan Chee Khoon, *Sabah's Triumph for Democracy*, Petaling Jaya: Pelanduk, 1986, pp. 63–83.

63 A. Kahin, "Crisis on the Periphery: The Rift Between Kuala Lumpur and Sabah," *Pacific Affairs*, vol. 65, no. 1, 1992, p. 32.

64 *FEER*, March 24, 1994, p. 23.

65 *NST*, September 10, 1978.

5 Human rights

1 Chandra Muzaffar, *Protector?*, Penang: Aliran, 1979, p. 1.

2 Interview with Tunku Abdul Rahman, May 1974.

3 Interview, July 1984.

4 J. Donnelly, "Human Rights and Human Dignity: An Analytic Critique of Non-Western Concepts of Human Rights," *American Journal of Political Science*, vol. 76, no. 1, 1982, p. 15.

5 *Freedom in the World* (annual), Lonham, MD: University Press of America; *New Straits Times* (hereafter *NST*), April 24, 1992.

6 D. Mauzy and R. Milne, "Human Rights in ASEAN States: A Canadian Policy Perspective," in A. Acharya and R. Stubbs (eds) *New Challenges for ASEAN: Emerging Policy Issues*, Vancouver: UBC Press, 1995, pp. 122–3.

7 Lim Kit Siang, *Malaysia in the Dangerous 80s*, Petaling Jaya: DAP, 1982, pp. 125–38.

8 Mauzy and Milne, op. cit., pp. 42–3.

9 US Department of State, *Country Reports on Human Rights Practices for 1996*, US Congress 105 Congress, 1st Session, Joint Committee Print, Report to the Committee on Foreign Relations US Senate and the Committee on Foreign Affairs US House of Representatives, Washington: US Printing Office, 1997, p. 714.

10 Tan Chee Khoon, "Without Fear or Favour," *Star*, September 12, 1984.

11 *Asiaweek*, October 17, 1980, p. 17.

12 H. Crouch, *Government and Society in Malaysia*, Ithaca and London: Cornell University Press, 1996, pp. 98–104; *Straits Times* (hereafter *ST*), July 11, 1976.

13 Khoo Boh Teik, *Paradoxes of Mahathirism: An Intellectual Biography of Mahathir Mohamad*, Kuala Lumpur: Oxford University Press, 1995, pp. 227–8.

14 *NST*, August 18, 1987. In refusing to call off the giant UMNO rally, Najib was quoted as saying, "The rally will release tension and hopefully things will get better after that," in *Far Eastern Economic Review* (hereafter *FEER*), October 29, 1987, p. 21. According to Mahathir, the rally was not meant to threaten anybody but "somebody tried to change it from an UMNO rally to a Malay rally against the Chinese," *ST*, November 17, 1987.

15 D. Mauzy, "Malaysia in 1987: Decline of 'The Malay Way'," *Asian Survey*, vol. xxvii, no. 1, 1988, p. 21.

16 *NST*, January 1, 1988.

17 *FEER*, January 7, 1988, pp. 13–14. The MCA's deputy president, Lee Kim Sai, a target of criticism by UMNO Youth, wisely followed advice that he should leave the country temporarily (*ST*, October 28, 1987).

18 G. Means, *Malaysian Politics: The Second Generation*, Singapore: Oxford University Press, 1991, p. 214.

19 Khoo, op. cit., p. 285.

20 US Department of State, op. cit., p. 715.

21 *Sunday Star*, December 16, 1994.

22 *Straits Times Weekly Edition* (hereafter *STWE*), February 10, 1996.

23 Lim, op. cit., pp. 160–75.

24 *Aliran Speaks*, Penang: Aliran, 1981, pp. 381–91.

25 *Malaysian Digest* (hereafter *MD*), vol. 13, no. 4, 1988, p. 7.

26 Means, op. cit., p. 36.

27 J. Jesudason, "Statist Democracy and the Limits to Civil Society in Malaysia," *Journal of Commonwealth and Comparative Politics*, vol. 44, no. 2, 1995, p. 349. For other recent developments, see J. Jesudason, "The Syncretic State and the Structuring of Oppositional Politics in Malaysia," in G. Rodan (ed.) *Political Oppositions in Industrializing Asia*, London: Routledge, 1996, pp. 143–5.

28 *ST*, May 17, 1988; *STWE*, March 2, 1996.

29 *MD*, October 31, 1981.

30 *FEER*, April 7, 1994, p. 21.

31 *FEER*, October 6, 1994, p. 9.

32 *ST*, December 4, 1987.

33 *ST*, March 26, 1988.

34 *FEER*, March 21, 1995, p. 13.

35 Crouch, op. cit., p. 86.

36 *ST*, March 12, 1988.

37 *Aliran Monthly* (hereafter *AM*), vol. 16, no. 2, 1996, pp. 2–10.

38 *FEER*, November 26, 1995, p. 24.

39 *STWE*, November 23, 1996.
40 US Department of State, op. cit., p. 717.
41 Election Watch, *Report on the Eighth Malaysian General Elections Held on 20th and 21st October 1990*, Kuala Lumpur: Percetakan Bintang, n.d., p. 23.
42 *NST*, October 19, 1990.
43 *STWE*, November 2, 1996.
44 *Solving Sarawak's Forest and Native Problems*, Penang: Sabahat Malaysia, 1990; M. Colchester, *Pirates, Squatters and Poachers: The Political Ecology of Dispossession of the Native Peoples of Sarawak*, London/Petaling Jaya: Survival International/INSAN, 1992.
45 *FEER*, March 3, 1992, p. 9.
46 *ST*, June 15, 1992.
47 G. Robinson, "Human Rights in Southeast Asia: Rhetoric and Reality," in D. Wurfel and B. Burton (eds) *Southeast Asia in the New World Order: The Political Economy of a Dynamic Region*, New York: St. Martin's Press, 1996, p. 93.
48 *NST*, November 7, 1996.
49 International Commission of Jurists, *Critique of the US State Department Report of 1991*, Geneva, 1992, p. 153.
50 In 1997 HAKAM blamed the government for having given little attention to respect for human rights (*AM*, vol. 17, no. 3, 1997, p. 28.)
51 Interview with the vice-chairman of the Indonesian National Commission on Human Rights, August 1996.
52 *AM*, vol. 17, no. 2, 1997, pp. 24–30. In opposing this conference, the government showed its support for Indonesia as a fellow member of ASEAN.
53 *Bernama* (official government news summary), "Operation," February 26, 1977, p. 2.
54 Khoo Boo Teik, "Malaysia: Challenges and Upsets in Politics and Other Contestations," *Southeast Asian Affairs 1997*, Singapore: ISEAS, pp. 179–80. The Bakun Dam, of course, was an example of a heavy industry project (p. 167).
55 *Star*, June 28, 1996.
56 *Star*, November 11, 1996.
57 *The Second Outline Perspective Plan 1991–2000*, Kuala Lumpur: National Printing Department, 1991, p. 5. In March 1997, officers of any company, found guilty of breaking environmental laws, could face a mandatory five-year jail sentence (*NST*, April 10, 1997).
58 *NST*, September 25, 1997, September 30, 1997.

6 Foreign policy

1 *Straits Times* (hereafter *ST*), November 18, 1959.
2 ASA, *Report of the First Meeting of Foreign Ministers*, Kuala Lumpur, 1961.
3 J. Saravanamuttu, *The Dilemma of Independence: Two Decades of Malaysia's Foreign Policy, 1957–1977*, Penang: Penerbit Universiti Sains Malaysia, 1983, pp. 74–5.
4 M. Leifer, *ASEAN and the Security of South-East Asia*, London and New York: Routledge, 1989, p. 7.
5 J. Saravanamuttu, "Malaysia's Foreign Policy in the Mahathir Period, 1981–1985: An Iconoclast Comes to Rule," *Asian Journal of Political Science*, vol. 4, no. 1, 1996, p. 1.
6 Interview with Datuk Seri Dr. Mahathir Mohamad, August 5, 1970.
7 *Malaysian Digest* (hereafter *MD*), November 1985, p. 1. The Commonwealth ranked low in Mahathir's priorities for relations with other countries. ASEAN countries came first, Islamic countries second and the non-aligned countries third. The Commonwealth countries came fourth, and all others after that (Khoo Boo Teik, *Paradoxes of Mahathirism: An Intellectual Biography*, Kuala Lumpur: Oxford University Press, 1995, pp. 74–5).
8 *MD*, November 1987, p. 1.

9 *New Straits Times* (hereafter *NST*, July 25, 1995; September 30, 1995; July 27, 1997.
10 *NST*, September 30, 1995.
11 Saravanamuttu, "Malaysia's Foreign Policy in the Mahathir Period," pp. 1–16, esp. p. 8.
12 *NST*, September 30, 1995.
13 *ST*, April 7, 1995; July 24, 1997.
14 J. Saravanamuttu, "ASEAN in Malaysian Foreign Policy Discourse and Practice, 1967–1997", *Asian Journal of Political Science*, vol. 5, no. 1, 1997, p. 48. Lee Poh Ping believes that the "glue" that held ASEAN together a few years back was the Vietnamese occupation of Cambodia, while the new "glue" is cooperation in AFTA. See *NST*, August 9, 1997. The new "glue" may have less adhering power, however.
15 Saravanamuttu, "ASEAN in Malaysian Foreign Policy Discourse," p. 40.
16 M. Leifer in *ST*, June 20, 1995.
17 D. Crone, "New Political Roles for ASEAN," in D. Wurfel and B. Burton (eds) *Southeast Asia in the New World Order*, New York: St. Martin's Press, 1996, p. 46.
18 *Christian Science Monitor* (hereafter *CSM*), July 30, 1997; *NST*, August 4, 1997; *Far Eastern Economic Review* (hereafter *FEER*), August 7, 1997, p. 26.
19 Saravanamuttu, "ASEAN in Malaysian Foreign Policy Discourse," p. 5, citing Roger Irvine, "The Formative Years of ASEAN: 1967–1975", in A. Broinowski (ed.) *Understanding ASEAN*, London: Macmillan, 1982, p. 32. Also see Zakaria Haji Ahmad, "ASEAN and the Great Powers", in K. Jackson, S. Paribatra and J. Soedjati Djwandono (eds) *ASEAN in Regional and Global Context*, Berkeley, CA: University of California Press, 1986, pp. 347–57, esp. p. 348.
20 Hoang Anh Tuan, "ASEAN Dispute Management: Implications for Vietnam and an Expanded ASEAN", *Contemporary Southeast Asia*, vol. 18, no. 1, 1996, p. 75. Also see Hoang Anh Tuan, "Vietnam's Membership in ASEAN: Economic, Political and Security Implications", *Contemporary Southeast Asia*, vol. 16, no. 3, 1994, pp. 259–73.
21 C. Thayer, "Vietnam and ASEAN: A First Anniversary Assessment," *Southeast Asian Affairs 1997*, Singapore: Institute of Southeast Asian Studies, 1997, p. 373; Sukhumbhand Paribatra, "From ASEAN Six to ASEAN Ten: Issues and Prospects", *Contemporary Southeast Asia*, vol. 16, no. 3, 1994, p. 253.
22 At the AMM in Manila in 1992, Indonesia supported inviting Myanmar as an observer, a preliminary step towards membership. See Amitav Acharya, *Human Rights in Southeast Asia: Dilemmas for Foreign Policy*, Toronto: University of Toronto–York University Joint Centre for Asia Pacific Studies, Eastern Asia Policy Papers No. 11, 1995, pp. 14–17. Again in late 1995, Suharto urged ASEAN to "hasten" its expansion. See *ST*, December 15, 1995. Walden Bello believes Myanmar's admission was pushed mainly by Indonesia (*Burma Debate*, March/June 1997, pp. 24–5).
23 *NST*, July 27, 1992, cited in *Aliran Monthly*, vol. 16, no. 10, 1996, pp. 10–11.
24 *The Australian*, April 28, 1997.
25 *ST*, July 24, 1997; *The Weekend Australian*, July 19–20, 1997.
26 *New Sunday Times*, July 20, 1997; *NST*, July 22, 1997; *ST*, July 22 and 25, 1997.
27 In the May 1993 elections, supervised by the United Nations Transitional Authority in Cambodia (UNTAC), of the four parties that won seats, Ranariddh's FUNC-INPEC won the most votes and seats – being two seats short of an absolute majority in the Assembly. However, Hun Sen's Cambodian People's Party, which won the second most votes and seats, and which also controlled the army and effectively controlled the state's bureaucracy, refused to accept the election results until a power-sharing formula was agreed to by UNTAC. The formula made Ranariddh the first prime minister in name, but very much second to Hun Sen in terms of governing power and armed strength. The co-prime ministers never trusted each other and there were bitter squabbles. As soon as UNTAC pulled out in November 1993, the power-sharing formula began slowly to disintegrate. See *FEER*, July 24, 1997, pp.

18–19, and August 21, 1997, p. 13. There is irony in the situation. For four years, ASEAN poured considerable energy into supporting the military and diplomatic efforts of three Khmer groups (Ranariddh's group, another non-Communist group, and the Khmer Rouge), backed by the United States and China, against the Vietnamese-installed Hun Sen government in Phnom Penh. After the December 1978 Vietnamese invasion and occupation of Cambodia, Malaysia and Indonesia were initially reluctant to oppose Vietnam, because they viewed Hanoi as a buffer against China. However, in the interests of ASEAN solidarity, and because Thailand was most affected as a "front-line state," they supported the views of the majority to oppose the Vietnamese occupation and Hun Sen's rule. Having secured the withdrawal of Vietnam, the Paris Peace Agreement (October 1991), and the staging of relatively free elections leading to a power-sharing arrangement, ASEAN now seems poised to accept Hun Sen's *de facto* undisputed rule.

28 Nate Thayer and Rodney Tasker, "Unfree, Unfair", *Far Eastern Economic Review*, August 13 1998, pp. 16–17. New York Times, July 26 1998.

29 J. Clad, "Regionalism in Southeast Asia: A Bridge Too Far?", *Southeast Asian Affairs 1997*, Singapore: Institute of Southeast Asian Studies, 1997, p. 5.

30 *The Asian Wall Street Journal*, July 21, 1997. Also see *Bangkok Post*, July 21, 1997.

31 F. Langdon, "Japan's Regional and Global Coalition Participation: Political and Economic Aspects", Working Paper No. 14, June 1997, Institute of International Relations at the University of British Columbia, p. 19.

32 *FEER*, July 20, 1989, p. 10.

33 N. Gallant and R. Stubbs, "APEC's Dilemmas: Institution-Building Around the Pacific Rim," *Pacific Affairs*, vol. 70, no. 2, 1997, pp. 203–18.

34 Langdon, op. cit., p. 12. Apparently, Australian Prime Minister Keating was instrumental in convincing Suharto to push for a free trade agreement (interview with Bob McMullan, Australian MP and former Minister of International Trade, May 7, 1997).

35 *ST*, February 12, 1995.

36 G. Sheridan, *Tigers*, St. Leonards, NSW: Allen and Unwin, 1997, p. 210.

37 Gallant and Stubbs, op. cit., pp. 214–15.

38 K. Nossal and R. Stubbs, "Mahathir's Malaysia: An Emerging Middle Power?", in A. Cooper (ed.) *Niche Diplomacy: Middle Powers in the Post-Cold War Era*, London: Macmillan, forthcoming, manuscript p. 21.

39 P. Searle, "Recalcitrant or *Realpolitik*? The Politics of Culture in Australia's Relations with Malaysia," in R. Robison (ed.) *Pathways to Asia*, St. Leonards, NSW: Allen and Unwin, 1996, p. 75.

40 R. Higgott and R. Stubbs, "Competing Conceptions of Economic Regionalism: APEC vs EAEC in the Asia Pacific," *Review of International Political Economy*, vol. 2, no. 3, 1995, p. 522.

41 Jusuf Wanandi, "ASEAN, The Wider Region and the World: The Political/Security Agenda", paper prepared for the 2nd ASEAN Congress in Kuala Lumpur, Malaysia, July 20–3, 1997, p. 4.

42 *FEER*, November 24, 1994, p. 18.

43 A prominent Malaysian quite close to Mahathir said it was just Indonesia's way of killing it through other means (interview, July 1997).

44 Saravanamuttu, "Malaysia's Foreign Policy in the Mahathir Period," p. 5.

45 Langdon, op. cit., pp. 27–8.

46 Higgott and Stubbs, op. cit., p. 523.

47 *Straits Times Weekly Edition* (hereafter *STWE*), December 7, 1996.

48 Searle, op. cit., pp. 61 and 71.

49 Ibid., p. 67.

50 *Sunday Times*, July 30, 1995; *ST*, July 25, 1997.

51 Langdon, op. cit., p. 28.

52 *ST*, April 26, 1994; *FEER*, July 20, 1989, p. 10,

53 See *Sunday Star*, February 2, 1997; *Sydney Morning Herald*, February 15, 1997; *FEER*, February 13, 1997, pp. 21–2, and February 27, 1997, p. 22. Also see Yeo Lay Hwee, "The Bangkok ASEM and the Future of Asia–Europe Relations," *Southeast Asian Affairs 1997*, Singapore: Institute of Southeast Asian Studies, 1997, pp. 35–6.

54 D. Camroux and C. Lechervy, "'Close Encounters of a Third Kind?': The Inaugural Asia–Europe Meeting of March 1996," *The Pacific Review*, vol. 9, no. 3, 1996, p. 442.

55 *ST*, April 8, 1995 and January 16, 1996; *The Australian*, February 19, 1997; Sheridan, op. cit., p. 54. Indonesia joined Malaysia in 1998 in vetoing Australia's membership bid.

56 *Malaysian Business*, January 1, 1997, p. 32.

57 *MD*, vol. 23, no. 9, 1996, p. 4.

58 See Zhou Mei, *Rafidah Aziz Sans Malice*, Singapore: Yuyue Enterprise, 1997, pp. 94–102 for a detailed account of Rafidah's behind-the-scenes coalition-building efforts. Also see *Globe and Mail*, December 29, 1996; *FEER*, December 12, 1996, pp. 38, 56–9.

59 See *FEER*, December 19, 1996, pp. 5, 28, 56–9; *MD*, vol. 23, no. 9, 1996, p. 4; *Singapore Bulletin*, vol. 24, no. 9, 1996, pp. 1–2.

60 *CSM*, December 2, 1996; *Globe and Mail*, December 9, 1996; *FEER*, December 12, 1996, p. 38.

61 *Vancouver Sun*, December 13, 1996; *FEER*, December 19, 1996, p. 5. A *FEER* article (December 26, 1996–January 2, 1997, pp. 121–2) concluded that the Asians let themselves be "bullied, cajoled and prodded" into accepting a Euro-American agenda.

62 *FEER*, December 26, 1996–January 2, 1997, p. 122.

63 *NST*, December 16, 1996. In an interview with the authors in July 1997, Rafidah noted that there was no mistake about the Declaration, and those who believed otherwise could not read.

64 *ST*, December 12, 1994.

65 Ibid., January 2, 1995.

66 *NST*, May 3, 1997.

67 S. Narine, "ASEAN and International Relations Theory," *Cancaps Bulletin*, no. 11, November 1996, pp. 9–10.

68 A. Whiting, "ASEAN Eyes China: The Security Dimension," *Asian Survey*, vol. xxxvii, no. 4, 1997, pp. 311–22; *FEER*, June 12, 1997, pp. 17–21.

69 Sheridan, op. cit., pp. 196–7.

70 Mahathir Mohamad and Shintaro Ishiharo, *The Voice of Asia*, trans. Frank Baldwin, Tokyo: Kodansha International and Kinokuniya Company, 1995, p. 124. This book was originally published in Japan, with the title *The Asia That Can Say No* (in Japanese, 1994).

71 M. Donnelly and R. Stubbs, "Japan and Southeast Asia: Facing an Uncertain Future," in D. Wurfel and B. Burton (eds) *Southeast Asia in the New World Order: The Political Economy of a Region*, New York: St. Martin's Press, 1996, p. 182.

72 Khoo, op. cit., pp. 48, 54, 63.

73 Saravannamuttu, *The Dilemma of Independence*, pp. 72–3; interview with Datuk Seri Dr. Mahathir Mohamad, August 5, 1970.

74 Khoo, op. cit., p. 88.

75 *NST*, October 19, 1995.

76 *Seventh Malaysia Plan, 1996–2000*, Kuala Lumpur, National Printing Department 1996, pp. 666–7, 680.

77 *FEER*, August 19, 1992, p. 17.

78 *NST*, May 3, 5, 7, 1997.

79 *STWE*, May 17, 1997.

80 *Star*, February 14, 1992.

81 *Foreign Affairs Malaysia*, vol. 16, no. 2, 1983, pp. 231–6.
82 In 1997 UMNO Youth, along with some NGOs, protested to the UN on the question, particularly on Israel's having designated Jerusalem as its capital (*NST*, June 30, 1997).
83 *ST*, July 27, 1995. For a general account of Malaysian concern over the Bosnian issue, see Shanti Nair, *Islam in Malaysian Foreign Policy*, London: Routledge, 1997, pp. 253–8.
84 Datuk Seri Dr. Mahathir Mohamad, "The Bosnia-Herzegovina Situation," *Malaysia's Defence and Foreign Policies*, Appendix 5, Petaling Jaya: Malaysian Strategic Defence Centre, Pelanduk, 1995, pp. 115–21.
85 United Nations, *Declaration and Programme of Action*, Vienna, 1993.
86 D. Mauzy, "The Human Rights and 'Asian Values' Debate in Southeast Asia: Trying to Clarify the Key Issues," *Pacific Review*, vol. 10, no. 2, 1997, pp. 215–19.
87 Speech by Datuk Seri Dr. Mahathir Mohamad at the Forty-Sixth Session of the UN General Assembly, New York, 24 September 1991.
88 Mauzy, op. cit., p. 229.
89 *NST*, May 12, 1994.
90 *Star*, September 24, 1994.
91 *FEER*, December 22, 1994, p. 20.
92 K. Mahbubani, "The West and the Rest," *The National Interest*, vol. 28 (Summer), 1992, pp. 3–12.
93 Tan Sri Musa Hitam, *NST*, June 22, 1993.
94 M. Leifer, "Anglo-Malaysian Alienation," *The Round Table*, no. 285, 1983, pp. 56–63.
95 M. Leifer, "Anglo-Malaysian Alienation Revisited," *The Round Table*, no. 331, 1994, pp. 347–5.
96 *Star*, April 12, 1991.
97 D. Camroux, *"Looking East"…and Inwards: Internal Factors in Malaysian Foreign Relations during the Mahathir Era, 1981–94*, Griffith University, Australia–Asia Paper No. 72, 1994, p. 41.
98 Sheridan, op. cit., pp. 203–8; Camroux, op. cit., p. 45, fn. 49.
99 Searle, op. cit., pp. 65–72.
100 A.B. Shamsul, "Australia in Contemporary Malaysia's Worldview," in Zania Marshallsay (ed.) *Australia–Malaysia Relations: New Roads Ahead*, Clayton, Victoria: Monash Asia Institute, 1995, pp. 71–2.
101 *STWE*, June 22, 1996.
102 *STWE*, April 5, 1997.
103 *FEER*, August 20, 1992, p. 17.
104 *FEER*, May 15, 1997, p. 26.
105 Liak Teng Kiat, "Malaysia: Mahathir's Last Hurrah?," *Southeast Asian Affairs*, Singapore: Institute of Southeast Asian Studies, 1996, p. 234.

7 The succession to Mahathir: Anwar Ibrahim

1 *Solidarity*, October 1971, p. 3.
2 For a conventional biography, see V. Morais, *Anwar Ibrahim: Resolute in Leadership*, Kuala Lumpur: Arenabuku, 1983. For a brief sketch, see D. Mauzy, "The Human Rights and 'Asian Values' Debate in Southeast Asia: Trying to Clarify the Issues," *Pacific Review*, vol. 10, no. 2, 1997, n. 12, p. 231.
3 *Asiaweek*, July 9, 1982, p. 14.
4 Anwar Ibrahim, *The Asian Renaissance*, Singapore: Times Books International, 1996.
5 *Sunday Star*, September 11, 1994.
6 *New Straits Times* (hereafter *NST*), June 25, 1994.
7 Anwar Ibrahim, *The Asian Renaissance*, pp. 48, 58.

8 *NST*, September 26, 1994.

9 *Aliran Monthly* (hereafter *AM*), vol. 16, no. 10, 1996, p. 7.

10 Anwar, *Asian Renaissance*, p. 49.

11 *Star*, December 9, 1994.

12 *Star*, June 20, 1994

13 *Straits Times Weekly Edition* (hereafter *STWE*), December 10, 1994.

14 *NST*, December 3, 1994.

15 *New Sunday Times*, May 13, 1994.

16 *Star*, August 9, 1996.

17 *STWE*, June 14, 1997.

18 *Far Eastern Economic Review* (hereafter *FEER*), October 6, 1996, p. 34.

19 *Asiaweek*, October 26, 1994, pp. 24–7.

20 *NST*, July 30, 1994.

21 *Star*, September 8, 1997.

22 *FEER*, July 31, 1997, pp. 17–20.

23 *FEER*, October 9, 1997, pp. 14–15; *New York Times*, September 22, 1997.

24 *FEER*, April 21, 1994, p. 20.

25 *NST*, December 12, 1995.

26 *Asiaweek*, January 12, 1994, pp. 24–5.

27 D. Camroux, *"Looking East"…and Inwards: Internal Factors in Malaysian Foreign Relations during the Mahathir Era, 1981–1994*, Griffith University, Australia–Asia Paper No. 72, 1994, p. 38.

28 *Straits Times* (hereafter *ST*), November 8, 1994.

29 *AM*, vol. 15, no. 9, 1995, pp. 6–7.

30 For an enumeration of anomalies and irregularities in the Daim-supported Bakun project, see E. Gomez and K.S. Jomo, *Malaysia's Political Economy: Politics, Patronage and Profits*, Cambridge: Cambridge University Press, 1997, pp. 110–16.

31 Asiaweek, May 30, 1997, pp. 4–6, 60.

32 *NST*, November 25, 1995.

33 *NST*, November 25, 1995.

34 *Asiaweek*, May 9, 1997, p. 30.

35 *Star*, August 7, 1996. A few years before, he said that his reading included story-books, economics, and books on management (Hasan Haji Hamzah, *Mahathir, Great Malaysian Hero*, Kuala Lumpur: Mediaprint, 1990, p. 20).

36 *Asiaweek*, May 9, 1997, pp. 30, 39.

37 *NST*, September 8, 1997.

38 G. Sheridan, *Tigers: Leaders of the New Asia-Pacific*, St. Leonards: Allen and Unwin, 1997, pp. 182–215.

39 *FEER*, May 11, 1994, p. 30.

40 *Asiaweek*, May 9, 1997, p. 39.

41 *Asiaweek*, June 12, 1994, pp. 24–5.

42 Khoo Boo Teik, *Paradoxes of Mahathirism: An Intellectual Biography of Mahathir Mohamad*, Kuala Lumpur: Oxford University Press, 1995, pp. 336–8.

43 *AM*, vol. 15, no. 9, 1995, pp. 7–8.

44 *ST*, October 9, 1995.

45 W. Case, "The UMNO Party Elections in Malaysia: One for the Money," *Asian Survey*, vol. 34, no. 10, 1994, pp. 916–30.

46 *The Australian*, April 16, 1995.

47 *NST*, September 20, 1995.

48 *NST*, November 27, 1995.

49 *NST*, November 30, 1995.

50 *Asian Wall Street Journal* (hereafter *AWSJ*), October 10, 1996.

51 *AWSJ*, October 11–12, 1996.

52 There had been rumors that Anwar, widely credited with a clean private life, had been involved in extra-marital sex. They were publicly denied by Mahathir (*FEER*, September 11, 1997, pp. 18–20).

53 *NST*, September 8, 1997.

54 *Star*, October 13, 1997

55 "Anwar – traitor or victim?", *The Straits Times Interactive*, September 4, 1998 on email to Southeast Asia Discussion List: seasia-l@list.msu.edu.

56 "Dear Mahathir", letter from Anwar to Mahathir dated 25 August 1998, *The Straits Times Interactive*, September 6, 1998, translated from Bahasa Malaysia and posted on the Internet, http://straitstimes.asia1.com/anwar/anwar4_0906.html.

57 *FEER*, July 30 1998, pp. 26–7.

8 Mahathir as Prime Minister

1 *Far Eastern Economic Review* (hereafter *FEER*), February 11, 1993, p. 21.

2 Khoo Boo Teik, *Paradoxes of Mahathirism: An Intellectual Biography of Mahathir Mohamad*, Kuala Lumpur: Oxford University Press, 1995, p. 322, citing *Asiaweek*, September 23, 1983, p. 31.

3 Interview with a Malay politician, July 1988.

4 J. Jesudason, "The Syncretic State and the Structuring of Opposition Parties in Malaysia," in G. Rodan (ed.) *Political Oppositions in Industralising Asia*, New York: Routledge, 1996, pp. 134–5.

5 *FEER*, October 29, 1996, p. 21.

6 R. Adshead, *Mahathir of Malaysia*, n.p., Hibiscus, 1989, p. 172.

7 Ibid., pp. 1, 7.

8 Interview with a Malaysian journalist, July 1986.

9 *Asiaweek*, July 31, 1987, p. 12.

10 *FEER*, February 11, 1993, p. 25.

11 *Straits Times* (hereafter *ST*), January 25, 1988.

12 *New Straits Times* (hereafter *NST*), March 6, 1976.

13 Interview with a speech-writer for Mahathir, July 1997.

14 *Asiaweek*, June 2, 1995, p. 52.

15 G. Sheridan, *Tigers: Leaders of the New Asia-Pacific*, St. Leonards: Allen and Unwin, 1997, p. 196.

16 *Asiaweek*, June 2, 1995, p. 52.

17 *Asiaweek*, May 9, 1997, p. 38.

18 *NST*, April 9, 1997.

19 Interview with a Malay businessman.

20 *ST*, February 22, 1973.

21 Mahathir Mohamad, *The Malay Dilemma*, Singapore: Donald Moore, 1970, pp. 162–4.

22 Mahathir Mohamad, *The Challenge*, Kuala Lumpur: Pelanduk, 1986, p. 1.

23 Hasan Hj. Hamzah, *Mahathir: Great Malaysian Hero*, Kuala Lumpur: Media Printext, 1990, p. 18.

24 Ibid., p. 25.

25 Ibid, p. 25.

26 Ibid., pp. 18–25.

27 *The Economist*, November 7, 1987, p. 17.

28 *FEER*, May 8, 1981, pp. 8–10.

29 Interview with a Malay politician, June 1986.

30 *ST*, September 7, 1990.

31 Prime Minister's Department, *Malaysia's Vision 2020: Understanding the Concept – Implications and Challenges*, Petaling Jaya: Pelanduk, 1993, p. 3.

32 Mahathir Mohamad, *Malaysia: The Way Forward*, Kuala Lumpur: Centre For Economic Research and Services, Malaysian Business Council, 1991.

33 "Vision 2020: The Way Forward" (keynote address by Mahathir Mohamad at the Vision 2020 National Congress, Petaling Jaya, April 29, 1997).

34 Ibid., pp. 2–3. *See also* Mahathir, *The Way Forward*, London: Weidenfeld and Nicolson, 1998.

35 *NST*, May 6, 1981.

36 *ST*, April 6, 1995.

37 Interviews, June–July 1997.

38 Khoo, op. cit., pp. 336–8.

39 *FEER*, September 4, 1997, p. 19.

40 *Opinion*, vol. 1, no. 11, 1968, p. 155 (Tan Sri Musa Hitam).

41 *Malaysian Business*, June 1, 1991.

42 *The Star*, May 2, 1997.

43 Jesudason, op. cit., p. 130.

44 Interview with a senior MCA officeholder, July 1997.

45 Khoo, op. cit., pp. 6–7.

46 Interview with a cabinet minister, July 1984.

47 Ibid.

48 Interview with Datuk Harun Idris, July 1988.

49 M. Esman, *Administration and Development in Malaysia*, Ithaca and London: Cornell University Press, 1972; M. Puthucheary, "The Administrative Elite," in Zakaria Haji Ahmad (ed.) *Government and Politics in Malaysia*, Singapore: Oxford University Press, 1987, pp. 94–110.

50 Riggs applied the term "bureaucatic polity" to describe Thailand and some other Asian states (F. Riggs, *Thailand: The Modernization of a Bureaucratic Polity*, Honolulu: East–West Center Press, 1966). His thesis was that, in the absence of a stable government with strong political will, the bureaucracy, not politicians, took many decisions, some calculated to benefit itself. There was too much continuity of government in Malaysia and too many initiatives by politicians for his model to be applicable there. Other descriptions of the state in Malaysia are concerned mainly with its actions to promote the interests of particular social classes. A good example is: J. Saravanamuttu, "The State, Authoritarianism and Industrialization: Reflections on the Malaysian Case," *Kajian Malaysia*, vol. 5, no. 2, 1987, pp. 43–76.

51 *NST*, April 8, 1994.

52 *NST*, June 29, 1997.

53 Khoo, op. cit., p. 14, n. 6.

54 *FEER*, April 14, 1988, p. 24.

55 V. Morais, *Mahathir: A Profile in Courage*, Petaling Jaya: Eastern Universities Press, 1982.

56 *NST*, April 8, 1994.

57 *New Sunday Times*, March 16, 1997.

58 Khoo, op. cit., pp. 217–18.

59 *FEER*, April 14, 1988, p. 22.

60 W. Case, "The 1996 UMNO Party Election: 'Two for the Show,'" *Pacific Affairs*, vol. 70, no. 3, 1997, p. 401.

61 *Star*, December 28, 1994.

62 *FEER*, September 24, 1997, p. 19.

63 *NST*, July 25, 1997.

64 *Straits Times Weekly Edition* (hereafter *STWE*), October 25, 1997.

65 *Aliran Monthly* (hereafter *AM*), vol. 17, no. 5, 1997, p. 9.

66 Mahathir Mohamad, op. cit., p. 141.

67 Ibid., p. 142.

68 *NST*, July 5, 1986.
69 *NST*, November 4, 1974.
70 R. Milne, "Malaysia: Beyond the New Economic Policy," *Asian Survey*, vol. xxvi, no. 12, 1986, p. 1368.
71 K. Nossal and R. Stubbs, "Mahathir's Malaysia: An Emerging Middle Power?", in A. Cooper (ed.) *Niche Diplomacy: Middle Powers in the Post-Cold War Era*, London: Macmillan, forthcoming, manuscript p. 21.
72 *FEER*, December 2, 1995, p. 77.
73 *STWE*, November 11, 1995.
74 *NST*, July 5, 1966.
75 *NST*, July 4, 1986.
76 J. Sachs, *New York Times*, November 3, 1997.
77 *FEER*, October 16, 1997, p. 15.
78 *ST*, January 7, 1998; *FEER*, January 8, 1998, p. 12.
79 *Sun* (Vancouver), November 4, 1997.
80 *Globe and Mail* (Toronto), November 25, 1997.
81 N. Graves, "Yearend: Malaysian Economic Miracle at an Impasse," *Reuters*, December 24, 1997, forwarded on email, December 26, 1997, by Bala Pillai (bala@malaysia.net) on "Sangkancil."
82 *FEER* September 10 1998, pp. 10–12.
83 Web-Exclusive, 1 September 1998, "An Open Letter to Prime Minister Mahathir from Paul Krugman," http://www.pathfinder.com/fortune/investor/1998/980907/malaysia.html; Vikram Khanna, "KL's Currency Move a High-Risk and Bold Gamble," *Straits Times Interactive*, September 3 1998, http:// straitstimes, asia1.com.
84 *The Australian*, September 5 1998.
85 "Sacked Anwar Vows to Campaign for Reform Across Malaysia," Agence France Presse, 4 September 1998, http://www.afp.com/go/english/coun...80904112512.ytw8qrae&name=malaysia.
86 For a list of inventive attempts to demarcate shades of difference in terms, see H. Crouch, *Government and Society in Malaysia*, Ithaca and London: Cornell University Press, 1996, p. 4.
87 Ibid., pp. 5–7. He correctly states that the "poles" analogy constitutes an over-simplification.
88 "Distracting" because of the need, conceptually, to distinguish between rights and democracy.
89 Crouch, op. cit., p. 7.
90 J. Jesudason, op. cit., p. 130.
91 *Opinion*, vol. 1, no. 6, 1969, p. 70.
92 *FEER*, September 18, 1969, p. 688.
93 *Solidarity*, vol. vi, no. 10, 1971, p. 15.
94 *NST*, October 14, 1995. For a contrast, see Anwar's view (p. 146).
95 *Star*, April 22, 1985.
96 W. Case, "Malaysia: The Semi-Democracy Paradigm," *Asian Studies Review*, vol. 17, no. 1, 1993, p. 82.
97 Case, "The 1996 UMNO Party Election," pp. 393–411.
98 Starting with Tunku's presidency. See Mahathir, *The Malay Dilemma*, pp. 8–10.
99 For a contrary view, see *FEER*, April 14, 1988, p. 24.
100 A main theme of R. Michels, *Political Parties*, trans. Eden and Cedar Paul, New York: The Free Press, 1962.
101 For Ghafar's explanation, including the protection that the changes would provide against the intervention of "foreign forces," see *ST*, October 29, 1988.
102 *NST*, October 11, 1996.
103 Khoo, op. cit., p. 303.

104 Thak Chaloemtiarana, *Thailand: The Politics of Despotic Paternalism*, Bangkok: Khadi Institute, Thammasat University, Social Science Association of Thailand, 1979.

105 J. Saravanamuttu, *The Dilemma of Independence: Two Decades of Foreign Policy, 1957–1977*, Penang: Universiti Sains Malaysia, 1983, pp. 3–5.

106 *STWE*, May 7, 1997.

107 *NST*, November 28, 1995.

108 Ibid.

109 M. Vatikiotis, *Indonesia Under Suharto: Order, Development and Pressure for Change*, London and New York: Routledge, 1994, pp. 152–4.

110 *AM*, 1997, vol 17, no. 8, pp. 19–20. Reputedly, in 1994, three of his sons sat on a total of 213 company boards.

111 *NST*, December 28, 1995.

112 For other criticisms, see *AM*, vol. 17, no. 11, 1997, pp. 4–6.

113 Interview with a business executive with political connections, August 1997.

114 Interview with Tan Sri Sanusi Junid, Menteri Besar of Kedah, August 1997.

Further reading

Recent History: Malaya/Malaysia

K.J. Ratnam, *Communalism and the Political Process in Malaya*, Kuala Lumpur, Oxford University Press, 1965. This describes how independence and "Westminster-type democracy" were transferred to Malaya, with a minimum of violence. A "success story," successfully told.

R. Stubbs, *Hearts and Minds in Guerrilla Warfare: The Malaysian Emergency, 1940–1960*, Singapore, Oxford University Press, 1989. A perceptive account of how British and Commonwealth troops helped Malayans/Malaysians defeat a major Communist insurgency, understatedly referred to as the "Emergency." The methods used are ably analyzed, showing how both the conditions and the strategies employed were conducive to a more favorable outcome than in Vietnam.

Mohamed Noordin Sopiee, *From Malayan Union to Singapore Separation: Political Unification in the Malaysia Region 1945–65*. This is essential background for understanding the tensions existing today between the Malaysian government and the states of Sarawak and Sabah, as well as for appreciating the misunderstandings which sometimes occur between two neighboring sovereign states, Malaysia and Singapore.

Politics: Malaysia

D. Camroux, *"Looking East" … and Inwards: Internal Factors in Malaysian Foreign Relations During the Mahathir Era, 1981–94*, Griffith University, Australia-Asia Paper, No. 72, 1994. This book is not confined to the "Look East" policy, but considers the bases of Mahathir's foreign policy generally. It has useful sections on Malaysia's policy towards Australia and on a comparison of possible Anwar foreign policies, as compared with Mahathir's.

—— "State Responses to Islamic Resurgence in Malaysia: Accommodation, Co-option and Confrontation," *Asian Survey*, 1996; vol. xxxvi, no. 9, pp. 852–68.

Gives an account of what the resurgence was about, an assessment of the principal resurgence movements, and the new governmental organizations set up to counteract them.

Chandra Muzaffar, *Protector?*, Pulau Penang, Aliran, 1979. The theme, taken from Malay history, is the unquestioning loyalty accorded to a leader, in return for protection. Chandra contends, giving examples, that this relation also applies to current political behavior in Malaysia.

—— *Freedom in Fetters*, Penang, Aliran, 1986. This is a scathing indictment of the powers of the executive under Mahathir and the weakness of the individual who has to contend with them. A year after its publication, the author himself was detained.

—— *Islamic Resurgence in Malaysia*, Petaling Jaya, Penerbit Fajar Bakti, 1987. This account, by a convert to Islam, deals not only with religious movements, but also with their social causes. It also shows that resurgence assumed several forms, which had varying political effects.

W. Case, *Elites and Regimes in Malaysia: Revisiting a Consociational Democracy*, Clayton, Australia, Monash Asia Institute, 1996. This book attempts, successfully, to show that elite agreement in Malaysia, encouraged by the British when the country was still Malaya, has persisted until the present. This is in spite of many changes and the high degree of authoritarianism now existing in Malaysia.

H. Crouch, "Industrialization and Political Change," in H. Brookfield (ed.), *Transformation with Industrialization in Peninsular Malaysia*, Kuala Lumpur, Oxford University Press, 1995, pp. 14–34. Crouch states, and amply illustrates, his thesis that industrialization was conducive to authoritarianism, not because it was planned but because individual leaders, incrementally, saw the advantage of introducing new authoritarian measures.

—— *Government and Society in Malaysia*, Ithaca and London, Cornell University Press, 1996. An excellent and current book. It is complementary to the present book. As shown by the title, it stresses society as well as government, while it does not enter so deeply into policy or the role of Mahathir.

—— "The Military in Malaysia," in V. Selochan (ed.), *The Military, the State and Development in Asia and the Pacific*, Boulder, Westview Press, 1991, pp. 121–38. This book is not entirely up-to-date, but the central question, which it answers, still applies; why is Malaysia one of the very few states in the area in which the military does not play a major role in politics?

J. Jesudason, "The Syncretic State and the Structuring of Opposition Politics in Malaysia," pp. 128–60 in G. Rodan (ed.), *Political Oppositions in Industrialising Asia*,

London and New York, 1996. The emphasis is on recent social and political changes, particularly the rise of the "new rich" and other class changes, and developments in the civil society. An understanding of the "syncretic state" is not vital for appreciation of the article.

Khoo Boo Teik, *Paradoxes of Mahathirism: An Intellectual Biography of Mahathir Mohamad*, Kuala Lumpur, Oxford University Press, 1995. The chief strength of this thought-provoking book is that Khoo's study of Mahathir's writings, including those earlier than *The Malay Dilemma*, is intelligently applied to his political actions. The only point of possible major disagreement is: can the term, "Mahathirism" be justified?

A. Kahin, "Crisis on the Periphery: The Rift Between Kuala Lumpur and Sabah," *Pacific Affairs*, vol. 65, no. 1, 1992, pp. 30–49. Kahin analyses the struggle of a local Sabah party, the PBS, which fought for more autonomy vis-à-vis the federal government, concentrating on events in 1991. It maintained power for only three more years. She ably demonstrates that, even with local support, it could not win against the superior resources of the federal government.

D. Mauzy, *Barisan Nasional: Coalition Government in Malaysia*, Kuala Lumpur, Maricans, 1983. A thorough study of Tun Razak's brilliant enlarged version of the "Alliance," maybe the best-known Asian example of "consociationalism."

—— "The Human Rights and 'Asian Values' Debate in Southeast Asia: Trying to Clarify the Key Issues," *The Pacific Review*, vol. 10, No. 2, 1997, pp. 210–36. This article does help to clarify the key issues (in a debate where Mahathir played a major role); Western and Eastern values; universality; the use of conditionality by the West; and the importance of good government.

G. Means, *Malaysian Politics: The Second Generation*, Singapore, Oxford University Press, 1991. The standard, and excellent, text. Time for a new edition, even if there may not be a sufficiently large third generation ready to take over.

Mahathir Mohamad, *The Malay Dilemma*, Singapore, Donald Moore for Asia Pacific Press, 1970. Mahathir's generalization about Malay traits in the 1960s, which led to his vision of the reconstruction of a "new Malay" for the following century. Essential reading.

—— *The Challenge*, Petaling Jaya, Pelanduk, 1986, translated from *Menghadapi Cabaran*, Kuala Lumpur, Pusaka Antara, 1976. Mahathir's thoughts on a number of subjects, including "polemics" (time-wasting arguments), the West, and corruption. Less well-known than *The Malay Dilemma*, but equally revelatory of the author.

R. Milne and K.J. Ratnam, *New States in a New Nation: Political Development of Sarawak and Sabah in Malaysia*, London, Frank Cass, 1974. Concerns the attempt to fit the new states into the existing Malayan framework, on the whole successfully, but with frictions described in the book.

R. Milne and D. Mauzy, *Politics and Government in Malaysia*, Singapore, Federal Publications, 1978. The emphasis is on politics rather than government. Features explored at length are: consociationalism; the early days of the New Economic Policy; and the formation of the Barisan Nasional.

Rais Yatim, *Freedom Under Executive Power: A Study of Executive Supremacy*, Kuala Lumpur, Endowment Publications, 1995. The author was a minister and a member of the, losing, Team B in the UMNO split of 1987, and afterwards studied law. The result is a book which covers all aspects of Mahathir's extension of executive power, written in terms of constitutional law supplemented by political experience (including experience of Mahathir).

A.B. Shamsul, "The Battle Royal: The UMNO Election of 1987" in Mohammed Ayoob and Ng Chee Yuen (eds.), *Southeast Asian Affairs 1988*, Singapore, Singapore Institute of Southeast Asian Studies, 1988, pp. 170–88. The most politically insightful account of what was behind the UMNO "split" of 1987.

G. Sheridan, "Mahathir and Anwar, the Malay Magician and the Sorcerer's Apprentice, ch. 7 in *"Tigers": Leaders of the New Asia-Pacific*, St. Leonards, Australia, 1997, pp. 182–215. Based on an interview with each, this is the best portrayal of Mahathir's mental agility yet published.

Zakaria Haji Ahmad, "Malaysia: Quasi-Democracy in a Divided Society," in L. Diamond, J. Linz, and S. Lipset, (eds), *Democracy in Developing Countries, Volume Three, Asia*, Boulder, Lynn Rienner, 1989, pp. 347–81. This is still the best treatment of an important theme; what are the possibilities of introducing democracy in a country which is not only in the process of development but is also ethnically-divided?

—— *Government and Politics in Malaysia*, Singapore, Oxford University Press, 1987. There are two contributions by the editor, "Introduction" and on the police. Other outstanding articles are: M. Ong on Parliament; Lee Kam Hing on "Chinese" parties; M. Puthucheary on the administrative elite; and J. Saravanamuttu on Foreign Policy.

Economics/Political Economy: Malaysia

A. Bowie, *Crossing the Industrial Divide: State, Society and the Politics of Economic Transformation in Malaysia*, New York, Columbia University Press, 1991. Bowie takes the general question – why and when do states use the industrializing strategies they do? – and applies it to Malaysia. He perceptively suggests that the answers lie in what ethnic issues are salient, and what the structural arrangements are for reaching ethnic settlements (in the case of Malaysia, "the bargain.") He refers to the role of Mahathir, although maybe he underestimates it.

E. Gomez, *Politics in Business: UMNO's Corporate Investments*, Kuala Lumpur, Forum, 1990. This was *the* pioneering study in this field. It disclosed a multitude of connections between the dominant party, UMNO, and business, at first mainly through formal links, later through less formal, and more clandestine, arrangements.

E. Gomez and Jomo, K.S., *Malaysia's Political Economy: Politics, Patronage and Profits*, Cambridge, Cambridge University Press, 1997. This book has a rather wider scope than the previous item, not being confined to UMNO. It is also concerned with the allocation of resources, and the government's ability to benefit some Malay capitalists by enabling them to gather "rents." Privatization provides numerous examples. There are eleven case studies.

Jomo, K.S., *A Question of Class: Capital, the State, and Uneven Development in Malaysia*, Singapore, Oxford University Press, 1986. More than half the book deals with the pre-Independence period. Yet it is useful for understanding later events. In spite of the title, the approach is eminently political, as is illustrated in the opening section on democracy and authoritarism.

J. Jesudason, *Ethnicity and the Economy: The State, Chinese Business, and the Multinationals in Malaysia*, Singapore, Oxford University Press, 1989. The title is almost long enough to outline the book's ample scope. An important feature in its broad sweep is the different methods which Chinese businessmen used in order to survive the restrictions of the New Economic Policy. This meant that many were not totally alienated from the regime.

K. Machado, "Japanese Transnational Corporations in Malaysia's State-sponsored Heavy Industrialization Drive: The HICOM Automobile and Steel Projects," *Pacific Affairs*, vol. 62, no. 4, pp. 504–31. Discusses the costs and benefits of Malaysia's attempt to gain advantages from Japan's technology, while acquiring the necessary know-how for itself. Mahathir's close personal interest in HICOM is made clear.

International Relations

M. Leifer, *ASEAN and the Security of South-East Asia*, London and New York, Routledge, 1989. The book deals with the issue of security in ASEAN for more than two decades after its foundation in 1967. It reviews the movement from the original idea of an economic organization to one seeking security, at first through "neutralization." During this period, habits of ASEAN cooperation grew, Vietnamese dominance was challenged, and plans had to be worked out for achieving a settlement in Kampuchea.

K. Nossal and R. Stubbs, "Mahathir's Malaysia: An Emerging Middle Power," in A. Cooper (ed.), *Niche Diplomacy: Middle Powers in the Post-Cold War Era*, London, Macmillan, forthcoming. The contribution examines Mahathir's desire to have an all-Asian group of countries which have something in common, as regards culture and attitudes and approaches towards economic development, to counter the West and provide Asia with a strong united voice in international trade negotiations.

D. Wurfel and B. Burton (eds), *Southeast Asia in the New World Order: The Political Economy of a Dynamic Region*, New York, St. Martin's Press, 1996. The main divisions of the subject-matter are according to the "regional environment", or the "policies of the external powers" toward the area. The former is more path-breaking, and includes: Linda Lim on ASEAN cooperation; D. Crone on new political roles for ASEAN; J. Clad and A. Siy on ecological issues; and G. Robinson on human rights. The Introduction (P. Evans), on economic and security issues, is also commendable.

J. Saravanamuttu, *The Dilemma of Independence: Two Decades of Malaysia's Foreign Policy, 1957–1977*. The author uses a sophisticated, yet logical, theoretical framework. He applies it to the transition, under Razak, from continuing foreign policy much as it was pre-1957, to one which was based on ASEAN's working together, seeking neutralization, and reaching an accommodation with China.

—— "Malaysia's Foreign Policy in the Mahathir Period, 1981–1995: An Iconoclast Come to Rule," *Asian Journal of Political Science*, vol. 4, no. 1, 1996, pp. 1–16. This continues the analysis of Malaysia given in the above reference. He justifies "Iconoclast" by citing the many novel elements in both Mahathir's domestic and foreign policies. The price of his rapid development policies, the author argues, was an increasingly authoritarian state structure.

—— "ASEAN in Malaysian Foreign Policy Discourse and Practice, 1967–1997," *Asian Journal of Political Science*, vol. 5, no. 1, 1997, pp. 35–51. In addition to recapitulating some main themes of the two previous references, Saravanamuttu surveys Mahathir's "iconoclasm" (or iconoclastic tendencies) in relation to ASEAN, and also examines his position on the EAEG/EAEC. In one important respect he believes that Mahathir preserved continuity in Malaysian foreign policy: ASEAN remains central as its main instrumentality.

Miscellaneous

Anwar Ibrahim, *The Asian Renaissance*, Singapore, Times Books International 1996. To condense the contents cruelly, the book has two main themes. The first is the reflowering of Asian culture in the last century or so, often minimized by those who are over-impressed by the economic success of some Asian countries. The other is, through dialogue, to reach a "common vision," shared by both East and West. The book testifies to the range and power of Anwar's mind.

J. Kahn and Francis Loh Kok Wah (eds), *Fragmented Vision: Culture and Politics in Contemporary Malaysia*. There is much of interest in this volume, but it is hard to find an overarching theme. Readers of this book are most likely to be interested in: H. Crouch on authoritarian trends; Khoo Kay Jin on Mahathir and modernization; Jomo and Ahmad Shabery Cheek on Islamic movements; J. Kahn on class, ethnicity, and diversity; Tan Liok Ee on two Chinese organizations which challenge cultural hegemony; and Francis Loh Kok Wah on the Kadazans' cultural revival.

J. Nagata, "What is a Malay? Situational Selection of Ethnic Identity in a Plural Society," *American Ethnologist*, vol. 1, no. 2, pp. 331–50. This is a seminal article which answers an apparently simple question in a satisfying way. The question is not just semantic or pedantic. In a plural society, such as Malaysia, the answer can determine which groups get what and when and which get less.

Rehman Rashid, *Malaysian Journey*, Petaling Jaya, Rehman Rashid, 1993. Reminiscences of a well-known Malaysian journalist. Useful from two points of view. It gives an insight into government–press relations and also contains entertaining anecdotes concerning politicians, including Mahathir.

Index